CREATION,
UN-CREATION, RE-CREATION

CREATION, UN-CREATION, RE-CREATION

A Discursive Commentary on Genesis 1–11

JOSEPH BLENKINSOPP

t&t clark

Published by T&T Clark International
A Continuum Imprint
The Tower Building, 11 York Road, London SE1 7NX
80 Maiden Lane, Suite 704, New York, NY 10038

www.continuumbooks.com

British Library Cataloguing-in-Publication Data
A catalogue record for this book is available from the British Library

ISBN: 978-0-567-59101-2 (Hardback)
         978-0-567-37287-1 (Paperback)

Typeset by Free Range Book Design & Production Ltd
Printed and bound in India by Replika Press Pvt Ltd

Mens Works have an age like themselves; and though they out-live their Authors, yet have they a stint and period to their duration: this only (the Bible) is a work too hard for the teeth of time, and cannot perish but in the general Flames, when all things shall confess their Ashes.

Sir Thomas Browne, Religio Medici *(1635)*

Contents

Preface

The threefold sequence indicated in the title implies that in order to understand creation in the biblical sense we must take into account not just an event at point zero but a mythic history, the history recorded in the first eleven chapters of Genesis. The theme of this history is the infiltration of evil into a world declared at the beginning to be good, an issue most resistant to explanation but an essential element in any theological or philosophical account of creation. The 'discursive commentary' of the subtitle is intended to describe a mode of exposition which goes beyond linguistic, historical and culture explanation, the stock in trade of critical exegesis, to dwell on the issues of theological and general human interest which confront the reader of these chapters at every turn. It also implies a willingness to draw on the vast pool of midrash-type commentary which these chapters have generated for centuries and continue to generate.

I wish to thank Robin Baird-Smith, Dominic Mattos, Anna Turton and the other people at Continuum for their courteous and expert co-operation in bringing the work to print. My thanks also to my son David, for help with a recalcitrant computer, and, as always, my gratitude to my wife Jean, for her companionship and support.

Except where otherwise indicated, translations of biblical texts are my own. Translations from the book of Isaiah are from my three-volume Anchor Bible commentary with kind permission of Yale University Press.

Joseph Blenkinsopp

Abbreviations

AB   Anchor Bible
ABD   D. N. Freedman (1992), ed., *The Anchor Bible Dictionary* (6 vols). New York: Doubleday
ANET   J. B. Pritchard (1969), ed., *Ancient Near Eastern Texts Relating to the Old Testament* (3rd edn). Princeton: Princeton University Press
Bib   *Biblica*
BK   *Bibel und Kirche*
BN   *Biblische Notizen*
BZ   Biblische Zeitschrift
CBQ   *Catholic Biblical Quarterly*
DDD   K. van der Toorn, B. Becking and P. W. van der Horst (1999), eds, *Dictionary of Deities and Demons in the Bible* (2nd edn). Leiden: Brill
EDSS   L. H. Schiffman and J. C. VanderKam (2000) *Encyclopedia of the Dead Sea Scrolls* (2 vols). Oxford: Oxford University Press
ErIsr   *Eretz Israel*
ET   English Translation
HTR   *Harvard Theological Review*
ICC   International Critical Commentary
JAAR   *Journal of the American Academy of Religion*
JAOS   *Journal of the American Oriental Society*
JBL   *Journal of Biblical Literature*
JCS   *Journal of Cuneiform Studies*
JJS   *Journal of Jewish Studies*
JNES   *Journal of Near Eastern Studies*
JPS   Jewish Publication Society translation of the Hebrew Bible
JSJ   *Journal for the Study of Judaism in the Persian, Hellenistic and Roman Period*

JSOT	*Journal for the Study of the Old Testament*
JSOTS	Journal for the Study of the Old Testament Supplement Series
JSP	*Journal for the Study of the Pseudepigrapha*
JTS	*Journal of Theological Studies*
KTU	M. Dietrich, O. Loretz and J. Sammartin (1976), eds, *Die keilalphabetischen Texte Ugarit* (Alter Orient und Altes Testament 24/1). Neukirchen Vluyn: Neukirchener Verlag
LCL	Loeb Classical Library
LXX	Septuagint
MT	Masoretic Text
NEAEHL	E. Stern (1993), ed., *The New Encyclopaedia of Archaeological Excavations in the Holy Land* (4 vols). Jerusalem: Magnes
NCB	New Century Bible
NRSV	New Revised Standard Version
NTS	*New Testament Studies*
OCD	S. Hornblower and A. Spawforth (1996), eds, *The Oxford Classical Dictionary* (3rd edn). Oxford: Oxford University Press
Or	*Orientalia*
OTS	Oudtestamentische Studiën
RB	*Revue Biblique*
REB	Revised English Bible
TDNT	G. Kittel and G. Friedrich (1964–76), eds, *Theological Dictionary of the New Testament* (8 vols). ET by G. W. Bromiley. Grand Rapids: Eerdmans
TDOT	G. J. Botterwick and H. Ringgren (1974–), eds, *Theological Dictionary of the Old Testament* (8 vols). ET by J. T. Willis, G. W. Bromiley and D. E. Green. Grand Rapids: Eerdmans.
UF	*Ugarit-Forschungen*
VT	*Vetus Testamentum*
VTSup	Supplements to *Vetus Testamentum*
WBC	Word Bible Commentary
ZA	*Zeitschrift für Assyriologie*
ZAW	*Zeitschrift für die alttestamentliche Wissenschaft*

CHAPTER 1

Humanity: The First Phase

Genesis 1–11: The Basic Story

According to the biblical chronology the story of the origins and early history of humanity in Genesis 1:1–11:26 (for convenience, Genesis 1–11) from the creation to Abraham, the first Hebrew, covers 1946 years. It comprises the following episodes: the creation of the world (heavens and earth) and its inhabitants (1:1–2:4); the first man and woman in the garden of Eden (2:4–3:24); their family history following the expulsion from the garden; the first murder; the families of Cain and Seth, surviving sons of the proto-parents (4:1-26); the ten generations from Adam to Noah; the mating of 'the sons of God' with 'the daughters of men'; their giant offspring; the announcement of imminent catastrophe (5:1–6:8); and the annihilation by water of all life on earth with the exception of Noah, his family – wife, three sons, three daughters-in-law – and the animals which survived with him in the ark (6:9–8:22). The deluge is the decisive break in the history, the watershed, following which a new humanity emerges with Noah's three sons and is established under a new dispensation (9:1-28). The spread of the new race over the known world is in keeping with the creation command to increase and multiply, but nevertheless leads to a major deviation: the first empire built by Nimrod, symbolized by the city and temple tower of Babel, emblematic of imperial pretensions and their religious legitimation (10:1–11:9). The list of ten generations of the line of Shem, Noah's son, ends with Abraham (11:10-26). It serves as a transition to the stories about Israel's three great ancestors: a very different kind of story.

This last section of the narrative in 11:10-26 marks the passage from mythic to historical time, though not historical in the way history is understood by historians today. The transition is signalled by a steep fall-off in human life expectancy which may be taken to indicate closure on the story of origins composed in the idiom of myth. Leaving aside the exceptional Enoch, who occupies the significant seventh place in the antediluvian genealogy and whose life span reflects the length of the

1

solar calendar (5:21-24), the ten patriarchs from Adam to Noah almost attained the 1,000 year mark. Adam, the first patriarch, lived for 930 years, Noah twenty years longer, and Methuselah holds the record for longevity with 969 years. In his monograph on *The Garden of Eden and the Hope of Immortality*, James Barr (1993a: 79–81) made the interesting suggestion that 1,000 years was thought to count as virtual immortality, which these ancient worthies almost but not quite achieved. This motif of the longevity of the denizens of the archaic world is well attested. As incredibly spectacular as these ages are, the life expectancy of the primaeval race in ancient Mesopotamia, or at least of its rulers, leaves the biblical figures well in the shade. Kings of Mesopotamian city-states before the deluge ruled for an average of 30,000 years (*ANET* 265), and the reigns of the ten antediluvian kings in the *Babyloniaca* of Berossus, from the Hellenistic period, were more than ten times longer on average (Burstein 1978: 18–19). The longevity theme is an example of the deliberate and conscious use of mythic topoi to make a point about the surpassing energy and power available in the first age of the world and, by implication, its gradual diminution in the course of human history. The diminution is in keeping with a basically deterrent attitude to technological progress in Mesopotamian thought. The idea was always to go back to remote antiquity for the wisdom and knowledge necessary for living well in the present. By the time of the last of the postdiluvian biblical patriarchs, Abraham's father Terah, the life span is down to 205 years (Gen. 11:32). This is an age which no one would ever attain again, not even Moses who died 120 years old, 'his sight undimmed, his vigour unimpaired' (Deut. 34:7).

The steep decline in longevity as we move from the archaic to the 'historical' period is also one of several indications that Genesis 1–11 was conceived as a distinct composition with its own structural and thematic integrity. Genesis 1–11 is, of course, an integral part of Genesis and the Bible as a whole, but this does not exclude the possibility of our reading it as a narrative with its own distinct coherence and identity, most obviously in the themes with which it deals. It is also differentiated by its use of symbolic names (Adam, Eve, Abel, etc.) and symbolic geography (Eden, Nod, etc.). Interest in origins is not confined to the first creation but is emphasized throughout in a list of 'firsts' – the first acts of worship of Yahweh (Gen. 4:26), the first population explosion (6:1), the first cultivation of the vine (9:20), the first empire-builder (10:8), and the first construction of a city with its temple tower (11:6).[1]

Consistent with this reading of these first eleven chapters is the almost complete lack of overlap and cross-referencing with the rest of the Hebrew Bible. Leaving aside the names listed in 1 Chron. 1:1-27, which are drawn from Genesis 1–11 anyway, neither the persons who feature in these chapters nor the stories about them occur elsewhere in biblical texts. Adam is a familiar figure

---

1   All with different forms of the same verb *hll* (hiphil and hophal).

from Paul's presentation of Christ as the new Adam, but outside of Genesis 1 and 5 he is never mentioned again in the Hebrew Bible.[2] The same for Eve, Cain, Abel, Seth, Lamech, Enoch, Shem, Japhet and Nimrod. Noah occurs only at Isa. 54:9, an allusion to the flood as a metaphor for Israel's exile,[3] and in Ezekiel's triad of ancient righteous ones, Noah, Daniel and Job, but this is a different Noah from the survivor of the flood (Ezek. 14:12-20). We begin to hear echoes of what transpired in Eden only in post-biblical writings including the *Book of Jubilees* (second century BC) and *The Life of Adam and Eve* (first century AD), and about the activity of the 'sons of the gods/sons of God' in *1 Enoch* (second century BC). Genesis 1–11, likewise, makes no mention of the history or prehistory of Israel. Israel is not even mentioned in the 'Table of the Nations' in Genesis 10, which purports to cover a broad arc of the world inhabited by the sons of Noah. In at least one instance, the origins of the worship of Yahweh, God of Israel, it contradicts the traditions represented in the book of Exodus. According to Gen. 4:26 people began to worship Yahweh during the lifetime of Shem and his son Enosh, but in Exodus the first revelation of the name of Israel's God was either at the burning thornbush in the wilderness or in Egypt (Exod. 3:13-15; 6:2-3). In other words, even though Genesis 1–11 came to be prefixed to the national history of the ancestors, the sojourn in Egypt and the rest, it has little in common with it.

By way of a footnote, we should question the common assumption that Abraham's mission to leave his country and kin and set off for another land (Gen. 12:1-3 or 12:1-4a) is the link connecting the archaic period with the history of the ancestors. This much-quoted passage does not refer back to the previous chapters – for example by substituting blessing for curse – as we might expect it to do if its function was to serve as a link. From the point of view of structure the passage belongs to the first or Terahite unit of the second *tôlĕdôt* (hereafter *toledot*) pentad in Genesis, to be discussed shortly. On closer inspection, moreover, it appears to have been inserted into the account of the vicissitudes of Terah and his family. It assumes that the destination of Abraham's journey is unknown ('a land that I will show you'), but the assumption is contradicted by the information already given, that Canaan was the destination from the beginning (*lāleket ʾarṣâ kĕnaʿan*, 11:31; repeated resumptively at 12:5). The age of Terah at death, noted immediately before 12:1-4a, and that of Abraham at

---

2   A possible exception is Job 31:33 where Job denies concealing his transgressions in his bosom *kĕʾādām*, which could be translated 'like Adam' (as JPS), except that Adam did not do that (see NRSV and REB: 'as others do').

3   The Noah of Ezek. 14:12-20 is not connected with the flood. The two individuals who bear the name Enoch (Gen. 25:4; 46:9; Exod. 6:14; 1 Chron. 1:33; 5:3) have no connection with the patriarch of Genesis 5, and the name *qayin* (Cain) in Num. 24:22 refers to a settlement in the Negev.

his departure from Harran, noted immediately after, would also seem to belong together (Crüsemann 1981).

Another clue to Genesis 1–11 as an originally independent text is the literary integrity and coherence manifested in its structure. Its most prominent structural feature is the introductory formula *'elleh tôlĕdôt* ('these are the generations') repeated five times. The Hebrew word *toledot*, always in the plural, is not confined to genealogical material but can also introduce straightforward narrative. In modern Hebrew, in fact, *toledot* means 'history'. But genealogies can themselves contain residual narrative material and generate more narrative, as we see in the additional information about Enoch in the antediluvian genealogy (Gen. 5:21-24) and about Nimrod, a mighty hunter before the Lord, among the descendants of Ham (Gen. 10:8-12). The *toledot* formulas and the sections they introduce in Genesis 1–11 are as follows:

Gen. 2:4	Heaven and earth (1:1–4:26)
Gen. 5:1	Adam and his line (5:1–6:8)
Gen. 6:9	Noah and the deluge (6:9-28)
Gen. 10:1	Noah's three sons and their descendants (10:1–11:9)
Gen. 11:10	Shem and his line (11:10-26)

One or two comments on this list may be helpful. The heading to the first of the series is somewhat anomalous since it comes not at the beginning but in the middle, between the creation account and the garden of Eden narrative. Some commentators have taken this first superscript to be the introduction to the garden of Eden story, but the latter does not deal with the heavens, only with the earth, and with one bit of it at that. Furthermore, the formula always introduces material of priestly–scribal origin which the garden of Eden story assuredly is not. In this one instance the formula was probably displaced to make room for the solemn prelude to the creation account in Gen. 1:1. The second heading, 'this is the book of the generations of Adam', raises the possibility, indeed the probability, that the Genesis 1–11 *toledot* were taken from a separate 'book' containing a list of names, perhaps originally deposited in the temple archives, somewhat similar to the bare listing of names corresponding to Genesis 1–11 in 1 Chronicles 1–9. If this is so, it must have been thoroughly expanded, 'narrativized' and reworked to fit its present context. The third and central panel of the pentad locates the deluge as the great divide between the archaic world, which according to the biblical chronology lasted 1,656 years, and the damaged world that survived the catastrophe, the one we inhabit. Like the first creation, this new world was inaugurated with a blessing and the command to reproduce and fill the earth (Gen. 9:1-7).

Since structure is an important way of conveying meaning, especially in ancient compositions, it seems that this fivefold arrangement was adopted to indicate the central thematic importance of the deluge by its position at the centre of the pentad. What this means is that the theme of Genesis 1–11 is not just creation but something more overarching, something like creation–un-creation–re-creation.[4] A similar arrangement obtains in the next long segment of Genesis dealing with the three great ancestors of Israel, their wives, and nearest kin. This segment is also arranged as a *toledot* pentad:

Gen. 11:27–25:11	Terah (Abraham)
Gen. 25:12-18	Ishmael/Arabs
Gen. 25:19–35:29	Isaac (Jacob)
Gen. 36:1–37:1	Esau/Edom
Gen. 37:2–50:26	Jacob (Joseph and his brothers)

The pattern is identical, except that the first, third and fifth units deal with the descendants of the eponymous ancestor (in parentheses) rather than the eponym himself. The entire narrative pivots on the central unit, the story of Jacob and his 20-year exile in Mesopotamia. As a kind of destruction and re-creation, this central *peripateia* corresponds structurally and thematically to the deluge in the preceding segment. The story, vividly told, inscribes the same theme of judgement followed by passage to a new identity and a new relationship with God.

The fivefold structure in Genesis 1–11 also imitates the structure of the Pentateuch as a whole, known in Judaism as 'the five fifths of the law'. That there was nothing inevitable about the fivefold division of the story from creation to the death of Moses related in the last chapter of Deuteronomy will be apparent when we note that this arrangement does not correspond to the most natural divisions in the narrative as a whole. The centrally important Sinai event is divided among three books, Exodus, Leviticus and Numbers. Israel arrives at Sinai in Exodus 19 and departs in Numbers 10, and the ritual prescriptions received by Moses and set out in great detail in Exodus, for example about the ordination of priests, spill over into Leviticus. Genesis, likewise, could just as well have concluded with the list of the 70 Israelites in Egypt (Gen. 46:8-27), making a natural link with the opening verses of Exodus which refer to the 70 and their leaders (Exod. 1:1-5). In other words, the material could have been set out in four, or six, or almost any number of sections. We can only speculate, but arranging the story from creation to the death of Moses as a pentad had the advantage for those responsible for the final edition of the Pentateuch, presumably temple priests, of locating Leviticus, by far the shortest of the five books, in the centre. This position intimated that its prescriptions for the holy life, and for the life of Israel as a holy people, were of central importance. The fivefold structure of the Pentateuch would therefore confirm our expectation that the *toledot* pattern in Genesis 1–11 will supply important clues to the intentionality and meaning of the work as a whole.[5]

---

4   As articulated by David Clines in *The Theme of the Pentateuch* (1997: 80–82).
5   For the time and circumstances of the division of the Pentateuch into five books, see Blenkinsopp 1992: 43–47.

On the chronological schema which is built into the *toledot* structure something will be said later in connection with the antediluvian list in 5:1-32.

Sources

If the distinctive character of Genesis 1–11 has often been overlooked or underestimated, the reason is perhaps to be found in the scholarly concentration on sources co-extensive with the Pentateuch or Hexateuch as a whole or at least a great part of either. The identification of sources has always been a matter of great concern in critical scholarship on the Bible in the modern period. To state the situation briefly, there is broad agreement that Genesis 1–11 results from the combination of two principal sources. What has come to be known as the Priestly source (siglum P) carries the main narrative line, provides a degree of continuity, uses distinctive and often formulaic language, and is concerned primarily with worship, the religious calendar, Sabbath (which even God observes, Gen. 2:2) and purity rules. This source refers to the deity as 'Elohim'. Elohim is a generic designation for deity rather than a personal name, which means that the God who in these chapters creates, with whom the righteous Enoch and Noah walk, who brings on the deluge and establishes the new order after it, maintains anonymity. Only with the appearance of Abraham on the scene do we hear a personal divine name for the first time when this deity is identified as El Shaddai, traditionally rendered 'God Almighty' (Gen. 17:1). Later still, the name Yahweh, the personal name of the God of Israel, is revealed to Moses. In the P narrative strand the revelation takes place in Egypt, and it is stated explicitly that the name is being revealed for the first time: 'I appeared to Abraham, Isaac and Jacob as El Shaddai, but I did not make my name Yahweh known to them' (Exod. 6:2-3). The alternative version of the revelation of the divine name Yahweh occurs in one of the key passages in the Pentateuch, the revelation of the I AM to Moses out of the burning thornbush (Exod. 3:13-15).

P – who will also be referred to in what follows less impersonally as the priest–scribe or the priest–author – is assigned responsibility in Genesis 1–11 for the initial creation account (Gen. 1:1-2:4a), the ten-member genealogies before and after the deluge (5:1-32; 11:10-26), an account of the moral corruption which led to the deluge followed by the initial instructions to Noah (6:11-22), one of the two strands of the deluge narrative (7–8), the new dispensation and covenant with the survivors of the cataclysm (9:1-28) and, by some commentators, the core of the Table of the Nations (10:1-32). It is less urgent in Genesis 1–11 than in later narrative to reach a decision about the long-standing debate as to whether P constitutes an independent narrative, that makes consecutive sense, or is intelligible only when read in conjunction with the other source material. The question hardly arises with the initial creation account in Gen. 1:1–2:4 and the new postdiluvian dispensation (9:1-19), and does not arise at all on the assumption, adopted here, that the material conventionally assigned to J is later than P.[6]

The source with which P has been combined, usually designated Yahwistic on account of the name Yahweh which it uses (siglum J),[7] is more focused on the human predicament and more characteristically lay than priestly and clerical in orientation. The question of chronological priority between P and J is disputed. It used to be one of the 'assured results of biblical scholarship' that J was much earlier than P, in fact from as far back as the time of Solomon or shortly thereafter. It can at least be said that this conclusion is no longer assured, indeed is no longer heard in critical circles, and that there is less resistance today to reading J as later than the P narrative material and perhaps composed as a kind of ongoing critical comment on it (Blenkinsopp 1992: 63–67). The chronological sequence of the sources is an important issue, but it will suffice for the moment to draw attention to the fact that in each unit of the *toledot* pentad J material follows P. We will assume, therefore, that this arrangement resulted from the deliberate choice of the author of Genesis 1–11.[8]

That Genesis 1–11 results from the combination of these two sources is still the ruling assumption in academic commentary, but like all such assumptions it leaves space for a hermeneutic of suspicion. We have already seen that the *toledot* book (*sēper*; so called at 5:1) gives the appearance of a distinct archival text, at whatever point it may have been incorporated into the narrative. Contrary to the current *opinio communis*, moreover, the antediluvian and postdiluvian genealogies in chapters 5 and 11 manifest none of the standard and well-known criteria for identifying the P source, and should not be assigned to it purely on account of P's alleged predilection for lists. Since the priest–author could not have composed the work without access to archives, there must have been no shortage of lists at his disposal. The point may be made by a glance at the beginning of the Adam *toledot* (Gen. 5:1-32) where the carefully structured genealogical formula is disturbed by an insertion referring back to the P creation account (Gen. 5:1b-2). In view of the fact that in the critical analysis of Genesis 1–11 the sources tend to overwhelm the idea of authorship, it would not be out of place to insist, once again, that Genesis 1–11 is not just a combination of two sources pasted together like two computer files but the production of an author who worked up P and J, together with other source material, into a compelling narrative.

6 For a defence of P's independent status, see Zenger 1983: 32–36; Weimar 1974; Koch 1987; Emerton 1988; Nicholson 1988.

7 The mediaeval Masoretes who equipped the consonantal text of the Hebrew Bible with diacritical marks indicating vowel sounds added the vowels of Adonai ('Lord') to the four consonants of the divine name (YHWH), which out of reverence was not used in common speech, to indicate that it should be pronounced Adonai. The result in translation was the linguistically anomalous form 'Jehovah'. Another reason for the siglum J is that source criticism originated in German-language scholarship, and in German the divine name is written 'Jahwe'.

8 More on sources in Pury 1989, 1992; more recently, Schüle 2006: 11–58.

Another reservation about recent source-criticism of the Pentateuch or Hexateuch narrative is in order. It would be generally admitted that, unlike P, J does not provide the reader with clear criteria allowing for the identification of one continuous narrative strand beginning in the garden of Eden and encompassing the so-called primaeval history (Genesis 1–11), stories about Israel's ancestors (Genesis 12–50), the sojourn in Egypt, the trek through the wilderness, and occupation of the land (Exodus, Numbers, Joshua). It is therefore not surprising to find a tendency in recent scholarship to emphasis vertical divisions, in other words, to read the Pentateuch as composed of distinct blocks of narrative material, the first of which is Genesis 1–11 (Rendtorff 1990: 33–34, 184–86).

Theme

This first narrative section of the Bible is generally described as a history ('primaeval history', *Urgeschichte*) since it narrates a sequence of events extending over almost two thousand years from creation to the failed attempt to build a city and temple tower. This characterization is deceptive in one respect, in that Genesis 1–11 comprises a series of originally distinct myths about cosmic and human origins – 'man's first disobedience' in Eden, Cain the first murderer, the invention of certain technologies among the descendants of Cain, the mating of superhuman beings with human women, primaeval giants, a universal deluge, a tower reaching to the heavens – all of these threaded together by the author who supplied continuity by means of brief narrative links and genealogical lists. The ostensibly historical form results from the tradition of writing histories of cosmic, national and ethnic origins in the Near East and Levant, and more specifically from the author's taking over the plot of *Atraḫasis* and related mythic narratives about the world of the gods both before and after the creation of human beings. At a less explicit level, this quasi-historical form conceals, not entirely successfully, a retrospective on the historical experience of Israel. Called into existence by its God in the no-man's-land of the wilderness, Israel is placed in the land; just as the first man, who was created outside of Eden, is placed in the garden (Gen. 2:7-8). Permanent residence in this pleasant abode is contingent in both cases on obedience to a commandment, but failure to observe the commandment leads to expulsion from the original habitat, the spread of sin through successive generations, the punishment of near-total annihilation,[9] and dispersion over the face of the earth. Both histories end in Mesopotamia with the descendants of the first ancestors and the survivors of national disaster facing an uncertain future (Gen. 11:1-9; 2 Kgs 25:27-30).

---

9   For inundation as a metaphor for defeat and subjugation see the Sumerian *Lament over the Destruction of Ur* (*ANET* 455–63) and Ps. 124:4-5. At Isa. 54:9-10 the phrase 'the waters of Noah' occurs in a context which refers to exile.

This narrative form was chosen as a way of articulating troubling questions of a religious nature. In a world created by a benevolent deity and declared – seven times – by that same deity to be good, how did humanity go so wrong as to bring an annihilating judgement on itself? How did evil infiltrate into humanity blessed by God? How is it that humanity, created in God's own image, so easily deviated from the moral order laid down in creation? How – this especially – do we account for gratuitous evil, evildoing for its own sake? Why is the history of humanity – in Edward Gibbon's summary statement – largely a history of crimes, follies and misfortunes?

In telling the story in such a way as to raise these and similar questions the author is faithful in general terms to the view of history implicit in the myths. In *Atraḥasis* the demographic expansion and increasing complexity of humanity results in the infliction of disasters vividly described – plague, famine, drought and climactically the great deluge. In Greek myth as related by Hesiod (*Theogony*, 507–14; *Works and Days* 42–105), which may have been familiar to the biblical author, the crafty Prometheus sided with humanity against Zeus by stealing fire, essential for working with metals and for other technologies, and was punished by being presented with Pandora, created ad hoc by Hephaestus and endowed with gifts by all the gods – hence her name. Pandora removed the lid from the jar in which the gifts were stored and all the evils which plague humanity were spread abroad. In both the Hesiodic and Genesis forms there is an intimation of deceptive forms of wisdom, of forbidden knowledge, and the ambiguous allure of unlimited technological progress, the problematic nature of which we are all now aware of.[10] It is also Hesiod who gives us the view of history as a process of irreversible decline in the metaphor of the four metals, beginning with the golden age, then silver and bronze, and finally iron. This last is the world of the author and our world: a world characterized by toil and suffering, mutual hostility, war, and the absence of justice (*Works and Days* 109–201).

On the question of how evil infiltrated into and undermined the good creation Genesis 1–11 has no one answer. In early Judaism (Wis. 2:23-24) and early Christianity (Rev. 12:9; 20:2) the snake in the garden of Eden is identified with Satan, which implies that evil originates in the superhuman realm. In one form or another, and with varying degrees of conviction, this idea has become part of the belief of most Christian churches and is expressed in prayer and ritual, for example, in the prayer of exorcism in the Roman Catholic baptismal ritual. This is hardly surprising since the overcoming of Satan is a central theme in the ministry of Jesus as described in the Gospels. It is therefore understandable that the doctrine of original sin, understood as the cornerstone of Christian anthropology, would be brought to bear on the interpretation of Genesis 2–3.

---

10 This theme is developed along original lines by Roger Shattuck in *Forbidden Knowledge* (1996).

But whatever may be said theologically in favour of the doctrine, it is not the best point of departure for interpreting Genesis 2–3. As Paul Ricoeur put it:

> The concept of original sin is not at the beginning but the end of a cycle of living experience, the Christian experience of sin. Moreover, the interpretation that it gives of this experience is only one of the possible rationalizations of the root of evil according to Christianity. (Riceour 1967: 4)

The narrative logic of the Eden story suggests a better alternative. In the first place, the snake is simply one of the animals that the Lord God had made (Gen. 3:1), even if one endowed with human speech. We may suspect that what the snake insinuates in its conversation with the woman simply externalizes what was already in her mind as she considered the tree and its fruit. As for the man, that God gave him a command with a penalty attached means that he already possessed the capacity to disobey, to choose his own course of action. Both man and woman were therefore created with the capacity for moral deviation. We will even hear from the mouth of Yahweh himself, as the clouds are gathering over doomed humanity, that every inclination of the human heart is set on evil continually (Gen. 6:5).

There is therefore no one answer to the question of the origin and first flowering of evil. Here, as in other matters, the text offers the possibility of different explanations. A more serious challenge to the view that moral evil can be understood exclusively from within human nature and its evolutionary history is the brief and baffling notice about divine beings ('sons of God/sons of the gods') mating with human women (Gen. 6:1-4). This text, which will claim our attention in Chapter 5, has generated an immense amount of speculation about fallen angels and other esoteric matters. It may be that the commingling of these 'sons of the gods' with human women was intended as one last description, in the familiar idiom of myth, of the old world in which gods and humans commingled and giants walked the earth, a world doomed to disappear for ever like that of the equally gigantic prehistoric antecedents of the Israelites in Palestine. But it is also possible that more than this was intended. In its more expansive form in the Enoch cycle from the second century BC, the myth of this divine–human commingling anticipates the early Christian belief in angelic rebellion against God and the existence of malevolent angelic beings who, in the words of the prayer, wander through the world for the ruin of souls. Talk about such spiritual agents of evil will seem counter-intuitive to many today, but the idea that evil cannot be explained without remainder from within the human condition, that influences and agencies from beyond these limits are at work in the life of societies and individuals, has been part of the belief structures of all three Abrahamic faiths from the beginning and remains so to this day. To that extent, Jews, Christians and Muslims have taken over a variation of the idea inscribed in the old myths of origins, the idea that humanity is caught up involuntarily in a history which antedates it and is basically not its own; one which results in conditions and situations which can render human life painful, morally disordered, even at times intolerable.

History or Myth?

The first eleven chapters of Genesis purport to be a history of early humanity. They include a lot of genealogical and chronological data which give the impression that the sequence of events takes place in real time: according to the biblical time chart, a little under two millennia. The principal characters have recognizably real names – Adam, Eve, Cain, Abel, Enoch and so on – and there are others with walk-on parts or who must be satisfied with a mention in one of the genealogies. It is not therefore surprising that this first section of the Old Testament/Hebrew Bible has been read for centuries, and continues to be read by many, as a historical record, either absolutely inerrant, or basically reliable perhaps with some allowance made for the deficiencies of ancient historians, including biblical historians.

This way of reading Genesis 1–11 is understandable since it deals with a number of episodes in sequence, but it can be misleading if it leads the reader to ask the wrong questions of the text, questions which the text is incapable of answering. But we should not find it strange that misconceptions about cosmic and human origins have been around for centuries and still are. Everyone, for example, even the brightest and best, believed for centuries that the earth was no more than a few thousand years old and was at the centre of the universe with the sun and constellations rotating round it. We have always been deceived, and continue to be deceived, by scale along both the spatial and temporal axis. The most recent estimate of the age of the universe at this writing is 13.7 billion years, and the lineage leading to *Homo sapiens* branched off from the other primates about 5 million years ago. Needless to say, both estimates are approximate and subject to revision, almost certainly upwards. In short, it should be obvious by now that questions about cosmology, palaeo-anthropology and related matters belong not to the Bible but to the relevant sciences.

The sequential order of incidents in Genesis 1–11, the kind expected in a history, is also deceptive. Several episodes presented as sequential – the man and woman in the garden, Cain and Abel, the mating of superhuman males with human females – were originally distinct origin stories in their own right which have been linked together into a sequence to serve the author's agenda. In somewhat the same way, the chronological order of the seven days of creation is in counterpoint to a logical order which is non-sequential, thus obviating the need to ask questions of a 'scientific' nature, for example, how there could be light before the creation of the sun. More will be said about this in the following chapter.

We speak of Genesis 1–11 as myth rather than history not just because it features such matters as a conversation between a woman and a snake, gods and humans consorting together, people who lived for almost a thousand years, and a flood that covered the entire earth including the highest mountains. Let us begin with the simple, obvious, but often neglected observation that we are dealing with a *text*, that we have access to the realia only through this text, and that the text must be understood in context. One important aspect of the context to be borne in mind is that Genesis 1–11 is an Israelite or, more precisely, a late-Judaean or early Jewish version of a literary mythic tradition which was already of venerable antiquity at the time the biblical author put stylus to papyrus. A necessary approach to reading with understanding and profit therefore entails the recognition that the author and the author's sources are dealing not with raw physical, historical or biographical data but with a literary tradition which they are remoulding to suit their own view of reality and their own theological agenda. This admission adds a level of complexity, but also of richness, to the task of understanding the text. Something should therefore first be said about these narrative traditions which provided models, or a kind of thematic grid, for Genesis 1–11. In what follows we confine ourselves to what lay within the cultural memory of the author of Genesis 1–11 and the author's public, absolving ourselves thereby of the task, and saving ourselves the tedium, of surveying even briefly the vast repertoire of myths of origins from beyond that range. We begin in Mesopotamia.

According to the ancient Mesopotamian scribal tradition, which was the dominant cultural and literary influence on Israel and early Judaism, normative value is always to be sought in the past. Everything necessary for society, including models for religious, political and legal institutions, was present in essence from the beginning. In this culture the idea of progress, which we tend to take for granted, is conspicuously absent. On the contrary, history documents a process of steady decline. At the risk of oversimplifying, much the same can be said of ancient Greece, as expressed in Hesiod's metaphor of metals in descending order of value – gold, silver, bronze, iron – a motif more familiar from Daniel's interpretation of the statue of the tyrant with head of gold, upper body of silver, lower body of bronze, legs of iron and feet of clay mixed with iron (Dan 2:31-33). In both ancient Mesopotamia and ancient Greece the past always weighed heavily upon the present.[11] We shall see that Genesis 1–11 has its own version of this disenchanted view of 'progress', the downward spiral of history.

According to Mesopotamian tradition, humanity's appearance on the scene was part of a history which stretched back into the time of the gods. The fullest, though still fragmentary, representative of this tradition is a work entitled *Atraḫasis*, written in Akkadian cuneiform and copied and recopied for more

---

11 On these ideas about origins and history in ancient Mesopotamia and Greece, see Groningen 1953; Speiser 1955; Oppenheim 1964; Van Seters 1983, 1995.

than a millennium, beginning no later than ca. 1700 BC. About two-thirds of this seminal text are now readable due to the patient work of cuneiform scholars (Lambert and Millard 1969). The story it tells runs more or less as follows. In the three-decker world common to the imagination of many peoples, ancient and modern, the god Anu ruled the upper level; Enki (Ea) the underworld, the waters under the earth; and Enlil was lord of Middle Earth, the world we inhabit. Enlil set the junior gods, the Igigi, to work digging irrigation canals essential for fertility in his domain. Resenting this imposition, they went on strike, laid down their tools, burned their equipment and threatened Enlil. The latter appealed to his fellow-deities, Anu and Enki, for support, but to his chagrin they expressed sympathy for the rebels. Since Enki, being lord of the underworld, was preternaturally cunning – like the snake in the garden of Eden and the snake which has a brief walk-on (or slither-on) part in *Gilgamesh* – he offered the suggestion that the mother-goddess Mami be petitioned to make creatures of a lower order called *lullu* who would take over the tasks of the junior gods, thus solving the problem. She agreed to do so with the assistance of the wise Enki, and proceeded to fashion seven male and seven female figures out of clay mixed with the blood of a sacrificed god. The gods then celebrated her achievement in creating these human prototypes by proclaiming her *Bēlet-ilī*, 'Mistress of the Gods'.

In due course, however – some 1,200 years later – the same pattern was repeated when the noise of the overcrowded and perhaps rebellious earth disturbed Enlil's rest.[12] This time Enlil came up with his own solution, which was to afflict the earth with plague and famine every 1,200 years in order to thin out the population. When these malthusian measures were thwarted by the machinations of Enki, Enlil sent a great deluge which covered the earth for seven days and nights. With the assistance of Enki, the royal hero Atraḥasis – the counterpart to Utnapishtim in *Gilgamesh* and Noah in Genesis – was rescued together with his family from death by water. This was displeasing to Enlil who, once again and finally, decreed measures calculated to keep the population in check with a view to avoiding a recurrence of the situation which occasioned the deluge in the first place. These measures included the celibacy of dedicated priestesses, infant mortality and probably also disease and pestilence, though the tablet is broken off at this point.

The story told in the fragmentary *Atraḥasis* myth can be filled out with the help of other Sumerian and Akkadian texts from ancient Mesopotamia. The tradition about the great deluge, the most prominent structural feature in the story,

---

12 The idea that the noise and tumult (*rigmum, hubūrum*) is meant to suggest rebellion was proposed by Pettinato (1968), but questioned by Lambert and Millard (1969: vi). Oden (1981) made the interesting suggestion that the noise and tumult represent the attempt to overcome the divine–human distinction, which he considered a key theme in *Atraḥasis*. On the theme of overpopulation, tumult and rebellion, see also Schwarzbaum 1957.

was familiar in Mesopotamia, Asia Minor and the eastern Mediterranean region from at least the third millennium BC. A tablet in the British Museum written in Sumerian and published almost a century ago by Arno Poebel describes a great flood which lasted for seven days and nights. Warned in advance, the Sumerian king Ziusudra (counterpart to Atraḫasis) built a huge boat in which he survived the disaster, and after sacrificing to the gods was elevated by them to eternal life (*ANET* 42–44; Jacobsen 1981). A list of eight antediluvian kings of Sumerian city-states whose combined reigns lasted 241,000 years, followed by 23 postdiluvians who reigned for only about a tenth of that time, postulates the same great divide in the early history of humanity (*ANET* 265–66; Jacobsen 1939). Another version of the list appears in a history of Babylon composed by Berossus, a Babylonian priest, about 280 BC and dedicated to the Seleucid ruler Antiochus I. Its original form is lost, but substantial sections have been preserved in Josephus and Eusebius of Caesarea's abridged version of an earlier historical work which drew generously on Berossus. Berossus lists ten kings before and ten after the flood, reminiscent of the biblical ten antediluvian and ten postdiluvian patriarchs, but of much greater longevity. He also supplies a lack in the king list by providing a brief description of the deluge, the salvation of Xisouthros (Ziusudra), his sacrifice on leaving the vessel and his departure to live with the gods (Burstein 1978: 18–21). In the great epic poem *Gilgamesh*, with which Berossus would almost certainly have been familiar, the story of the deluge is told to the hero by Utnapishtim to explain how he, and he alone, had been granted immunity from death by the gods, and why Gilgamesh must return to his city to face his allotted task and destiny in a world bounded by death (Heidel 1949: 80–93; Dalley 1989: 109–20; George 1999: 88–99). Finally, a single, fragmentary tablet from the excavations at Bronze Age Ugarit (Ras Shamra) with about fifteen lines written on both sides, contains part of the flood story but nothing not previously known (Lambert and Millard, 1969: 131–33).

The Greek mythic–historiographical tradition was also familiar with the deluge as the critical juncture in the early history of humanity. It is not in Hesiod, writing in the eighth century BC, for whom the Trojan war marked the end of the age of myth, but about two centuries later Hecataeus of Miletus mentions Deucalion, survivor of the deluge together with his three sons. These are presented as ancestors of the three branches of the Hellenic race, analogous to Noah's three sons. About a generation after Hecataeus, Hellanicus of Lesbos traced the history of Attica back to the flood, dividing his account of origins into antediluvian and postdiluvian epochs, the former beginning with the first man Phoroneus (Jacoby 1957: 1–47, 104–52; Van Seters 1983: 10–15, 22–28). Later uncritical and fanciful versions of the flood story, for example, those in Apollonius and Ovid, add little if anything of value.

For the ancient Greeks, the world of the gods was even more chaotic and violent than that of the ancient Babylonians. As its title indicates, Hesiod's *Theogony* deals with the genesis of gods rather than humans. The appearance of humans on the scene in this work is no less incidental than in *Enuma Elish*, the canonical Mesopotamian creation account to be considered shortly. Chaos is primordial, more so than the generation of numerous gods from Ouranos (Sky) and Gaia (Earth). Chaos also persists, represented in one of several versions by the baneful progeny of Night – another triad with the names Abyss, Darkness and Fate. In another version a fourth offspring, War-Without-End, is also part of the picture. This is the world with which the ancient Greeks were familiar, the world of the Homeric epics in which warfare, violence and deceit are endemic. No less than in the Mesopotamian texts, the world of the Greek gods is a world of violence, bloodshed and treachery. With the connivance of his mother Gaia, Kronos castrates his father, devours his own children as they come from the womb and is himself in due course treacherously supplanted by Zeus, the only survivor of this infanticidal cannibalism. The theme of rebellion, the attempt to usurp the privileges of the high gods, is represented by the war between the Olympians and Titans. It ends with the subjugation of the latter and the creation of humans from their ashes.

It is important to note that what is common to all these myths of origins is the belief that humanity appears on the scene as an episode in a narrative already in progress, one which they do not own, which they do not control and in which they are involuntarily involved. In *Atraḫasis*, the creation of human beings is a by-product of hostility and bad feeling between gods. Plague, famine and flood result from a decision repeated several times over a period of thousands of years by the boorish Enlil. The final decision to destroy by a deluge is in fact called 'an evil deed' (*ši-ip-ra le-em-na, Atraḫasis* II viii 35). Enlil is also malevolently at work in *Gilgamesh*. He hates and possibly envies the hero (*Gilgamesh* XI 35–40), and when it is all over is reproved by Ea for inflicting a great deal of indiscriminate destruction and collateral damage on humanity (XI 177–88).

In keeping with common practice in antiquity, the title of the canonical Mesopotamian creation myth, *Enuma Elish*, is taken from the opening line: 'When on high the heaven had not yet been named'.[13] In this cosmogonic myth human beings also feature as minor and incidental characters. Briefly summarized, the story begins at a time when there was neither sky nor earth. Gods are generated from the mingling of the male Apsū and the female Tiāmat, representing subterranean fresh water and the salt water of the ocean respectively. The familiar pattern is then reproduced with variations: the lesser gods disturb Apsū with their noise, he decides to destroy them, but is himself pre-emptively disposed of by the magical wiles of Enki. To avenge her husband's death Tiāmat declares total war on the lesser gods and appoints a monstrous being, Kingu, as her commander-in-chief. Panic-stricken at the prospect of having to face Tiāmat in battle, the junior gods appoint Enki's son, the heroic Marduk, later the imperial deity of Babylon, as their

13 Translations of the text by Heidel (1951: 18–60), Speiser (*ANET* 60–72) and Dalley (1989: 228–77) are readily available. An edition of Mesopotamian creation myths, some of them previously unpublished, is at this writing being prepared by Professor Wilfred Lambert.

leader. He defeats Tiāmat, is appointed supreme deity, creates sky and earth out of her body and human beings out of clay mixed with the blood of the sacrificed Kingu. The purpose of this new creation of low-status beings is essentially the same as in *Atraḫasis*, to take over the service of the high gods, especially their cult, a task originally assigned to the minor deities.

Like the Greek myths, *Enuma Elish* attests to the primordiality of chaos or the abyss (the *tĕhôm* of Gen. 1:2), before any gods or humans existed. The generation of the gods takes place in an atmosphere of horror, violence and treachery. Tiāmat gives birth to a brood of monstrous beings including poisonous reptiles and lethal scorpion-men (*Enuma Elish* I 140–41). Apsū, who plotted the destruction of his offspring, is himself treacherously killed, Tiāmat is dismembered, Kingu is slaughtered to provide blood, the vital element, for the creation of *lullu*, a lower order of beings. Violence, malevolence, evil do not, therefore, originate with humanity. All humanity does is propagate and perpetuate them. In this world view there can be no question of a 'fall'. Chaos is present *ab initio*.

These ancient stories were not written to entertain. Those who first set them down in writing may have been curious about the remote past, but historical curiosity was not their main purpose in writing. Rather, the creation of narratives, fictive genealogies of gods and mortals, and dramas featuring characters and situations set in the remote past provided their authors with a vehicle for thinking through basic issues, for expressing convictions and ideas about life in the present, the life of their societies and, no doubt, their own individual lives as well. We should expect to find something comparable in the biblical history of cosmic and human origins. When we speak of these events taking place in mythic time, we are thinking of myth not as the opposite of factuality or history but as a way of addressing and exploring matters of concern for the life of the individual in any society, at any period of history, and in the first place for our own lives at this point in history. Mythic narratives of the Genesis 1–11 kind were written, and possibly recited, not primarily to give information about the past but to add value and resonance to life in the present. They can address a challenge to our modern self-understanding, our way of being in the world, if we are receptive to them, as they did for Plato for whom such narratives provided a way of 'philosophizing by means of myth' (*Republic* 27:1). We can, if we think it worth our while, read these stories in the expectation of understanding better and coping better with the contrarieties, contradictions and ills of human existence, the tasks and burdens it places on us, and the negative and destructive tendencies within us and around us.

Creation Beyond Point Zero

When we speak of creation in the idiom of either myth or science, we tend to think of it as an event, whether a 'once off' act of a deity or a cosmic singularity. The distinctive *literary* character of Genesis 1–11, however, suggests a different way of thinking about it, one which is captured in the common designation 'primaeval history'. For biblical scholars and the general reader, the horizon is generally limited to Genesis 1:1–2:3a and 2:3b–3:24, often referred to somewhat misleadingly as the first and second accounts of creation. But a more ample understanding of creation corresponding to the entire narrative scope of Genesis 1–11 can be argued. The first and most pragmatic consideration in favour of this way of approaching the subject is the fact that Genesis 1–11 corresponds to, and in important respects is dependent on, a pre-existent extended narrative myth of cosmic and human origins not limited to the initial technomorphic act. The narrative pattern will by now be familiar: conflicts and accommodations in the world of the gods, the creation of human beings and the world they are to live in, solutions to problems in the world of the gods, the spread of humanity throughout the world, the disturbance of the order of creation leading to an annihilating judgement, and a new beginning in changed circumstances. The basic pattern is therefore: creation–un-creation–re-creation. On this showing, creation is not exclusively, and not even primarily, about absolute beginnings. The Creator is not to be thought of after the manner of William Paley's divine clockmaker who winds up the cosmic clock and leaves it to run on its own. The emphasis in Genesis 1–11 is on creating order along the temporal and spatial axis, setting apart a space in which humankind can not only survive but flourish, and dealing with the outcome of these initial creative acts. In more traditional theological terms, creation entails also divine providence. Less traditional is the idea, suggested by the author of the garden of Eden narrative, that there is even an element of trial and error as the Creator discovers the consequences of bringing into existence not automata but human beings with the capacity for making their own moral decisions and following their own devices and desires. This is an idea to which we must return at the appropriate point of the commentary.

Once we have reached this juncture, the question is how to reconcile the creation of a world declared by the Creator to be really good with the spread of deviance and moral disorder of such magnitude as to lead the Creator to regret his creation and decide on the need for a new beginning. At this point we come up against the impenetrable mystery of the absolute freedom of God. But what can be said is that without taking into account the infiltration of evil into the created order as a primary theme throughout Genesis 1–11 and its long tradition of interpretation there can be no adequate theology of creation.

The theme of Genesis 1–11 is therefore creation, but creation understood as a more complex phenomenon with several phases or, alternatively, viewed from different perspectives and angles of vision. These are of necessity presented sequentially, but there is reason to suspect that the narratives about the first murderer (Cain), the first intrusion from the superhuman world (the 'sons of the gods') and the first empire-builder (Nimrod), and possibly others, were originally independent myths of origins which have been threaded together to depict the growing power of evil as a counter to the creation declared redundantly (seven times) at the beginning to be good. In their different ways, the Mesopotamian and Greek myths of origins on the one hand and the biblical version on the other embody the idea that there can be no creation, however good, without allowing for the possibility of disorder, deviance and evil. Sirach (ben Sira) may have had this in mind in bringing a brief meditation on the creation of humanity to a conclusion as follows:

> Good is the opposite of evil,
> Life is the opposite of death,
> Thus, the sinner is the opposite of the godly.
> Consider all the works of the Most High;
> they come in pairs, one the counterpart of the other. (Sir. 33:14-15)

The anonymous author known as Deutero-Isaiah makes the same point more problematically in terms of divine causation. Yahweh is the one who

> forms light and creates darkness,
> brings about well-being and creates woe. (Isa. 45:7)

The continual re-emergence and re-assertion of forces antithetic to the good creation is without a doubt the major theme of Genesis 1–11, and no theology of creation can afford to leave it out of account.

The dramatic element in these chapters revolves therefore around the divine–human relationship which sets the pattern for the future, for our history, and is therefore a *creatio continua*. Traditional exegesis tends to state this relationship theme in terms of sin and judgement, crime and punishment, which, while not mistaken, does not do full justice to the theological nuance and originality of Genesis 1–11. In the first place, we should not be surprised that the Creator Deity can and does change his mind in dealing with the vicissitudes of the human actors in these chapters. Did Yahweh not choose Saul as king only to regret his decision (1 Sam. 10:1, 24; 15:11)? And when the people of Nineveh repented, did God not change his mind about the disaster he said he would inflict on them and not do it (Jon. 3:10)? So it was at the beginning. The man and woman in Eden go their own way, disobey, but are not put to death as threatened. After being suitably clothed for their new life, they are thrust into the 'real world' out of the mythic Edenic existence, and in fact continue living for little short of a thousand years (Gen. 5:5). God talks to Cain and warns him; but after he too goes his own way and kills his brother, he is not put to death as the law will require. Instead, he is assigned a nomadic existence and equipped to survive the blood feud by means of the mark or sign. In the line of Cain's descendants the sinners are also the innovators and inventors, offset by warnings against the ambiguities and allure of technological progress. Only after the intrusion into the human scene of preternatural evil in the form of non-human agents and the ensuing moral corruption is the flood decreed. After the earth dries out things continue to go wrong, but God makes a fresh start with a new creation initiated with the promise of his concern for all humanity, indeed all living things, to whom he gives the first law and the first covenant. Throughout this somewhat disjointed but ultimately coherent story we the readers feel the tension between our expectations and our encounter with the intractable demands of living in the real world, between the mythical world of timelessness which we are to leave behind and the real world, the damaged world, into which we, like the first parents, have been thrust.

CHAPTER 2

In the Beginning

The Priest–Scribe's Version

Compared with the Mesopotamian and Greek origin myths, the most striking feature of the first chapter of Genesis, apart from its sobriety of tone, is its hebdomadal or seven-day structure. This original and unprecedented arrangement must have been the result of a definite decision since the entities to be created number more than six. There are, in fact, eight word-acts in the course of the six-day creation: two on the third day and two on the sixth day, the Tuesday and Friday of the creation week respectively. Some doubling-up was therefore called for in order to achieve this arrangement. Another feature, one which rules out a straightforward chronological reading of the chapter, is that the first day corresponds to the fourth, the second to the fifth, and the third to the sixth, resulting in the following scheme:

Day 1	*Day 4*
light	sun, moon, stars
separation of light from darkness	day and night
Day 2	*Day 5*
firmament, lower and upper waters	aquatic and winged creatures
Day 3	*Day 6*
dry land	land creatures
separation of water from dry land	humans
vegetation	vegetation as food

Cross-linkage places the created entities in the environment appropriate for them. The heavenly luminaries correspond to the creation of light; aquatic and winged creatures to the creation of the vault of the sky which separates the upper rain-producing source from the oceanic abyss below; and land creatures including human beings correspond to the emergence of dry land. Vegetation is then designated as food for all creatures including humans. Since this first creation was a kingdom of peace and concord neither human being nor animal killed for food; all living creatures had a vegetarian diet. The wolf lay down with the lamb and the lion ate straw like the ox (Isa. 11:6-7).

The chronological order of creation was therefore not a concern of the author, a conclusion which permits us to set aside the kinds of 'scientific' questions so often asked by readers of this chapter, for example, how light could be created before the sun. The narrative logic of this account moves on a different level. It can be stated more or less as follows. In the beginning, there is the primordial darkness like the darkness of empty space (Gen. 1:2). Then, after the creation of undifferentiated light on the first day, Elohim (the Deity) performs the first of seven acts of separation and differentiation resulting in night and day, the unusual order (evening before morning) signifying that this is the liturgical day.[1] After the creation of the firmament on the second day, dry land emerges on the third day to serve as a platform from which the heavenly bodies, to be created on the fourth day, could be observed and their movements recorded. That the heavenly luminaries were created to enable the calculation of the festal calendar is stated explicitly (Gen. 1:14), and the festal calendar was essential for the orderly worship of God throughout the week, ending with the Sabbath, and throughout the year, with its festivals. Its importance is fully in evidence in early Jewish texts, especially where differences arose about calendric matters. For example, Ben Sira, a defender of the traditional lunar calendar, mentions only the phases of the moon as determining the festal calendar (Sir. 43:6-8), whereas for the author of *Jubilees* the calendar is calculated exclusively with reference to the sun (*Jub.* 2:8-10).

Only when all this is in place does God create humanity, male and female, and the means to sustain them. The author wishes to exhibit in this way the possibility of order by sanctifying human existence along the temporal axis (the liturgical calendar) which is inseparable from the spatial axis (the cosmos as temple), as time is inseparable from physical extension. On this view, human beings are created and sustained for the worship of God, and the world is created as a cosmic temple in which that worship takes place, a theme for which parallels can be found in Mesopotamian myth. The author of Job reproduces this cosmos–temple symbolism where he depicts the liturgy accompanying the laying of the foundation stone:

---

1   In traditional Christian practice the liturgical day begins with First Vespers the previous evening; the same with Sabbath, Passover and other festivals in Jewish liturgical practice.

> Where were you [God asks Job] when I established the earth?
> Tell me, if you are so clever!
> Who fixed its measurements? Surely you know!
> Who stretched the measuring line upon it?
> On what were its foundations sunk or who laid the cornerstone
> When the morning stars sang together,
> And all the sons of God shouted for joy? (Job 38:4-7)

The scene is the ceremony accompanying the laying of the foundation stone of the cosmic temple, recalling the ceremony at the dedication of the second Jerusalem temple accompanied with joyful hymn-singing.[2] The singers in the Job passage are the heavenly luminaries, the stars and planets represented as deities ('sons of God') who, following an ancient belief, make music as they move in their orbits. The trope has a long life. As the three youths in the fiery furnace sing the praises of God (in the apocryphal *Prayer of Azariah* 1:41), the stars of heaven are invited to sing along. Much later, in *The Merchant of Venice*, Lorenzo voices the same theme as he and his well-beloved Jessica contemplate the night sky: 'There's not the smallest orb which thou behold'st/ but in his motion like an angel sings' (V i 60–61).

The formulaic language of the priest–scribe who authored this account of creation provides essential clues to intention and meaning, a point which the reader can easily verify. One example is the repetition of the language of distinction and difference. The verb for distinguishing or separating (Hebrew stem *bdl*) occurs five times and the word for species or kind (*mîn*) ten times in this chapter. The author no doubt had in mind the laws of clean and unclean (in Lev. 11), though it is not clear that this distinction applied in the first creation. While the rationale for the levitical rules about clean and unclean in matters of diet and social contacts will seem opaque to many today, they served to maintain the good order set up in the first creation week, with different kinds (*mînîm*) of creatures assigned to their respective habitats. We see, then, how the author's interest is more in exhibiting order emerging out of chaos than in providing information about absolute beginnings. This task of preserving order is passed on to humanity, one of the ways in which the human being, male and female, fulfils the high destiny of being created in the divine image.

Gender distinction is noted explicitly only in the solemn account of the creation of human beings, written in a kind of high recitative (Gen. 1:26-28). In this climactic passage, the word *ʾādām*, always used in the singular, is a collective noun ('humanity'). A rabbinic tradition, no doubt influenced by the contribution of the jesting Aristophanes to the debate about love in Plato's *Symposium* (189–191D), speculated that in the beginning God created a hermaphroditic being, later divided into male and female (Rabbi Jeremiah ben Leazar in *Gen. R.* 8:1).

---

2   Ezra 3:10-11. A common image, e.g. Pss 24:2; 89:12; 102:26; 104:5; Prov. 3:19.

But unlike the account of human origins which follows in Genesis 2–3, this version does not present sexual differentiation as problematic. It is simply the essential presupposition for fulfilling the command to increase and multiply.

The formulaic expression especially relevant to our exploration is the sevenfold repetition about the goodness of what has been created, with its climax in the assertion that God saw that it was *really* good (Gen. 1:31). In view of the violence which both precedes and follows the creation of humanity in the Mesopotamian and Greek origin stories, with some of which the Genesis author was surely familiar whether living in Babylon or Judah, we might well read this emphasis as polemical; and we would find confirmation in the corruption and violence which, according to the same priest–author, brought on the annihilating punishment of the deluge (Gen. 6:11-13). With the murder of Abel, the violence and disorder in the world of the Mesopotamian and Greek gods is transferred to the human level, if with significant modifications. Nothing of this kind disturbs the majestic process of creation for the author of Genesis 1.

Since the early modern period commentators have attempted to reconstruct a prehistory for the priest–author's magisterial account of cosmic and human origins. It may be assumed that the author, a learned priest, would have been familiar with myths of cosmic and human origins in circulation at that time. While adopting some of the conventions associated with these cosmogonies, he would obviously have avoided genealogies of gods and the idea of creation as the sequel to victory over the forces of chaos, familiar in Mesopotamia, Greece and ancient Canaan. This left the option of either creation by the spoken word – originally a form of magic – or by making objects – the technomorphic model. Some commentators have argued that the Genesis account represents a combination of these two procedures. They have noted that in some instances – light, dry land, vegetation – there is only the spoken word, while in others – the firmament, the sea monsters, and humans – God creates by making or dividing. But there are occasions where God is represented as both uttering a word and performing an action, namely, with the heavenly luminaries and living creatures. In any case, the account is perfectly integrated and intelligible as it stands, whatever sources the author may have drawn his inspiration from, and it is unclear why creative speech and action should be incompatible in one and the same narrative context. The distinction between a *Tatbericht* and a *Befehlsbericht*, between an account of creation by doing and by commanding, seems therefore to be an unnecessary hypothesis.[3]

Critical opinion on the date of composition of the priest–author's history, as distinct from the great amount of legal–ritual material incorporated into it, places it in the period of neo-Babylonian hegemony, from the destruction of

---

3   Perhaps the best known representative of the hypothesis is von Rad 1934: 11–18, 167–71. In his commentary, however, he is unsure whether the two kinds of creation can be separated (von Rad 1961: 51–52).

Jerusalem by the Babylonians in 586 BC to the fall of Babylon to the Persian and Medes in 539 BC. Equally feasible, however, would be the early years of Iranian–Achaemenid rule when the return to Judah of Judaean deportees or their descendants first became possible. In favour of this somewhat later date would be the presentation in P of Abraham as the ideal immigrant, and the prediction, only in the P account of Israel's ancestors (Gen. 17:6; 35:11), that kings would issue from Abraham's line (Blenkinsopp 2009). The latter part of the roughly half-century of Babylonian domination following the liquidation of the Judaean state, when it was possible realistically to anticipate the end of Babylonian rule, marks the *floruit* of the anonymous author of Isaiah 40–48, whose prophetic sayings have much in common with the P creation account. Time and again in these chapters the power of the God of Israel to direct the course of world affairs, with special reference to contemporary events and the career of Cyrus in particular, is established by the power of the same deity manifested in the creation of the world.[4] For the first time, the God of Israel is presented consistently as a creator deity, one indication of which is the frequent use of the key verb *bārā'* ('create') – twice as often in these chapters as in Gen. 1:1–2:4. Read and interpreted together, Genesis 1:1–2:4 and Isaiah 40–48 provide the essential core of a biblical theology of creation.

By way of appendix, mention should be made of the hypothesis of Persian–Zoroastrian influence on Second Isaiah and, by implication, on the priest–author's account of creation in Genesis. Writing almost half a century ago, Morton Smith argued that Second Isaiah was pro-Persian propaganda disseminated by Persian agents circulating in Jewish diaspora communities in Babylonia during the last years of the neo-Babylonian empire. On this basis he speculated that the creation theology in Isaiah 40–48 was inspired by Zoroastrian ideas.[5] Leaving aside the scenario of agents fomenting sedition among deported Jews, which cannot be ruled out but is unsupported, Smith's thesis is weakened by having to rely on a text from the Gathas (Yasna 44), a canonical collection of hymns committed to writing only under Sassanid rule which are notoriously difficult to interpret and practically impossible to date. More persuasive was his citation of the proemium to Achaemenid inscriptions which places the activities of rulers in a cosmological and protological framework. The earliest example and prototype, from the inscription on Darius I's tomb at Naqsh-e Rustam, reads as follows:

> A great god is Ahuramazda, who created this earth, who created yonder sky, who created man, who created happiness for man, who made Darius king, one king of many, one lord of many. (Kent 1953: 138)

---

4 Isa. 41:2-5, 25-29; 42:5-9; 44:24-45:7; 45:12-13. Cyrus is named at 44:28 and 45:1.
5 Smith 1963. Zoroastrian influence is extended to Gen. 1:1 by Bremmer (2005). The alleged evidence for Zoroastrian influence on pre-Hellenistic Judah is critically surveyed and evaluated by Barr (1985).

The problem here is that this formula, which bears some resemblance to the creation statements in Genesis and Isaiah 40–48 (see especially Isa. 45:12, 18) is attested only from the time of Darius I (522–486 BC), and therefore too late to influence either Isaiah 40–48 or the priest–author. Cyrus, founder of the Achaemenid dynasty (559–530), may have been an adherent of the Zoroastrian faith (Boyce 1988), but we would not suspect it on reading his famous cylinder inscription from 538 BC in which the Babylonian Marduk is the supreme deity who commissioned Cyrus to take Babylon and restore its cult. A better grounded hypothesis, and one in keeping with a background in the late neo-Babylonian period, would be to read what the author of Isaiah 40-48 has to say about the incomparability of Yahweh as Creator God as a kind of mirror-image of the ideology inscribed in the *akitu* festival in honour of Marduk who declares 'I am, and there is none other' (Isa. 47:8, 10; cf. *Enuma Elish* VII 14, 88). It was on the fourth day of the New Year *akitu* festival that the *Enuma Elish* myth was recited, perhaps accompanied by a ritual drama (Blenkinsopp 2000: 105–10).

The Sixth Day (Genesis 1:26-28)

On the sixth day of the creation week there was much to do before *erev shabbat* (Sabbath eve, Gen. 1:24-31). First, the earth had to bring forth living creatures according to their several categories – wild animals, domestic animals, reptiles and so on. These are created indirectly by God since the earth is to bring them forth; in other words, they are to come into existence by the natural means of reproduction. The creation of humanity is then introduced by a uniquely deliberative decision:

> God said, 'Let us make humanity (*'ādām*) in our image, after our likeness. Let them rule over the fish of the sea, the birds of the sky, cattle, and over the entire earth and all creeping things that creep on it.'

> So God created humanity in God's image
> In the image of God he created them,
> Male and female God created them.

> God blessed them and said to them, 'Be fertile, increase, fill the earth, master it, and rule over the fish of the sea, the birds of the sky, and all living things that creep on the earth.' (Gen. 1:26-28)

The emphasis in this compact passage is indicated by the solemnly intoned recitative of the central statement – more apparent in Hebrew than in translation – and the inclusive verbal repetitions in which it is wrapped, pointing to the relation of humanity to other life forms, a matter of great importance in Genesis 1–11 as it is for us today. And since the command to have dominion has encouraged the idea that the Jewish and Christian Scriptures have contributed to the degradation and extinction of species, it should at least be noted that where the corresponding Hebrew verb (*rādāh*) occurs, the emphasis is generally on the humane exercise of authority (e.g. Lev. 25:43; Ezek. 34:4).

The numerous articles, dissertations and monographs written to answer the question what it means for God to create humanity in God's image and likeness would fill a small library.[6] It will suffice to mention a few of the leading options. Since the first man himself fathered a son 'in his image, after his likeness' (Gen. 5:3), it may be that the likeness consisted in the beauty and perfection of the human form, like the first man 'full of wisdom, perfect in beauty' in a poem of Ezekiel's (28:12).[7] This idea was richly elaborated in midrashic descriptions of the first man. *Genesis Rabbah*, for example, tells us that when the ministering angels first saw Adam they took him to be a divine being (*Gen. R.* 8:10). According to the author of the Wisdom of Solomon (2:23) God created the human being in the image of God's own being (*idiotēs*), or perhaps of God's own eternity (*aidiotēs*). For Philo (*On the Creation* 69–71), the image is reproduced in the incorporeal soul, the human intellect and the human being's capacity for freedom. Somewhat similar is Augustine's opinion that the image resides in the human power of reasoning and understanding (*Confessions* XIII 32). Or perhaps the divine image refers to the commission to represent God on earth as God's viceroy, monarch of all he surveys, in keeping with the Mesopotamian idea of the king as the icon, representative and vicegerent of his deity. Something of this can be heard in the psalm which praises God for making the human being little less than a divine being and crowning him with glory and honour (Ps. 8:6). Such an interpretation would, moreover, be entirely compatible with the idea of creation as bringing order out of chaos, since in the ancient Near East the ruler was the essential point of reference for cosmic and social order. Or perhaps, since we must make an end, *imago dei* refers to the human being's capacity for dialogue, as a being who can be addressed by God. This relational rather than anthropological understanding of the image and likeness, the distinctive contribution of Karl Barth (*Church Dogmatics* III/1), has been much discussed and evaluated both positively and negatively.

Before looking for an answer in keeping with our resolve to stay within the narrative logic of the text, let us consider the matter within the scope of the priest–author's work as a whole and its cultural and religious background. With respect to the latter, we cannot fail to be struck by the high evaluation of the worth and dignity of the human being, male and female, in Gen. 1:26-28 when compared with Mesopotamian myths of anthropogenesis, and it would not be

---

6   For references, see Schmidt 1964: 127–49; Westermann 1984: 147–61; Jonsson 1988; Schüle 2006: 84–101.
7   Gunkel 1997: 113–14; von Rad, 1961: 55–58; Miller, 1972.

surprising if a polemical note underlies this aspect of the P creation account also.[8] The same high evaluation is implied in the only other allusion to the image in Genesis – apart from the Adam genealogy referred to earlier (Gen. 5:3) – where it has been appended to the legal dictum banning the shedding of human blood in Gen. 9:6:

> The one who sheds the blood of a human being
> for a human being his blood shall be shed;
> for in God's own image God made the human being.

What is ostensibly a judicial principal (the *lex talionis*) is thereby given a theological underpinning, in the sense that acts of violence visited on the other, especially extreme forms such as slavery, torture and homicide, constitute a desecration or defacing of the image of God in the victim.

In a more general sense, the first simple but immensely important observation to be made is that all humanity, *without distinction*, bears this qualification, including those millions living in parts of the world of which the author could have had no idea at all. The historical perspective will narrow down to Israel once Genesis 1–11 is linked with Genesis 12–50 and the story of Israel as a whole, but this statement has priority both chronologically and theologically. In the mind of the author it provides the indispensable context for whatever is said about Israel later on. This is the first and most important of several indications in this author's work of a broadly humanistic and universalistic perspective. Emboldened by Ezekiel's account of the visionary chariot throne (Ezek. 1) we might venture further. When the divine figure seated on the throne emerges in all its blinding splendour, it is comforting that the profile, the outline glimpsed through the dazzling light, is that of a human being. Humanity is created in God's image; God appears to the seer in the likeness of a human being, bespeaking a mysterious connaturality between God and humanity.[9]

The history of the interpretation of the *imago dei* is extraordinarily rich in theological insight, but we must not overlook what it means when read in its textual and cultural context. What, then, does it mean for God to create humanity in God's image, after God's likeness? Like its cognate in other Semitic languages (e.g. Akkadian *ṣalmu*), the Hebrew term for 'image' (*ṣelem*), can refer to a replica of a cult object or ex voto (1 Sam. 6:5, 11), a painting (Ezek. 16:47; 23:14), or even an evanescent or phantom figure, a silhouette, the shadowy image of a person (Pss 39:7; 73:20). More commonly, however, it

---

8   Phyllis Bird (1981), argues that, in describing the creation of the first human beings, the biblical author adopts the analogy of the king as the one who stands in a special relation to the divine world, and does so in order to counter the common Mesopotamian idea of humanity created to serve the gods.

9   'On the semblance of a throne there was the semblance of the likeness of a human being' (*dĕmût kĕmarʾēh ʾādām*, Ezek. 1:26).

denotes a statue, especially a statue of a deity, what in biblical terms is called an idol (e.g. Num. 33:52; 2 Kgs 11:18; Amos 5:26). The word translated 'likeness' (*dĕmût*), on the other hand, often has a more general and abstract meaning. The abundant iconographical repertoire available shows how the identity and function of the deity are exhibited by symbolic correspondences, whether garments, headdress or objects emblematic of the deity in question held in the hand. For obvious reasons, the religious function of the image is often deliberately misrepresented in biblical polemic. For its devotees, however, the image is a powerful object which focuses the psychological and spiritual energies of the worshipper and re-presents the deity, in other words, makes the deity present. A close analogy is the invocation of the deity's name. To invoke the name solemnly in an act of worship is to make present and available the power of the deity; hence the close parallelism between the image and the name in the Decalogue. An analogous instance is the calling out of the name of the demon in rituals of exorcism as a means of making it present and subject to the control of the exorcist, a practice we still memorialize when we say 'speak of the devil and he will appear'.

We saw earlier that the best estimate of the date of the priest–author's narrative places it either during the relatively short-lived neo-Babylonian empire or shortly thereafter. This was also the *floruit* of the author of Isaiah 40–48, from which we deduce that it was a time when polemic against the cult of images was in full spate. It is therefore perhaps not coincidental that this author goes well beyond previous anti-iconic polemic in satirizing the manufacture, display and care of statues of deities, especially those of the imperial Babylonian deity Marduk and his son Nabū (Isa. 40:18-20; 41:6-7; 44:9-20; 45:16-17, 20-21; 46:1-2, 5-7). At one point, he may have had the devotees of Marduk and their procession to the *akitu* house during the great New Year festival in mind:

> Those who lavish gold from the purse,
> who measure out silver on the scales,
> hire a goldsmith who makes it into a god,
> whom they then bow down to and worship.
> They hoist it on their shoulders and carry it;
> they set it down in its place; there it stays.
> It doesn't move from its place. (Isa. 46:6-7)

Taking account of these and similar passages in Isaiah 40–48 suggests that creation in the image of God implies polemic against the cult of other images, idolatrous images, in the sense that the human being is to be the only replica and representative of God on earth.

The creation of humanity in Gen. 1:26-28 comes about, exceptionally, not through a word-act but as the result of deliberation: 'let us make humanity'.

The Mesopotamian versions generally feature a collaborative effort among gods – Marduk with his father Ea (Enki), the Igigi, or the goddess Aruru;[10] or, in *Atraḫasis*, the mother-goddess Mami assisted by the wise Enki, lord of the nether regions. Some commentators think this may have occasioned the use of the deliberative plural in the Genesis version, while others appeal to the theme of discussion and debate in the heavenly council. The example most quoted is Isaiah's vision in which Yahweh asks 'whom shall I send and who will go for us?' whereupon Isaiah pre-empts discussion by volunteering his services (Isa. 6:8). Inevitably, early Christian writers referred it to the Trinity. The explanation may be simpler. We use the deliberative plural regularly in internal dialogue, as in deciding on our own on a course of action ('Let's do it!'), and this may be all that is implied in this instance.

In summary, in Gen. 1:26-28 contrast with the mythic cosmogonies, theogonies and anthropogonies surveyed earlier is much more in evidence than the similarities. No material (blood, earth, clay) is used, and the purpose of creation is expressed in relation to other life forms on the earth, animals and vegetation, rather than in relation to antecedent problems in the divine world. The term ʾādām is a collective noun referring to humanity in general, unlike the ʾādām of the garden of Eden story who is a male character, an actor in a drama involving a man, a woman and a snake.[11] Unlike the account in *Atraḫasis* (seven males and seven females), the Genesis version does not say whether the first creation involved one man and woman or several and, unlike Genesis 2–3, sexual differentiation is not presented as problematic. It is simply a necessary precondition for fulfilling the command to increase and multiply, for the beginnings of life in society. Most importantly, far from being a by-product of or a solution to problems in the world of the gods, a sort of afterthought, humanity is at the centre of things, blessed by God and declared to be really good.

> You made him little less than divine,
> crowning him with glory and honour;
> you made him master of your handiwork,
> you placed everything at his feet. (Ps. 8:6-7)

---

10 *Enuma Elish* VI 1–38; see Heidel 1951: 46–47, 63.
11 The designation ʾādām occurs 24 times in Gen 2:4–3:24, always with the article apart from the first occurrence at 2:5 and with the possible exceptions of those cases where the noun carries a prepositional prefix (2:20; 3:17, 21). ʾādām, which never occurs in the plural, can mean simply 'humanity' or 'human being', but in the garden of Eden narrative it refers, with the possible exception of 2:5, to an individual human male and does so even after the appearance of the female. The more gender-specific ʾîš is used in tandem with ʾiššâ, 'woman'. This point will be developed in the following chapter.

What Was There before God Spoke (Genesis 1:1-2)

The creation account in Genesis 1 begins, in the first two verses, by stating what was there from the beginning, before God pronounced the first word, 'let there be light' (Gen. 1:3). These verses may be translated as follows:

> When God began to create the sky and the earth, the earth being a shapeless mass, darkness lying over the surface of the abyss, and a great wind swirling over the surface of the water, then God said ...

This parsing of Gen. 1:1-2 may be unfamiliar but is linguistically and exegetically justified as an alternative to the translation which became standard in Judaism and Christianity, reinforced by the Septuagint version ('In the beginning God made the heaven and the earth') and the first verse of the Fourth Gospel ('In the beginning was the Word ...', Jn 1:1). There is, naturally, no one authoritative version, but the following translation of vv. 1-2 according to the traditional understanding would be generally recognized and accepted:

> In the beginning God created the heavens and the earth. The earth was a shapeless mass, darkness lay over the surface of the abyss, and the Spirit of God was hovering over the surface of the water.

By construing the opening sentence as a main clause rather than a subordinate temporal clause, this version provided warrant for a theology of creation from nothing (*creatio ex nihilo*), the standard and orthodox theological understanding of creation in early Judaism and Christianity. Creation out of nothing can be argued on philosophical and theological grounds,[12] it was accepted in Judaism before Christianity (see e.g. 2 Macc. 7:28, where it is explicitly stated), and if not explicitly formulated in the New Testament is hinted at indirectly (Rom. 4:17; 1 Cor. 1:28; Heb. 11:3). All this notwithstanding, it has been known at least from the Middle Ages – for example, in the commentary of the eleventh-century Jewish scholar Rashi – that from the linguistic and exegetical point of view this reading of Gen. 1:1-2 is not the preferred option in strictly exegetical terms. This conclusion is acknowledged in several major modern translations (NRSV, JPS, NAB, NEB, but not REB). Since the Hebrew text was consonantal, vowels could be added to justify reading the first sentence as a main clause, as in the traditional reading, or the first verse could be parsed as a subordinate temporal clause, with the main clause beginning either with v. 2 (as in NRSV and NAB) or in v. 3 (as in JPS). A further clarification of a more technical nature should be added. The first word, *bĕrēʾšît*, comprises a noun (*rēʾšît*, 'beginning') with a prepositional prefix,

---

12   e.g. G. May 1994; Schwarz 2002: 172–75; Copan and Craig 2004. The weakest part of this last-named study is the section dealing with 'The Old Testament Witness'.

therefore ('in the beginning'), which normally forms part of a genitival phrase ('in the beginning of something') as in all other occurrences in the Hebrew Bible, for the most part dealing with the beginning of a reign (Jer. 26:1; 27:1; 28:1; 49:34).[13] The reading most consistent with classical Hebrew usage would therefore, translating literally, run as follows: 'In the beginning of God's creating the sky and the earth', with the principal clause to follow.[14]

Decisions about translation must also take account of literary context, and from this perspective it is clear that the alternative proposed is to be preferred. Genesis 1 belongs to the genre of cosmogony, narratives about world origins, and ancient cosmogonic myths in that culture area begin by describing the way it was at the time of the first creation, only then proceeding to the creation itself. In the canonical Babylonian creation myth *Enuma Elish*, for example, the list of what was or was not there at the beginning, or what had or had not been done, occupies the first eight lines of the first tablet. Only then are the first gods created (Heidel 1951: 18). The same pattern is adopted at the beginning of the garden of Eden story. A subordinate clause lists three things absent at the beginning – vegetation, rain and agricultural workers – and one thing present – a mysterious source of water coming up from the ground (Gen. 2:4b-6). It should not surprise us that the priest–author retains this narrative feature, if in a more subdued and tacit form, adapting the genre to his own theological agenda.

It is in any case a mistake to coerce an ancient text to conform to what is essentially a philosophical and theological theory. As we read on, we see that the author is thinking of creation as the production out of chaos of an ordered, liveable environment for the human race. A creation account is necessarily narrative, and it is characteristic of narrative that one event follows another. Creation follows chaos, but chaos is logically rather than chronologically prior to order. We shall see how the description of the great deluge as an event of un-creation reveals that chaos is a recurring possibility; it is inseparably constituent of physical reality. In this respect, therefore, Genesis 1 follows the same pattern as the Mesopotamian and Greek myths of origin. Unlike *Enuma Elish* and creation myths originating in Canaan, however, the biblical version does not represent creation as the sequel to a victory of the Creator Deity over the forces of chaos, not explicitly at any rate, but the holding in check of life-threatening forces – chaos, darkness, the storm wind. If we wish, we may read this as the first victory in a war which is destined to be prolonged as long as humanity lasts.

What, then, was there at the beginning, before the first word was spoken? The image presented with great economy in Gen. 1:2 epitomizes a situation diametrically contrary to the ordered creation as the author envisages it.[15] There

---

13 *bĕrēʾšîtāh*, 'in its beginning', with reference to the season for figs, is no exception since it is also genitival.
14 On the syntax of Gen. 1:1-3, see Rochenmacher 2002.
15 On the *Vorwelt* of P's creation account see Bauks 1997, 2001.

was the shapeless, chaotic mass from which the earth would be summoned into existence (the *tōhû wābōhû*), the primaeval watery abyss (Hebrew: *tĕhôm*), and a great wind (*rûaḥ ʾĕlohîm*) swirling over the surface of its waters; all this in complete darkness and silence. We, the readers, must try to think our way into what the author imagined behind what he has put down in writing. The primaeval substance from which the earth was to emerge on the third day as a habitable space was a dark mass without shape or form. For the transformation to take place this mass must be visible, hence God's creative activity begins with the first word-act by which light was created. Order could then emerge in response to the seven remaining word-acts of Elohim, the anonymous deity. In Genesis 1, therefore, we are dealing with the creation of the *visible* world as a habitat for humanity. This limitation was recognized in the midrash which insisted that Torah and the Throne of Glory existed before the creation of the world (*Gen. R.* 1:4); indeed, that Torah served as a blueprint for God in the creation (*Gen. R.* 1:1, 8; Schäfer 1971). This might remind the Christian reader that we cannot lay the burden on this one account of validating either the doctrine of *creatio ex nihilo* or the credal belief in God *factorem ... visibilium omnium et invisibilium* ('Maker ... of all things visible and invisible').

The point has been made, and may be repeated, that the word-acts follow less an outwardly chronological than an internally logical order. The emphasis is on order evoked and summoned out of chaos rather than on a series of absolute beginnings in chronological sequence. In the Mesopotamian and Greek cosmogonies the emphasis is much the same. The concluding scene in *Enuma Elish* is the establishment of political order through Marduk's kingship and of religious order through worship offered to him in his Esagila temple tower in Babylon. The final act in Hesiod's account of beginnings is the triumph of Zeus over Typhon and the establishment of peace, justice and social order through the rule of Zeus and the maintenance of his cult (*Theogony* 823–35, 881–85). Like his predecessors in Mesopotamia and Greece, our priest–author is composing a *narrative*, hence unavoidably expressing in a chronological sequence what is essentially an ontological truth, a conviction about the way the world is, about the fragility of order, and the persistent threat of disorder and chaos, physical and moral.[16]

The shapeless mass (*tōhû wābōhû*) seems to have been imagined as occupying the space between the upper and lower waters, but to have been indistinguishable from them. The space was created by a vault or firmament – the sky (Gen 1:6-8) – which suggests that this mass was, in effect, that part of the *tĕhôm* (the abyss) destined to be transformed. We can only speculate about the contours of the physical universe as conceived by our Mesopotamian, Greek and Hebrew forebears and, in spite of our vastly increased cosmological knowledge, we are

---

16 This aspect of what the Old Testament has to say about creation has been developed in interesting directions by Jon D. Levenson (1985).

still speculating about its contours today. The earth seems to have been imagined as a flat, habitable platform wedged in between the upper and lower waters and perhaps also closed in with water, like a great river circling the land mass. Ambivalence about 'the great wind' or, in the traditional version, 'the spirit of God', results from the semantic range of the corresponding Hebrew expression *rûaḥ ʾĕlōhîm*. Depending on the context, *rûaḥ* may be translated 'breath', 'wind' or 'spirit', and *ʾĕlōhîm* (or *ʾēl*) in a genitival phrase can serve as a superlative.[17] Hence the expression in Gen. 1:2, taken by itself, could imply that the agent in question is God's breath (as Pss 18:16, 33:6), or the spirit of God (as in the traditional interpretation) or a great wind. In the context, this last seems the most appropriate.

The *tĕhôm* may be related to the same Semitic root as the proto-goddess Tiāmat, representing the chaotic salt waters of the ocean from whose body the earth was formed. In Babylonian myth the nether depths, the primaeval sea, is the Apsū, the domain of Enki (Ea). For the earth to be, and remain, habitable, there had to be boundaries which the threatening waters of the abyss could not violate. We hear personified Wisdom proclaiming that she was present when God prescribed limits which the sea (or the abyss, or the Apsū) was not to transgress (Prov. 8:29). A liturgical hymn praises God for the same reason:

> You set a boundary that the water might not transgress
> lest it return and cover the earth. (Ps. 104:8)

The author of Job has the Creator God confining the threatening primaeval waters with dense and impermeable clouds (Job 26:8), and the pseudepigraphal *Prayer of Manasseh* (line 3) makes the same point using the language of exorcism and magic:

> You who bound the sea by your word of command
> Who closed up the abyss (*tĕhômâ*),
> sealing it with your fearful and glorious name.

Yet the waters did return and covered the earth in the deluge, described as an act of un-creation, a returning of the earth to its unformed, watery *materia prima*. The description of how the annihilating deluge came about confirms our understanding of the way it was in the beginning, before God spoke the first word:

---

17 Three examples with respect to *ʾĕlōhîm* or *ʾēl*: Mount Bashan described as 'a mighty mountain' (*har-ʾĕlōhîm*, Ps. 68:16); the local inhabitants flatter Abraham by addressing him as 'an awesome prince', literally 'a prince of God' (*nĕśîʾ ʾĕlōhîm*, Gen. 23:6); the king of Babylon is said to aspire higher than 'the mighty stars' (*kôkĕbê ʾēl*, Isa. 14:13).

> All the fountains of the great abyss (*tĕhôm rabbâ*) were broken open, the
> windows of the sky were opened. (Gen. 7:11)

Then, as the deluge came to an end and the water retreated, the process was
reversed:

> The fountains of the abyss and the windows of the sky were stopped up, and
> the downpour from the sky was checked. (8:2)

During the deluge, therefore, the habitable space wedged in between the
threatening waters above and below was eliminated and replaced by chaos-come-
again. Another indication of the deluge as un-creation is that the wind which, in
Gen. 1:2, was swirling over the waters, is the means by which the flood waters
were made to subside – 'God made a wind blow over the earth and the waters
subsided' (Gen. 8:1). We are also meant to understand that the duration of the
deluge, variously calculated in the biblical version, was a time of darkness and
the silence of God. God speaks before and after but not during the cataclysm.
Then, finally, according to the priest–author, the earth re-emerged from the flood
waters on the first of the month, namely, New Year's Day, the New Year's Day
of the new creation corresponding to the first creation (8:13).

Analogy between the beginning and the end of life on earth, between
protology and eschatology (*Urzeit gleicht Endzeit*),[18] the threat of un-creation,
an undoing of what God had done at the beginning of time, is a major theme in
those apocalyptic writings which anticipate an imminent end of history. The most
familiar images are of monstrous beings, creatures of nightmare, embodiments
of disorder and violence, which threaten the narrow foothold of ordered life on
the beleaguered earth. In one passage, this day of final reckoning, in biblical
terms the Day of Yahweh, will witness the decisive combat of the Creator God
with Leviathan and the Sea Dragon:

> On that day:
> Yahweh will punish with his sword
> grim, mighty, and strong,
> Leviathan the pursuing serpent,
> Leviathan the twisting serpent,
> and he will slay the dragon in the primaeval sea. (Isa. 27:1)

In Daniel's dream-vision the seer witnesses the churning up of this sea as four
monstrous forms emerge and take shape (Dan. 7:2-3). The Christian apocalypse
depicts a war to end all wars waged in heaven against the hydra-headed monster

---

18 'The beginning time corresponds to the end time'. This was the theme of a still famous
    monograph of Hermann Gunkel, *Schöpfung und Chaos* (1895).

from the cosmic sea (Rev. 12–13). The theme is stated with more specific reference to the Genesis narratives in what is probably an apocalyptic, or proto-apocalyptic addition to Jeremiah (Eppstein 1968; Carroll 1986: 168; McKane, 1986: 106–108). Key words from Genesis 1 are in italics:

> I looked on the *earth*, and it was a *shapeless mass*,
> on the *sky*, and it was without *light*.
> I looked on the mountains, and they were shaking,
> and all the hills moved to and fro.
> I looked, and there was no *human being* (*'ādām*),
> and all the *birds of the sky* had fled ...
> before Yahweh, before his fierce anger. (Jer. 4:23-26)

What the seer witnesses, in vision, is the final undoing of creation, the collapse of the physical order following moral collapse, an eventuality we can imagine without difficulty today. The message is as much about the persistent power of evil in the world here and now as it is a prediction of a final catastrophic event in the future.

The Abyss and its Denizens

From what has been said so far it will be clear that the six-day *visible* creation cannot be the whole story. There remains the problem of accounting for what was there before the creation week, the shapeless mass (*tōhû wābōhû*) from which earth and sky emerged, and which, according to the biblical world view, is still residually present and active as a threat to the created order, a threat which became deadly reality in the great deluge. The Jewish and Christian traditions have also been aware from the earliest times that Genesis 1 does not account for the origins of spiritual reality in the form of intermediate, created beings both benign and malignant. Can the answer be found in the interstices of the six days of Genesis 1, as some early Jewish authors believed, or was there a creation before the work of the six days? Augustine's reply to those who asked what God was doing before the creation of sky and earth, that he was preparing hell for people who ask such questions – the only joke in his *Confessions* (11:12) – will not deter us, especially since Augustine himself asked such questions, as we shall see.

The author of Genesis 1, a learned priest and scribe familiar with Mesopotamian and Levantine myths of origins, has so thoroughly demythologized the different narrative elements of the creation story – for example, by substituting the *tĕhôm* for Tiāmat and by eliminating the use of physical material in creation (mud, blood, etc.) – that we have to work hard to detect the mythological *arrière-fond* of his account. Though below the surface, the mythic substratum nevertheless contributes much to the consistency and power of the narrative.[19] The mythic dimension is, however, much more explicit in those poetic compositions in which the abyss is populated by monstrous personifications of disorder and violence hostile to the ordered life of humanity. The imagery and theme of these texts are not always easy to interpret, but some of the mythic substratum which is suppressed or tacit in Genesis 1 can be recovered from them. Typical is a hymn praising the Creator God as follows:

> God is my king of old,
> working salvation in the midst of the earth;
> by your power you stirred up the Sea,
> you shattered the heads of the Dragons in the waters.
> You crushed the heads of Leviathan;
> you gave him as food to the wild creatures ...[20]
> Yours is the day, yours also the night;
> you set in place the luminaries and the sun.
> You fixed all the bounds of the earth;
> you formed summer and winter. (Ps. 74:12-17)

Affinity with the victory of Marduk and the celebration of his eternal kingship in *Enuma Elish* is not difficult to detect. It will remind us that in that culture creation was generally part of a more complex mythic pattern featuring conflict of the deity with the forces of chaos and disorder and concluding with the construction of a temple for the victorious god. In *Enuma Elish*, Marduk's temple is built over the Apsū, the abyss, and the climax is the solemn enthronement of the deity followed by creative or recreative acts (*Enuma Elish* VI 51–65). Echoes of this more complex pattern can be picked up in those psalms which celebrate the enthronement of Yahweh (Pss 47, 93, 96–99). According to one of these liturgical poets Yahweh is enthroned over the abyss, the subterranean flood waters: 'The Lord sits enthroned over the flood, the Lord sits enthroned for ever' (Ps. 29:10).

While the Mesopotamian literary grounding is fundamental in all this, it has become evident since the publication of the Ugaritic mythological texts from the Late Bronze Age that much of the mythological language in biblical poetry transmits a Syro-Palestinian or Canaanite version of the pattern. In the Baal cycle from Ugarit, Baal, son of the supreme deity El, defeats and kills Yamm (Sea) with a little help from his bloodthirsty sister Anath and with the aid of magical weapons. A house (i.e. a temple) is built for him and he is solemnly enthroned

---

19 Since myths are often expressed through ritual action, the question arises whether Genesis 1 was composed for recital in a ritual, as *Enuma Elish* was recited on the fourth day of the *akitu* New Year festival. Some commentators have suggested the celebration of the kingship of Yahweh at Sukkoth (Tabernacles), a plausible hypothesis but evidence is lacking.

20 REB, more adventurously: '[you] threw him to the sharks for food'.

as ruler of the gods. An apocalyptic-sounding passage in Isaiah replicates almost verbatim the point in the Ugaritic Baal cycle at which Baal is praised for having slain 'Lotan [identical with Leviathan] the pursuing serpent, the twisting serpent, the seven-headed monster':

On that day
Yahweh will punish with his sword
grim, mighty, and strong,
Leviathan the pursuing serpent,
Leviathan the twisting serpent,
and he will slay the Dragon [Tannin] which is in the Sea. (Isa. 27:1)[21]

Here and elsewhere (Isa. 51:9-10; Job 28:14) the sea is identical with the abyss, the *tĕhôm* of Gen. 1:2. In another late Isaianic passage the seer asks rhetorically:

Was it not you that hacked Rahab in pieces,
that ran the Dragon through?
Was it not you that dried up the sea,
the waters of the Great abyss? (Isa. 51:9-10)

The abyss or, in the Ugaritic–Phoenician–Canaanite tradition, the sea, is therefore the domain of monstrous creatures, dragons (*tannînîm*) and the seven-headed Leviathan. But in Hebrew lore, unlike Ugarit, the sea (Hebrew: *yām*) is not personified. In Psalm 74, cited earlier, it is stirred up in order to bring to the surface the monstrous beings lurking within it, and a similar image is presented in Daniel's dream-vision of the emergence of monsters from the sea (Dan. 7:2-3). Something analogous is the case with the 'Song at the (Papyrus) Sea' in Exodus 15, thought by some scholars to be one of the oldest poems in the Hebrew Bible. In this poem Egypt, not the sea, is the enemy (Exod. 15:5,8).[22] As noted earlier, in biblical poetry the sea is confined within its proper bounds in keeping with the language of the creation and flood narratives, a point with a certain resonance in an age of global warming.

You set a boundary that they may not transgress,
lest they once again cover the earth. (Ps. 104:9)

---

21 For the Ugaritic text see *ANET* 130–31; Coogan 1978: 106. For the Baal cycle as a whole see *KTU²* 1.2.iv; 1.3.iii; 1.5.i.
22 'The sea is not personified or hostile, but a passive instrument in Yahweh's control. There is no question here of a mythological combat between two gods. Yahweh defeats historical, human enemies' (Cross 1973: 131–32). The same can be said about Isa. 51:9-10 in which the sea is dried up in order to reveal Rahab and Tannin.

If this mythical sea is not itself personified, it is the abode of monstrous creatures of malevolent will which embody the threat of terminal disorder directed against the inhabitants of dry land, a threat which is checked but not eliminated by the first creation.[23] The best-known of these creatures is Leviathan (*litānu* in the Ugaritic texts), an immense, serpentine creature, seven-headed like the Hydra slain by Heracles.[24] According to a later opinion, Leviathan was female like Tiāmat, the salt-ocean goddess, while its male counterpart, Behemoth, was a land creature (*1 En.* 60:7-9, 24). Yet later tradition mitigated the terror and threat by representing Leviathan as a source of protein for the elect (2 Esd. 6:49-52; *2 Bar.* 29:4; Targum on Gen. 1:21). Closely associated, if not actually identical with Leviathan under different names, are the Dragon (Tannin) and Rahab. The former is perhaps the product of a mythicization of very large aquatic creatures (whales, narwhals, sharks) no doubt known to Eastern Mediterranean peoples from early times. Such *tannînîm* were created on the fifth day of the first week (Gen. 1:21) and are admonished by the psalmist to praise God (Ps. 148:7). The great Tannin is however a creature of a quite different kind, a monstrous being which opposed God in the cosmic war preceding the six-day creation (Isa. 27:1; 51:9) and will no doubt 'raise its fabulous green head' (a phrase of Robert Graves) at the end of the age. The same role and much the same characteristics are assigned to Rahab (Ps. 89:11; Job 9:13; 26:12; Isa. 51:9), though both Tannin and Rahab are historicized as personifications of Egypt and its Pharaoh.[25]

These embodiments of blind malevolence and disorder, denizens of the Abyss, present before the creation of earth and sky, symbolize aspects of human experience which evade rational control, confound our philosophies and theologies, and raise the sharpest and most persistent questions about the endemic downward spiral of evil and the countervailing power and benevolence of the God we worship. Nowhere does this come to clearer expression in terms of moral dilemma and disorder than in the book of Job. The prologue (Job 1–2) makes it clear that what will happen to Job – the abject physical and mental suffering, the loss of self-esteem, the collapse of a sense of moral rationality – is determined from outside his world, in the assembly of the 'sons of God' where the deity and his attendant, the Satan acting as *agent provocateur*, make their wager and prepare their laboratory experiment. They know the reason for what is about to happen, we the readers know, but Job does not. It will not surprise us that the theme of creation and the forces hostile to the creation feature so often in a debate which attempts to make sense of the suffering of one who, like the ancient patriarchs, is blameless, upright, and God-fearing

---

23 On these monstrous creatures see Kaiser 1959; Day 1985; Levenson 1985.
24 Pss 74:12-14; 104:26; Job 3:8; 26:13; 40:25; Isa. 27:1. For details and further references, see Uehlinger 1999.
25 Ps. 87:4; Isa. 30:7; Ezek. 29:3; 32:2; on which see van der Toorn 1999; Heider 1999.

(Job 1:1). Job begins by cursing the night of his conception and the day of his birth, and he does so in terms of a reversal of creation into non-being, of light into darkness (3:1-10). Sea – or perhaps the sea monster – and Leviathan are conjured up to put out the light of the heavenly luminaries and remove the day of his birth from the calendar. He expresses the wish that

> They may curse it who cast spells on the Sea,
> who are skilled to conjure up Leviathan. (3:8)

The image is perhaps based on the belief that the cosmic sea serpent can, by magic, be conjured up and coerced to cause an eclipse either by swallowing the sun or the moon or wrapping its coils around them.[26] There hangs over the book the threat of a moral void, an absence of rationality and meaning, in a world which at the beginning, as Job affirms, was suspended over nothingness, non-being (26:7).[27] Job ends in humility and acceptance, but not before putting this mythological theology of creation and counter-creation, being and non-being, to the test of personal experience.[28]

If these counter-forces to creation are not completely beyond the reach of the divine power, we might want to ask how, in the biblical scheme of things, they came into existence. It is of course possible that they represent a partially unresolved and unassimilated element of the theology of the priest–author. It is possible, but should not be too easily assumed since this author knows that these forces continue to threaten the rationality and order laid out in the first creation week. In fact, the threat became terminal after 1,656 years according to the Genesis chronology with the violent dissolution of the earth into the primaeval watery mass in the great deluge. This is part of a larger issue not often raised in commentary on Genesis 1. Is the creative activity of the first week all that can be said about creation? What of the origin not only of the *těhôm* and its monstrous surrogates but of spiritual entities, angels and demons, whose existence is uncontested in Jewish, Christian and Islamic tradition but of whom nothing is said in the creation story?

26   G. R. Driver cites an Aramaic incantation 'I will cast spells upon you with the spell of the Sea and the spell of the dragon Leviathan' (1955: 72). See also Albright (1938: 227), who understands 'sea' (*yām*) in this text against the background of Ugaritic *yammu*, the sea monster.
27   'God spreads the vault of the sky over the void/God suspends the earth over nothingness' (Job 26:7). The void over which the vault of the sky (*sāpôn*, 'north', 'northern sky'; cf. Isa. 14:13) is spread is the *tōhû* reminiscent of the *tōhû wābōhû* of Gen. 1:2. In the parallel line the Creator suspends the earth over *bělî-māh*, a hapax legomenon, literally, 'without anything', 'nothingness', 'non-being'.
28   See Ricoeur on 'the tragic myth' (1967: 306–46).

The Praise of the Creator God in Psalms

A more positive view of creation understood both as event and as a way of thinking about the world can be found in the hymns. Psalm 8 ('Lord, our sovereign, how glorious is your name throughout the world!') praises Yahweh God whose name, therefore whose creative power, is manifested throughout the world and acknowledged in the contemplation of the sky, the moon and stars.[29] The same power also restrains the adversary and avenger (v. 3b, MT) which, in the context, would most naturally refer to that forces hostile to the created order prefigured in the chaos or great deep encountered at the beginning of the creation narrative (Gen. 1:2). The hymn then moves from the cosmic to the human level and, in the spirit of Gen. 1:26-28, though not necessarily dependent on that text, wonders at the dignity, little short of divine, conferred on the human being, appointed overseer of creation.

Psalm 19 ('The heavens tell the glory of God'), another psalm of praise and wonder, is more a meditation than a prayer addressed to the Creator God. The heavens tell the glory of God, the great dome of the sky proclaims his handiwork, and the succession of day and night sends forth the same message, day passing it on to day and night to night. The message reaches from one end of the world to the other even without the use of human language (vv. 2-5a).[30] The sun moves majestically from one end of the sky to the other and nothing is hidden from its heat (vv. 5b-7). At this point of the poem there is a sudden shift from the contemplation of nature to the law of God. The poet identifies this law with six different terms all of which are familiar from the Israelite legal tradition, and we may be sure that the devout Israelite, hearing or praying this psalm, would take the law in question to be the Torah. This may be so, but nothing more specific with respect to the content of the law is mentioned. All we are told about it is that it is revealed by God, it revives the soul, confers wisdom on the simple, is upright and rejoices the heart, is pure and enlightening, is true, unsullied, abiding for ever, more desirable than the finest gold, sweeter than honey and the honeycomb (vv. 8-11). More to the point, the juxtaposition in this psalm of the natural order proclaiming the glory of God as Creator in the first half of the poem with an encomium on the law of God in the second half suggests that the law in question is understood in a more general if undefined sense to be divine

29   Psalm 8 seems to have served as inspiration for that splendid hymn 'O Lord our God when I with awesome wonder / consider all the world Thy hands have made / I see the stars, I hear the rolling thunder / Thy power throughout the universe displayed.'

30   There is a linguistic problem in v. 5a where MT reads 'Their line (*qawwām*) goes forth in all the earth' which seems improbable; cf. NRSV, 'their voice' (*qôlām*), and NEB, 'their music' supported by James Barr in his discussion of this psalm in *Biblical Faith and Natural Theology* (1993: 87n.), though REB now has 'their sign'. 'Their music' could refer to the ancient belief in 'the music of the spheres'; cf. Job 38:7, the morning stars singing together.

instruction universally available to anyone open to accepting it. In that case, it could be read as a remote preparation for what will be said later about natural law in Wisdom 13 and Paul's Epistle to the Romans (1:18–2:16).

Psalm 104, ('Bless the Lord, O my soul'), presents a particularly interesting instance of the combination of creation as primordial event with God's creative activity in preserving and sustaining the created order. The psalm begins and ends with praise of the Creator God (vv. 1, 31-35). The first part of the poem is a description of the creation of sky and earth interestingly different with respect to order and technique from the priest–author's version in Genesis 1. The creation of the sky reads as follows:

> You spread out the sky like a tent,
> you laid the beams of your upper chambers in the waters;
> you make the clouds your chariot, riding on the wings of the wind;
> you use the winds (spirits?[31]) as your messengers,
> your ministers are a flame of fire. (Ps. 104:2-4)

As in Genesis 1, the dome of the sky holds back the upper waters, allowing for a habitable space supported by piles driven down through the lower waters, the *těhôm rabbâ*, the great deep or abyss. The 'upper chambers' refer to the abode of God, and the depiction of the divine charioteer incorporates a theme familiar from North-West Semitic myth and iconography (cf. Yahweh 'rider on the clouds', Ps. 68:5a emended text). The messengers (*malʾākîm*, also 'angels') and ministers (*měšārětîm*, usually with the meaning 'liturgical ministers') could then be an allusion to spiritual beings the creation of whom is missing from Genesis 1. What the psalm has to say about the creation of the earth differs in some respects from the imagery of Genesis 1:

> You set the earth on its foundations
> so that it might never be moved,
> You covered it with the abyss as with a garment,
> and the waters stood above the mountains.
> Then at your rebuke they fled,
> at the sound of your thunder they took to flight.
> They flowed over the mountains,
> down into the valleys
> to the place you ordained for them.
> You established a boundary they were not to pass,
> never again to cover the earth. (Ps. 104:5-9)

---

31 *rûhôt*, usually translated 'winds', could also be translated 'spirits', like the spirit who served in Yahweh's heavenly court in the vision of the seer Micaiah (1 Kgs 22:21-22).

At the beginning the earth, supported on piles or columns, is entirely covered by water. Creation then consists in causing the water to run off leaving the earth, mountains, valleys and everything else exposed and ready for human and animal habitation. The watery chaos is then confined within bounds to prevent it encroaching on the habitable world, a process which is reversed in the account of the great deluge to which, however, this psalm makes no reference. Water is therefore a source of the greatest danger, a truth we have come to appreciate more keenly in recent years, but it is also the source of abundant fertility and growth, part of the life-sustaining order together with the heavenly bodies and the succession of day and night which dictate the life cycles of animals and human beings. Similarity with the Aten Hymn ascribed to Pharaoh Akhenaten, formerly Amenhotep IV (1367–1350 BC), has long been recognized. In this hymn the Aten has a creative and sustaining role in human affairs comparable to *ḥokmâ* (wisdom) in the psalm. A brief excerpt from the prose translation of Sir Alan Gardiner will make the point:

> How manifold are they works. They are mysterious in men's sight. Thou sole god, like to whom there is none other. Thou didst create the earth after thy heart, being alone, even all men, herds, and flocks, whatever is upon earth, creatures that walk upon feet, which soar aloft flying with their wings ... Thou settest every man in his place, and makest their sustenance, each one possessing his food, and his term of life counted; tongues made diverse in speech and their characters likewise; their complexions distinguished, for thou hast distinguished country and country. (Gardiner 1999: 219)[32]

In the hymn and the psalm all of this evidence of order and harmony is presented as an extension of an initial and benevolent creative act, attributed in the hymn to the divine sun disc, in the psalm to divine wisdom:

> How manifold are your works, O Lord,
> in wisdom you have made them all! (Ps. 104:24)

The divine wisdom active in creation is also acknowledged in the Qumran hymns of praise (e.g. *Hodayot* IX 7, 13–14) which have much more to say about the creation of spiritual beings – angels, luminaries, astral spirits – than the canonical psalms (*Hodayot* V 13–19; IX 10–12). The theological ambience of these psalms would, however, call for a closer study than can be undertaken here (Nitzan 2002).

---

32 Gardiner's translation may be compared with that of John A. Wilson, *ANET* 369–71.

Transcendent Wisdom

In Psalm 104 the psalmist praises God for his creative works by means of which, here and now, God provides for the innumerable living creatures on land, sea and air including, since this is the second creation and we are no longer in Eden, the lions roaring for their prey and seeking their meat from God (v. 21). Creation is therefore seen as an ongoing activity, a process rather than simply a first moment in time. All of this, the psalmist concludes, has been brought about through wisdom (v. 24). 'Wisdom' is one of those slippery terms that can mean different things in different contexts. At an early stage it connoted in both Hebrew and Greek (*hokmâ* and *sophia* respectively) a particular skill like that of the metal smith (Exod. 31:1-11), stonemason (1 Chron. 22:15) or carpenter (*Iliad* 15:412). It could also be attributed to a person of intelligence, knowledge and judgement, one to whom people could have recourse for counsel. Biblical examples would be 'professionals' like the wise woman of Tekoa (2 Sam. 14) and Ahithophel whose counsel was as if one consulted a divine oracle (2 Sam. 16:23). To these we may add ben Sira, scribe, teacher and intellectual (Sir. 38:24-25; 51:23), one of those who, so he himself informs us, maintain the fabric of the world (Sir. 38:34). By his time, the early second century BC, the Greek philosophical tradition had been long established. Socrates tells Phaedrus that only God can be called wise, but someone like Homer or Solon could be called a lover of wisdom, that is, a philosopher (*Phaedrus* 278D). For Aristotle, wisdom was the highest of the intellectual virtues, but it could also apply to one endowed with consummate skill, like the sculptor Phidias (*Nichomachean Ethics* VI vii 1–7; X vii 1). For the Stoics the sage (*sophos*) was the ideal of virtue, and members of the school expatiated at great length on his attributes (Arnim 1905: 216; 1903: 544–670).[33]

Coming back to the late-Judaean or early Jewish environment: texts of a more didactic and reflective nature, usually categorized as 'wisdom writings', often speak of elements of order and beauty behind the apparent chaos of the everyday experience of the world. Job receives no theoretically satisfying answer to his agonized appeal for redress and for *meaning* even more than redress. He is brusquely reminded that he is incapable of making sense of the world because he fails to understand natural phenomena, surveyed over an extremely broad range, in the light of their origins. He is invited to learn to look at the world around him as testifying to the ongoing creative and sustaining activity of a wise deity (Job 38–41). The reminder is not developed into a clear and coherent demonstration, but some light can be thrown on it by turning to the poem on inaccessible wisdom in Job 28. In its context in the book the poem is ascribed to Job, but it makes a poor fit with Job's mood. It anticipates the eventual denouement and

---

33 For a thorough account of the terms *hokmâ* and *sophia* see, respectively, Müller and Krause 1980 and Wilckens and Fohrer 1971.

follows a passage (Job 27:13-23) which argues strenuously that the wicked get their comeuppance in this life, a conclusion which Job has expended a great deal of energy and passion in denying. It is therefore in all probability an independent poem, one of the great poems of the Hebrew Bible certainly, which has been inserted at this point. It opens with the powerful metaphor of mining for precious metals, indicative of the great price that must be paid for the acquisition of wisdom, working long hours underground, far from the haunts of everyday life.

> That path no bird of prey knows,
> and the falcon's eye has not seen it.
> The proud wild animals have not trodden it,
> the lion has not passed over it. (Job 28:7-8)

The question which forms a kind of refrain to the poem:

> Where then can wisdom be found,
> where is the place of understanding? (Job 28:12, 20)

is addressed to all parts of the cosmos, including the deep (*tĕhôm*) and the primaeval sea (*yamm*) neither of whom has an answer. Even death that presides over everything has heard only a rumour of it (Job 28:22). The conclusion is that only God is the source of wisdom since only God was present at the creation (28:23-27).[34] The answer therefore shades off into mystery.

There seems to be a conviction behind much that is said in these writings that transcendent wisdom, reflecting the divine nature, is, in principle, detectable in the order and beauty of the phenomenal world, most clearly and strikingly, for both the ancients and ourselves, in the regularity of the movements of the sun, moon, planets and stars. Divine wisdom, says the learned ben Sira, is poured out on all creation including all human beings who are open to it (Sir. 1:9-10). The principle which governed creation at the beginning remains constituent of the fabric of physical reality in the world (Sir. 1:1-10), so that all creation is arranged according to an order (*kosmos*, 16:26-30) or plan (*logismos*, 43:23). The same idea is expressed in Wisdom in terms of the Stoic concept of an immanent divine power which pervades the world:

> She reaches mightily from one end of the earth to the other,
> and orders everything well. (Wis. 8:1)

This way of looking at the physical world, which antedates its different philosophical formulations, leads inevitably to assigning a role to wisdom in

---

34   The final verse, 'The fear of the Lord is wisdom / and to turn from evil is [true] understanding' (Ps. 28:28), rather undermines the point of the poem and has probably been added.

the initial creation, an extremely important development for the early Christian understanding of the cosmic role of Christ and creation in general.

Wisdom, First-Created, First-Generated

The work of the six days deals only with the visible creation beginning with the first word which summoned light out of darkness (Gen. 1:3). As in Plato's *Timaeus* (28B–30A), in which the phenomenal, orderly world is the result of God acting on chaos, the passive principle, the Genesis creation account is essentially an eliciting of order out of chaos while leaving unexplained the origin of what was there before this first word was spoken. The abyss (*těhôm*) remains somehow part of the structure of visible reality. It reappears catastrophically with the deluge and, as some apocalypticists believed, and still believe, will erupt once again at the end of the age – a not entirely incredible belief at a time of melting ice caps and global warming. The visible creation is therefore not the sum total of the created order, no more than the visible mass of the universe is all that there is, indeed, only a small part of what there is if the astrophysicists are right about the extent of dark energy and dark matter. The origin of spiritual substance, of spiritual agents both benign and hostile to God's creation, an essential element of Jewish, Christian and Muslim belief,[35] is not part of the Genesis 1 narrative. Unless we are to conclude that they are uncreated and therefore co-eternal with God, their origins either remain to be discovered between the lines of Genesis 1 or there is a creation apart from and prior to the work of the six days.

Augustine's interpretation of Gen. 1:1-2 in *Confessions* XII is an interesting example of attempting to cope with the difficult task of interpreting the first three verses of the Bible. The problem which interested him was that the creation of heaven is mentioned twice: before the work of the six days (1:1) and again on the second day (1:6-8). But since the latter is the visible heaven, created after light on the first day, the former must be a different and therefore invisible and spiritual heaven. Augustine found the solution to this puzzle in Ps. 113:24 in LXX (113:16 in the Vulgate, 115:16 in the MT) which reads, 'The heaven of heavens is the Lord's / the earth he has given to the children of men'.[36] This *caelum caeli* (Augustine did not read Hebrew and knew only little Greek) he took to be a created, intellectual being (*aliqua creatura intellectualis*) which, while not co-eternal with God, participated in God's eternity by contemplation of the divine essence (*Confessions* XII 9, 13). The earth given to humanity

---

35 The Nicaean creed professes faith in God *factorem coeli et terrae, visibilium omnium et invisibilium*, 'Maker of heaven and earth, of all things visible and invisible'.

36 LXX and Vulgate differ from the Hebrew text which reads 'The heavens are the Lord's heavens' (NRSV) or 'The heavens belong to the Lord' (REB).

would then refer to the entire material world, including the sky created on the second day. But then, having reached this conclusion influenced by his deep immersion in neo-Platonism, he goes on to concede that the heaven and earth of Gen. 1:1 may refer to spiritual and material formlessness – and therefore for Augustine timelessness – awaiting the creative word (*Confessions* XII 17). Subsequently, it seems, he lost interest in his hypothesis and preferred to think of angels as the highest order of spiritual creation.[37]

We meet angels at every turn in biblical narrative, in psalms and other poems, but nowhere are we informed about their origin. The only clue might be a text discussed earlier, God's address to Job (38:2-7) describing the laying of the foundation stone of the cosmic temple, with the 'sons of God' and the morning stars, divine or angelic beings, participating in the ceremony with joyful song. The silence of the biblical tradition leaves us some space for imaginative re-creation. Our sense of the superiority of the spiritual to the material would tend to make us think of spiritual creation necessarily prior to the work of the six days, but this may simply be a product of our unavoidable tendency to think in terms of temporal succession, of explaining by constructing a narrative, following the example of the author of Genesis 1. In re-imagining the creation, the author of *Jubilees* places the origin of the angels of the presence and the lower orders who preside over natural phenomena on the first of the six days (*Jub.* 2:2). The *Slavonic Enoch* (*2 Enoch*), a text full of strange and hallucinatory images, perhaps from the first or second century AD, places the creation of myriads of angels and the fall of the rebellious angel Satanail on the second day (*2 En.* 29 [J]), while a rabbinic opinion held that angels must have been created together with other winged creatures on the fifth day (Ginzberg 1955: 20–21). But might we not, in more sober fashion, imagine these spirit-entities, creatures of light, coming into being with the vast explosion of light on the first day? Or might it not be possible to think of the spiritual as, somehow, co-existent and co-efficient with the visible, material world, as some also of our poets have speculated?

The one biblically well-attested creation before the six days is that of personified Wisdom, antidote to the negative forces which oppose the good creation. This representation, the point of departure for one of the most important theological trajectories in early Judaism and Christianity, calls for attention in any serious theological study of the biblical creation account. We begin with the poem about Wisdom, firstborn of creation, in Prov. 8:22-31:

Yahweh created me as the beginning of his work
before any of his deeds of old.
Ages ago I was fashioned,

---

37 Augustine's debt to Plotinus, especially *Enneads* II 4 and III 6, is emphasized by O'Connell 1969: 145–57. I have also been helped by reading Knuuttila 2001: 103–15.

from the beginning, from the origins of the earth.
When there were yet no deeps I was brought forth,
no springs with water abounding;
before the mountains were laid down,
before the hills I was brought forth;
before he made the earth and its open spaces
or the world's first clods of earth.
When he set the sky in place I was there,
when he marked out a circle on the face of the Deep.
When he fixed the cloud-cover above
and made strong the fountains of the deep;
when he issued a statute for the sea
that its water not transgress his command;
when he strengthened the foundations of the earth –
I was with him, his delight and joy,
jubilant day after day,
rejoicing in his presence all the time
rejoicing in the world he had made,
jubilant with the human race.

The poem has probably been interpolated into Wisdom's public discourse to her 'children' which consists in moral exhortation of a fairly mundane nature, quite unlike the imaginative and arcane language of the poem itself. Allusion to Wisdom's 'way' immediately before and after (vv. 20, 32) would have provided the catchword for the insertion which opens with an allusion to Yahweh's 'way', that is, his creative activity.

The verb *qānāh*, translated 'create' in 8:22, has the more usual meaning 'to acquire', as elsewhere in the book where the acquisition of wisdom, understanding and knowledge is inculcated (e.g. Prov. 1:5; 4:5; 23:23). This sense would not be appropriate here at the beginning of the poem since no Jewish author would refer to Yahweh acquiring wisdom. The composition of the poem and its insertion into the book cannot easily be dated, but its literary type and themes suggest the century of Ptolemaic rule over the province of Judah (ca. 310–200 BC), on which more will be said shortly.[38]

What is Wisdom claiming in this statement about her origins and her relation to God? In the first place, primordiality. She came into existence before the earth with its many sources of water, its mountains and hills, its entire material substance. We saw earlier that this literary trope is characteristic of the theogony, the birth and genealogy of a god or goddess, exemplified in *Enuma Elish*. This feature helps to explain why the author speaks in a

---

38 On the date see Toy 1899: 171–79; Knox 1937; Fox 2000: 48–49, 279–89.

deliberately ambiguous way about Wisdom's origins. We have just seen that the verb *qānāh* more often than not means to acquire by personal effort or purchase but also, by extension, to create.[39] But it can also mean to acquire by begetting, by giving birth, as in the joyful cry of Eve at the birth of her son Cain, 'I have acquired (*qānîtî*) a male child with (the help of) Yahweh' (Gen. 4:1). That this is the tacit element in Wisdom's opening statement is confirmed immediately afterwards when she speaks of the time of her birth (Prov. 8:24, 25), and it is consistent with her portrayal at the end of the poem as God's delight and joy in whose presence she rejoices – or, depending on the translator – plays, frolics or sports. This kind of language towards the end of the poem, intimating that Wisdom is God's beloved daughter, would seem to rule out the alternative understanding of the obscure term *ʾāmôn* in v. 30 as an artisan commissioned to assist in the work of creation, in much the same way that Moses commissioned Bezalel, a skilled worker full of the spirit and wisdom, to make the wilderness sanctuary (Exod. 35:31). In his commentary on Proverbs 1–9, Michael Fox describes the hapax legomenon *ʾāmôn* as 'one of the great puzzles of the Hebrew Bible' (2000: 285).

Personification is one of the key literary devices in the book of Proverbs. The teachings of the sage are wisdom personified, and since Hebrew *ḥokmâ*, like Greek *sophia*, is feminine, wisdom can have the attributes of a good, virtuous, and desirable woman. The editor who arranged the aphoristic material in the book placed the personification in high relief by bracketing the seven collections of aphorisms with a discourse about the woman Wisdom at the beginning (Prov. 1–9) and an acrostic poem in praise of an idealized feminine figure at the end (31:10-31). Elsewhere in the Hebrew Bible cities and countries are frequently personified (Virgin Daughter Zion, Virgin Daughter Babylon, etc.), but in contrast to Greek practice (e.g. *eris*, *nemesis*, *tuchē*) personification of abstract qualities is relatively rare in classical Hebrew literature. An interesting parallel to the self-description of Wisdom in Prov. 8:22-31 can be found in the Egyptian mythic biography of the goddess Maʿat, daughter of the sun god Re. As his favourite child, she came down to humanity at the beginning of time as the embodiment and preserver of cosmic order (*maʿat* in Egyptian) and the guardian of justice. Without her benign influence even the gods could not survive, and the world would collapse into chaos and ruin. She is therefore the counter-force to those monsters of the abyss, embodiments of chaos, hostile to the good creation, discussed earlier. The parallelism between this goddess figure and the woman Wisdom in Proverbs is close enough to suggest the possibility that the author, especially if writing under the rule of the Egyptianized Ptolemies, was making reflective use of this popular myth. If so, he would be adopting, in a more concentrated form, a practice attested throughout the collections of aphorisms in Proverbs where the sage's teaching is described as the

39 See Gen. 14:19 and 22, where God Most High (*ʾēl ʿelyôn*) is identified as creator of heaven and earth (*qōnēh šāmayim wāʾāreṣ*); also Deut. 32:6, and the description of the supreme deity El as 'creator of earth' (*qn ʾrṣ*) in the Ugaritic mythological texts.

tree of life (11:30), the fountain of life (13:14), a house with seven pillars (9:1). This way of addressing philosophical and moral issues is comparable to Plato's use of myth, for example the Myth of Er at the end of the *Republic*, or the allegorizing of myth by the Stoics as a way of presenting their teachings.

A further stage in this figurative presentation of wisdom can be found in the moral treatise composed in the early decades of the second century BC by Jesus ben Elʿazar ben Sira, a work known in the Latin Bible as Ecclesiasticus, the church book, incidentally the first biblical (or deuterocanonical) book in which the author identifies himself (Sir. 50:27). The literally and no doubt deliberately central statement of Ben Sira's book (Sir. 24:1-22) is the self-praise of Wisdom speaking in the persona of the *Ḥokmâ*–Sophia of Prov. 8:22-31. In the presence of the divine assembly, Sophia (let us give her her more familiar Greek name) relates how she proceeded from the mouth of God at the beginning of time before anything else was created; how she came down among humanity in search of a resting place; and how her quest ended when she took up residence in Jerusalem (Sir. 24:1-12). From there she issues her invitation to her devotees in sumptuous and erotic terms – eating, drinking, honey and the honeycomb, and the like – to make the point that wisdom is the supreme object of desire and its acquisition the supreme goal of living (Sir. 24:13-22).

There is broad agreement that Sophia's discourse in this passage is modelled on the aretalogy, that is, the self-praise of a deity which details the deity's attributes, achievements and (generally miraculous) powers. In view of the time and circumstances of composition, the deity whose self-praise has inspired Sophia's paean would be the great Egyptian goddess Isis, closely associated with Maʿat. The cult of Isis, 'mistress of life and mistress of the heavens', whose principal sanctuary at Philae at the first cataract of the Nile was a centre of pilgrimage, enormously popular throughout the Ptolemaic empire and down into the Roman period. Several of her aretalogies have survived. One of the best known can be recovered from the famous scene in which, in the course of an initiation ceremony, the goddess addresses the hapless Lucius before bringing about his transformation from asinine to human form in the *Metamorphoses* of Apuleius (11: 5):

> I [am] the mother of the universe, mistress of all the elements, and first offspring of the ages; mightiest of deities, queen of the dead, and foremost of heavenly beings; my one person manifests the aspect of all gods and goddesses. With my nod I rule the starry heights of heaven, the health-giving breezes of the sea, and the plaintive silences of the underworld. My divinity is one, worshipped by all the world under different forms, with various rites and by manifold names.[40]

A much briefer example is reported by Diodorus Siculus (I 27.3–4) in which Isis proclaims herself eldest daughter of the god Kronos. In a third, inscribed on a

---

40   The translation is that of J. Arthur Hanson, *LCL* 453.

column in Memphis, she lists her titles and speaks of her role in the creation of the world:

> I divided the earth from the heaven;
> I showed the path of the stars;
> I ordered the course of the sun and moon.

Like Maʿat, with whom she was inevitably identified, Isis was the ultimate guarantor of justice and the embodiment of cosmic and social order. It was no doubt these attributes which led ben Sira, in his commentary on the poem (24:23-29), to identify pre-existent Wisdom with the Jewish Torah:

> All this is the book of the covenant of the Most High God,
> the law which Moses commanded us. (24:23)

The implication is that the law of Moses is the supramundane principle of moral order in the form in which it has been made available to Israel. In presenting an indigenized form of a non-Jewish liturgical genre, that is, aretalogy, the author is therefore claiming for the Jewish law a universal significance and respectability, and by so doing he no doubt also aimed to answer charges of intellectual obscurantism and xenophobia directed at Judaism which were in the air at that time.

The way in which ben Sira identifies the Law with Wisdom, *tôrâ* with *ḥokmâ*, is adumbrated in Deuteronomy where the law is the equivalent for Israel of the wisdom claimed by other peoples (Deut. 4:6). The identification will lead almost inevitably to the idea of the Law's pre-existence. The way was prepared by the self-predication of wisdom personified in Proverbs 8, and the statement in the same book that wisdom was the means or agency by which God created the world (Prov. 3:19). Hence it seemed justified to claim, with Rabbi Akiva, that Israel was blessed 'for to them was given the instrument with which the world was created'. According to another baraita (*Gen. R.* 1:4), the *tôrâ* was the first of six entities which preceded the creation of the world, an affirmation based on Prov. 8:22. The same point was made in a more roundabout way by a piece of exegetical virtuosity attributed to Rabbi Hoshaya, a contemporary and fellow-citizen of Origen in Caesarea. By linking 'in the beginning' of Gen. 1:1 with 'the beginning of his way' of Prov. 8:22, the key word being *rēʾšît* which appears in both places, Hoshaya concluded that God consulted the Torah before creating the world. Hoshaya elaborated as follows:

> In human practice, when a mortal king builds a palace, he builds it not with his own skill but with the skill of an architect. The architect moreover does not build it out of his head, but employs plans and diagrams to know how to arrange the chambers and the wicket doors. Thus God consulted the Torah and created the world. (*Gen. R.* 1:1)

Another third-century sage, Rabbi Simon, took this a step further, perhaps a step too far, in affirming that God read the whole of Genesis (which, *ex hypothesi*, God had written) and then created the world (*Gen. R.* 3:5), an idea which we imagine would have appealed to Borges.[41]

The idea of the created world as the reproduction of a model or archetype, borrowed from the Platonic theory of ideal forms, also served for Philo as a hermeneutic tool for interpreting the biblical account of creation. An intimation of this approach is his statement that 'wisdom is God's archetypal luminary and the sun is a copy and image of it' (*On the Migration of Abraham* 40). In his treatise *On the Creation of the World* it is stated more explicitly: 'When God proposed to create this visible world, he first made the intelligible world (*kosmon noēton*) as a model, in order that employing an immaterial and most godlike pattern he might produce the material world, a younger copy of the elder.' He followed up this Platonic idea of creation with an analogy similar to that of Rabbi Hoshaya:

> When a king proposes to found a new city he employs an engineer who surveys the ground, forms a plan in his mind, and makes a model of stone or wood (*On the Creation of the World* 16–17).

The material, visible world is real only by virtue of its correspondence to an ideal in the mind of God.

The pre-existence of Wisdom and her role in creation were therefore familiar in Jewish circles well before the advent of Christianity, including at Qumran (Harrington 2000). In the earliest Christian writings, and probably also in early Christian liturgies, we see how this wisdom trajectory served to nourish reflection on the transcendence and cosmic significance of Christ. Pre-existent Sophia therefore prepared the way for the pre-existent Word, thence for the pre-existent Christ. This opens up a broad, many-faceted, and immensely important theological issue on which a great deal has been written. It must suffice here to point briefly to one aspect of what would be part of a Christian theology of creation (Wilken 1975; Bouteneff 2008). In his first extant letter to the Christians in Corinth, written in the early 50s, Paul identifies Christ as the wisdom of God (1 Cor. 1:24) and the one through whom all things came to be (1 Cor. 8:6). A similar affirmation is made in the opening paragraph of the Epistle to the Hebrews: God created the universe and maintains it through God's all-sustaining Word (Heb. 1:2-3). For the Fourth Gospel, composed towards the end of the first century, Christ, is the Word of God, and therefore also the word spoken at the creation. All things came to be through him, and without him nothing created came to be (Jn 1:1-3). Here and elsewhere in early Christian writings the pre-existence of Wisdom is propaedeutic to belief in the pre-existence of Christ.

---

41 For other rabbinic speculations on the creation story, see Ginzberg 1955, 1961; and on the primordiality and perpetuity of the law, Moore 1927: 1:263–80.

The fullest and most revealing statement on this subject is found in what most scholars identify as an early Christian doxological hymn adopted to its present context. The lines relevant for our purpose read as follows (Col. 1:15-17):

> He is the image of the invisible God,
> the firstborn of all creation;
> for in him everything in heaven and on earth was created,
> things visible and invisible,
> whether thrones or sovereignties, authorities or powers.
> All things were created through him and for him;
> he exists before all things,
> all things are held together in him.

The language of this hymn reproduces much of what had already been claimed for pre-existent Wisdom's intimate association with God in the work of creation. Christ is the image (*eikōn*) of the invisible God as Wisdom is the *eikōn* of God's goodness and a reflection of eternal light (Wis. 7:26). Implicit in this statement is an allusion to the *imago dei*, the affirmation that all human beings are created in the divine image (Gen. 1:26-28) or, with the author of the Wisdom of Solomon, that 'God made us as an image (again, *eikōn*) of God's own nature' (Wis. 2:23). Christ as the firstborn of creation and the mediator of all God's creative activity likewise corresponds to what is said about Wisdom in the texts referred to earlier. The insistence on Christ's mediating position in relation to the invisible, cosmic 'powers and principalities', the 'gods who rule the world' (Wis. 13:2), here and throughout the Pauline corpus (Rom. 8:38; 1 Cor. 15:24; Eph. 1:21; 3:10; 6:12; Col. 2:10, 15), arose from the need to counter unacceptable opinions about how these powers related to the risen and glorified Christ but also, in part, from the failure of Genesis 1 to account for *invisibilia* as well as *visibilia*. Finally, the statement that the creation is held together in Christ parallels the praise of Wisdom as the source of order in creation, the principle that holds all things together (Wis. 1:7), reaching mightily from one end of the earth to the other, and ordering all things well (Wis. 8:1).

Summary

The priest–author's creation account takes its place in a long tradition of reflection on cosmic and human origins in the ancient Near East and the eastern Mediterranean. According to this tradition, the creation of humanity is part of a history antedating humanity's appearance on the scene, a history in which disorder and violence are much in evidence. In Genesis 1 the goodness of the creation and the dignity of the human being, male and female, is repeatedly emphasized, probably in deliberate contrast to that history. There is, however, a residue of this inherited mythic aetiology of physical and moral evil in the biblical account of what was there at the beginning, before the creation week, namely, the formless void, the abyss. Since it was from this dark, shapeless mass that the creative word of God summoned the visible world, the latter could retain traces of its origins; its primal matter remains inseparably part of its fabric. That this is so is evident from the narrative of the deluge in which the world reverted to the chaos from which it emerged, and did so consequent on the moral corruption of its inhabitants. The same perspective is expressed figuratively in psalms and other poetic compositions in which monstrous creatures, hostile to human life and the order which alone makes life worth living, threaten the foundations of rationality. The creative process by which order emerged out of chaos is therefore reversible. The threat of disorder and chaos, of evil both moral and physical, is never far away.

This reading of Genesis 1, especially of the first two verses of the chapter, does not entail a dualistic view of origins analogous to Zoroastrianism or those dualistic Gnostic sects which flourished in many parts of early Christianity. To speak of chaos as pre-existent is the inevitable outcome of the narrative model adopted by the author and, more basically, of the narrative and sequential character of Genesis 1 itself. The priest–author's recital provides clues to the kind of world and the kind of human society which can counter the persistent threat of physical and moral chaos without ever eliminating it. In the following chapters we will see how this understanding of the creation myth is given concrete expression in the history of early humanity down to and beyond the near-total annihilation of the deluge.

CHAPTER 3

The Story of the Man, the Woman and the Snake

The Eden Myth

If the priest–author's account is creation from the top down, this very different narrative is creation from the bottom up. A first clue to the difference is the reversal of order in the introductory sentence which links the second with the first account of origins. The link reads as follows:

> These are the generations [*toledot*] of *the heavens and the earth* when they were created. (Gen. 2:4a)
> On the day that the Lord God made *the earth and the heavens* ... (2:4b)

thus launching the story of the primaeval earth and the garden. The perspective now is local rather than cosmic. Instead of a shapeless mass, darkness and a great wind (Gen. 1:1-2), there is an earth without vegetation and inhabitants (2:5). The deity who presides over events is no longer anonymous, and no longer creates (*bārā'*) by uttering a word, but 'makes' (*'āśāh*) the earth and the sky, moulds a figure out of clay like a potter and brings it alive, plants a garden, walks about in it, makes things grow, anaethetizes the male in order to produce a female from his body, and talks to this first couple who appear on the scene fully grown.

Hence, this second story about origins has practically nothing in common with the one preceding it and nowhere refers to it. The juxtaposition of the two narratives nevertheless challenges the reader to look for connections. Until the early modern period, Genesis 1–3 was read continuously as one account of cosmic and human origins. This approach, which is of course still followed, is quite understandable, but taking account of the differences between Gen.

54

1:1–2:4a and 2:4b–3:24 also has a long pedigree and can lead to productive conclusions. One way of viewing the juxtaposition of the two accounts would be to read the second as offsetting the optimism and undisturbed serenity of the first by introducing an element of ambiguity and psychological realism, and especially by speaking more directly about how things went wrong right from the beginning of human life in society.

The Eden narrative is the first of the series of episodes in Genesis 1–11 which explore aspects of the same problem from different perspectives. The disturbance of the created order in Eden is replicated in the following episodes in different contexts and modalities corresponding to the increasing complexity of human society. This, in turn, permits further insight into the darker regions of the human spirit.

Old Testament scholars have generally taken the garden of Eden story, here given an alternative title which highlights its principal human and animal *dramatis personae*, to be the initial segment of the Yahwistic source (J). According to critical orthodoxy, this source extends throughout Genesis, Exodus and Numbers, according to some even further. In one respect, however, this 'assured result of modern scholarship' looks rather less assured on closer inspection. From the early days of critical biblical study, one of the principal criteria for distinguishing sources in the Pentateuch has been the more or less consistent use of different divine designations in different sources, in the case of the J source the name Yahweh (out of reverence sometimes written consonantally as YHWH). In the garden of Eden episode, however, the title Yahweh Elohim is used exclusively throughout (20 times), with the one interesting and possibly significant exception of the brief conversation between the snake and the woman in which both refer to Elohim (3:1-5). This may have been because, in what is probably part of the same source, the name Yahweh was known and invoked only two generations later (Gen 4:26). At any rate, in Genesis 2–3 the name Yahweh by itself never occurs. In assessing this matter of sources due weight should also be given to the fact, alluded to earlier, that neither the proto-parents nor the episode in which they act out their drama is named or referred to elsewhere in the Pentateuch or, for that matter, in the Hebrew Bible. The mythic garden of Eden is mentioned in some late texts, and a passage in Ezekiel laments the fate of the king of Tyre in Eden, but otherwise Eden is referred to only as the site of splendid trees not of human beings. In the book of Job, Eliphaz can ask Job, in sarcastic fashion, whether he is the firstborn of humanity (Job 15:7), but this is the generic *Urmensch* not the specific *ʾādām* of Genesis 2–3.

The history of interpretation of Genesis 2–3 from about the middle of the nineteenth century has been dominated by what is called 'literary criticism' (*Literarkritik*), but in actual practice consists largely in the identification of sources, breaking down the narrative into its component parts, assumed to have been taken by the author/editor from different sources written or oral, with the

putting them back together often considered optional.[1] The principal occasion
for this procedure in the case of Genesis 2:4–3:24 is the presence of repetitions:
the man is placed in the garden twice (2:8, 15); the woman is given a name twice
(2:23; 3:20); the man and woman are clothed twice (3:7, 21) and then sentenced
twice, with expulsion (3:22-24) and the pains and trials of ordinary living (3:16-
19). The most troublesome instance, however, is that there are the two trees in
the middle of the garden, one of which must necessarily be de trop (2:9, 17; 3:3).
Since the mid-nineteenth century if not earlier, these repetitions have played a
large part in persuading a number of scholars that the Yahwist author must have
incorporated fragments of existing oral or written material or have conflated
two originally distinct texts – a creation story and a paradise or 'golden age'
story. The task of this kind of literary criticism would then be to disengage and
expose the process by which these *disiecta membra* were put together to make
the narrative as we have it (Anderson 1978).

This line of enquiry can certainly be of value if pursued without excessive
pedantry and zeal, but rather than approaching a fascinating story like that of the
man, the woman and the snake as a work of *bricolage*, a matter of cutting and
pasting, it might be better to think of the author, often referred to – sometimes
misleadingly – as the redactor, doing what all competent authors do, namely,
incorporating ideas, traditions, motifs from the great store present in the cultural
memory of the society of which he was a part,[2] including the vast repertoire of
traditional narrative and myth. This is not to deny the possibility of editorial
additions, omissions and adjustments, either by a later hand or that of the author
himself. Most commentators agree on at least two instances in Genesis 2–3: the
passage about the river and its four tributaries (2:10-14) and the gloss at 2:24 on
the phrase 'flesh of my flesh' in the previous verse, referring it to the institution
of marriage. Leaving these aside, it should be obvious that repetitions need not
imply a combination of sources. The man and the woman cover themselves with
fig leaves, but this is no more than a provisional measure; they are later given
apparel more suited to their new life outside the garden. The verdict on the man
and the woman is not a punishment distinct from the expulsion into a harsher
world, but simply a description of what life outside the garden will entail. With
regard to the most problematic case, that of the two trees in the middle of the
garden, we could begin by pointing out that we know it is in the middle of the
garden only from the woman's conversation with the snake, in the course of
which she also misrepresents the prohibition (3:2-3). This may be a deliberate
misrepresentation by the woman or a subtle touch of the author rather than

1   For an older example see Begrich 1932. Recent surveys of scholarship in Westermann 1984:
    186–97; Stordalen 2000: 187–98.
2   The default masculine pronoun is used, but the author's gender is unknown. In *The Book of J*
    (1990) Harold Bloom speculated that J may have been a woman *d'un certain âge* at the Judaean
    court in the tenth or ninth century BC.

indicating authorial inattention, sloppy editing or a combination of sources. But in any case the Tree of the Knowledge of Good and Evil, which we may with some licence call the Tree of Ambiguous Wisdom, was in its relation to the Tree of Life an irreplaceable element in the narrative plot.

No alert reader will fail to notice how different from the first creation account is the language of this second narrative. There is movement, there are real characters we can recognize, whether divine, human or animal, and there is dialogue. It is clearly the product of a quite different milieu. If we wish to look further into the intellectual and literary milieu in which the narrative was generated, we might begin by noticing that much of the terminology is characteristic of, and in some cases exclusive to what is sometimes called 'late wisdom', the principal biblical representatives of which are Proverbs and Job.[3] It is also in these circles that we find an extensive use of the themes and the kinds of metaphorical language and mythical motifs which have gone into the construction of the garden of Eden story. Examples would be eating as a metaphor for sexual activity (cf. Prov. 6:30; 30:20), the arcane mysteries surrounding the movement and life cycle of the snake (cf. Prov. 30:2), and the Tree of Life, especially where it occurs as a symbol for wisdom (cf. Prov. 3:18).

The anonymous author of Job, writing no earlier than the fifth century BC,[4] provides clues to the kind of environment which produced not only the episode in question but the entire so-called J narrative strand in Genesis 1–11. This author, clearly a layman, does not reflect the world view of temple and priesthood. The fictional Job is presented as a sage (4:3; 15:2; 29:21) who exhibits interest in the natural world and the origins of natural phenomena. He also betrays some knowledge of astronomy (9:9; 38:31-32) and, where the occasion offers, makes use of mythological topics and figures. At one point Eliphaz, Job's Arabian interlocutor, asks him sarcastically whether he is the firstborn of the human race (15:7). The author of the dialogue and debate never refers to God as Yahweh, the personal name of Israel's God. Job's realistic and disenchanted view of human limitations, and the limitations of the moral capacity of struggling human beings in particular, fits well with the tone of the J narrative in Genesis 1–11 in general. It is Yahweh, after all, who reflects that the inclinations of the human heart tend towards evil from youth onwards, and does so both before and after the disaster (Gen. 6:5; 8:21).

---

3   Examples at the level of vocabulary: *ʾēd* ('spring, mist') 2:6; Job 36:27; *neḥmād* ('delight') 2:6, cf. Prov. 21:20; Ps. 9:11; *ʿēṣ haḥayyîm* ('tree of life') 2:9; 3:22, 24, cf. Prov. 3:18; 11:30; 13:12; 15:4; *ʿarûm* ('cunning') 3:1, cf. Job 5:15; 15:5; Prov. 12:16; *taʾăwâ* ('desirous object') 3:6, cf. Prov. 13:12 with reference to the Tree of Life; *haśkîl* ('to confer wisdom'), 3:6, cf. Prov. 13:12; Job 33:20; *tĕšûqâ* ('longing'), 3:16, cf. Song 7:11. This overlap in vocabulary was noted by Alonso-Schökel (1962) and Mendenhall (1974); on which see Blenkinsopp 1992: 64–66.
4   Driver and Gray 1921: lxv–lxxi; Rowley 1976: 21–23. Pope (1965: xxx–xxxvii), however, dates the dialogue to the seventh century BC.

A narrative which has interesting features in common with the story of the man, the woman and the snake, taken together with the closely related story about Cain and Abel, is the history of the succession to David's throne ending with the accession of Solomon (2 Sam. 11–20 + 1 Kgs 1–2), one of the great masterpieces of ancient Hebrew prose. Reading this narrative in tandem with the story of the man, the woman and the snake will, despite the difference in genre and length, place in higher and clearer relief themes common to both and help the reader to get a sense of the tone of the Genesis narrative. The Succession History falls into four episodes or novellas:

1   David's adultery with Bathsheba and cold-blooded murder of Uriah her husband, the birth of their child, the king's repentance followed by the death of the child, and the birth of Jedidiah (Solomon), their second child destined to mount the throne against all the odds (2 Sam. 11–12).

2   The rape of Tamar, Absalom's sister, by Amnon her half-brother, the crown-prince, and his subsequent murder by Absalom, Tamar's sister; Absalom's three-year exile brought to an end by a stratagem involving a 'wise woman', and his readmittance to the court after a further two years (2 Sam. 13–14).

3   Absalom's rebellion, supported by the counsellor Ahithophel who gives him wise advice which he ignores, ends with Absalom's death in battle, Ahithophel's death by suicide and the re-establishment of David's rule (2 Sam. 15–20).

4   During the last days of David's life Adonijah, a fourth son, makes a bid for the succession but is outwitted by Solomon's supporters, including his mother; Adonijah imitates Absalom by making the big mistake of attempting to possess David's concubine Abishag and is executed; the result: 'The royal power was firmly established in Solomon's hands' (2 Kgs 2:46).

The highly distinctive literary character of this piece sets it off in sharp contrast from the more annalistic and much less colourful history surrounding it. With its vivid characterization, psychological insight, its eye for significant and striking detail, and especially its use of dialogue, it reads more like a novel, or a series of novellas, than a straightforward history. Certainty is unattainable, but the fact that it has features in common with late wisdom and little in common with the history of which it is a part points to a later insertion into the history of the kingdoms.[5] By the same token, it has interesting similarities with the Genesis 2–4 narrative in spite of the great disparity in length. Not only does it share with

---

5   See Whybray (1968), who reads it as didactic and sapiential and draws attention to parallels with Egyptian novellas, but without raising the insertion issue. Van Seters (1983: 277–91), argues for an insertion on the grounds of incompatibility with the Deuteronomistic Historian's ideology.

the Genesis text the literary characteristics mentioned above, including brief and vivid dialogue, but the same themes recur impressively in both. Perhaps the most prominent of these is the theme of ambiguous wisdom represented by the counsel of wise, or seemingly wise, counsellors whose advice leads to ruin and death. Jonadab, 'a very wise man' (2 Sam. 13:3) – wise in the same way as the snake in the garden was wise – advises Amnon how he may by deceit have his will with his half-sister Tamar, but the advice leads to Amnon's death at the hands of Absalom and other ruinous consequences. David is persuaded to allow Absalom to return from exile by the skilful speech of the wise woman of Tekoa, but returning is the prelude to his rebellion and death (2 Sam. 14).[6] In the course of the rebellion, Absalom follows the advice of his counsellor Ahithophel to occupy David's harem, an act which leads to his death and Ahithophel's suicide (2 Sam. 16:20-23). The situation is basically identical in Genesis 3, though with different actors: the woman and the 'wise' snake[7] following whose advice leads to expulsion from the garden and loss of immunity from death.

The woman from Tekoa tells a fictitious story to David about her two sons one of whom killed the other when they were out in the fields, was himself in danger of death as a result, but was protected from blood vengeance by a higher power, that of the king. This skilful 'story within the story' or *récit à cadre* is the deliberate fictional counterpart of the double fratricide in real time in the Succession History (Absalom kills Amnon, Solomon kills Adonijah), but it also precisely replicates the plot and some of the terminology of the Cain and Abel episode in Genesis. A close reading of this superb narrative will reveal other similarities. Take, for example, the way in which the woman praises David for his wisdom like that of the angel of God to discern between good and evil (2 Sam. 14:17, 20).

A final observation on these parallels. The Succession History has something of the character of a *chronique scandaleuse*. Each of its four chapters opens with an act of a sexual nature which has tragic consequences. David's adultery with Bathsheba leads to the death of their child and to David passing sentence of death on himself ('that man must die!', 2 Sam. 12:6), a sentence which, like the sentence on the man in Eden, was not carried out. The rape of Tamar by Amnon leads to his death at the hands of Absalom (2 Sam. 12:14). Absalom's seizure of David's harem is the point of no return in his rebellion leading to his defeat and death (2 Sam. 16:20-23). Finally, Adonijah signs his own death warrant by requesting Abishag, David's concubine, for himself (1 Kgs 2:15-17).

---

6   Judging by this instance, and that of another wise woman from a town in the north (2 Sam. 20:14-22), these female specialists had the verbal skill to serve as consultants in cases requiring advocacy. Parallels from other cultures might suggest that this function grew out of another specialization, that of midwifery (cf. French *sage femme*).

7   The J author no doubt described the snake as ʿ*ārûm*, cunning, rather than *ḥākām*, the usual term for 'wise', in order to permit the play on ʿ*ărûmmîm*, 'naked', in the previous verse.

The sexual element is much less overt in the garden of Eden story. It should not be exaggerated but it is there nevertheless, expressed in the theme of nakedness and clothing, innocence and shame, and perhaps also sexual activity expressed as eating, a euphemism familiar to the didactic literature of Israel and that of other lands (e.g. Prov. 6:29-31).

The Scenario

Genesis 2–3 begins in the manner traditional with myths of origins by stating what was and was not there at the moment of creation (2:4b-6). An example of this feature, similar to *Enuma Elish* noted earlier, is a bilingual (Sumerian/ Akkadian) text discovered in 1882 in Abu Habba in southern Iraq, the ancient Sumerian city of Sippar. This text, known under the title *The Creation of the World by Marduk*, dates from the neo-Babylonian period (6th century BC), therefore roughly contemporary with Genesis 1. The first eleven lines are a list of what was not there at the beginning: no temples, cities, houses, no people to occupy them, and no trees or vegetation; not even the Apsū (the great deep) had been created. All the land was under water and there was a spring (*inu*) bubbling up from the depths, the counterpart to the mysterious ʾēd of Gen. 2:6, variously translated stream, spring, mist, moisture (Heidel 1951: 61–66). Only then does the creation by Marduk begin, including people, animals and the physical environment in which they are to live (lines 20–27). We find the same conventional exordium in both biblical accounts of origins (Gen. 1:1-2; 2:4b-6), but in other respects the second version is quite different from the first. In the first place, in Genesis 2–3 the earth is already there from the beginning though uninhabited. The order in which creation takes place is also different since in the second account a human being is created before the wild animals and birds – and presumably also before aquatic creatures which are not mentioned. This version begins by displaying an environment without vegetation. There was a source of ground water or moisture, the above-mentioned ʾēd, but it was insufficient to promote growth since no human labour was available to put it to use by digging irrigation canals, and the Lord God had not yet sent rain. The setting is therefore local and not on the cosmic scale of Genesis 1.

Compared with Genesis 1, contraction of the field of vision is especially observable in the description of the river from whose source in Eden four great streams branched out to the four quarters of the known world (Gen. 2:10-14). Most commentators agree that this passage was inserted by a scribe eager to supply topographical information lacking in the original. Its learned, didactic style sets it apart from the surrounding narrative, and the resumptive repetition immediately following about the placing of the man in the garden of Eden (Gen. 2:15, cf. v. 8) corresponds to a technique often used by interpolators. If that is so, the insertion may have been intended as an explanation of the obscure ʾēd referring to a source of ground water (2:6). This word, which occurs elsewhere only in Job 36:27 where its meaning is no more transparent than in Gen. 2:6, has given rise to a great deal of discussion which need not be detailed here (Westermann 1984: 200–201; Van Seters 1992: 123). Of the four rivers two, the Tigris and Euphrates, are well known. The interpolator tells us that the Pishon flows through Havilah (cf. Gen. 10:7, 29; 25:18), a land rich in high-quality gold, gum resin, and carnelian or onyx, all of which suggests Arabia. The Gihon flows through the land of Cush, a toponym which elsewhere refers to the lands south of the first cataract of the Nile, though a broader reference including Egypt and Lybia may have been intended. Josephus goes further afield by identifying the Pishon with the Ganges and the Gihon with the Nile (*Jewish Antiquities* I 38–39). The important point seems to have been to emphasize the amazing fertility of Eden in which the mighty headwaters originated, and a further inference would be that Eden is on a mountain, which would agree with other designations of a fertile reserve of a deity: the garden of God on the holy mountain in which the king of Tyre is placed (Ezek. 28:11-19), and the cedar forest on the magical mountain guarded by Humbaba and penetrated by Gilgamesh and Enkidu (*Gilgamesh* IV). The rich symbolism of the river bringing life and fertility to the earth is taken up towards the end of the visionary experience recounted in Ezekiel 40–48 (47:1-12) with the river flowing from the temple, the abode of God, down to the Dead Sea. The same theme of healing and life-giving water flowing from the temple appears in Psalms and other biblical texts (e.g. Pss 46:4; 65:9; Joel 3:18; Zech. 14:8). In a much later vision, the seer of Patmos is shown the river of the water of life, bright as crystal, flowing from the throne of God and the Lamb, and on its banks the Tree of Life whose leaves are for the healing of the nations (Rev. 22:1-2).

Like a potter, Yahweh Elohim formed a figure out of wet clay and breathed into its nostrils the breath of life (Gen. 2:7). The result was a living creature, an adult male, according to one rabbinic opinion a 20-year old adult male (*Gen. R.* 14:7), or perhaps 30 years old since this is, as Sir Thomas Browne informs us in *Religio Medici*, 'the perfect age and stature of man'. This first act of creation took place outside the garden. Yahweh Elohim first fashioned the man and then planted a garden over to the east full of all kinds of beautiful fruit-bearing trees in which he placed the ʾādām, the man, as its caretaker (Gen. 2:8-9, 15). The first man is therefore created to serve Yahweh Elohim as humans were formed out of the same material substance to serve the gods in *Atraḥasis* and other Mesopotamian myths. One commentator has even suggested comparison with the famous legend of Rabbi Loew of Prague with his golem made out of clay and animated by magical incantations to serve the purpose of protecting the Jewish community threatened with a pogrom (Greenstein 2002).

When we first hear of it, the garden is *in* Eden (Gen. 2:8), and shortly afterwards we are told that the river flowed from Eden to water the garden (2:10). The Yahwist author is deliberately vague about the location of Eden. All he will tell us is that it is 'over in the east' (2:8), which is not very helpful. His reticence has not, however, deterred the curious from attempting a more precise positioning, whether in the Isles of the Blessed beyond the western ocean (Josephus, *Jewish War* II 155), or in Bahrain, in the Persian Gulf off the east coast of the Arabian peninsula. This locality, a great favourite of an earlier generation, has been identified with the ancient Dilmun, described in a Sumerian mythological text as the luxuriant garden of the god Enki:

> The land of Dilmun is pure,
> The land of Dilmun is clean ...
> The land of Dilmun is most bright. (*ANET* 38)

The name of the garden may therefore have been transferred from the region in which it was thought to be situated, but it is generally agreed in any case that the name Eden is symbolic rather than topographical. In substantival form, the North-West Semitic stem *ʿdn* can refer to luxurious garments (2 Sam. 1:24), rich food (Jer. 51:34), sexual pleasure (Gen. 18:12; *Genesis Apocryphon* II 9, 14) and spiritual joy (Ps. 36:9), while in verbal form, in Middle Hebrew and Syriac, it has the meaning to delight or luxuriate in some object.[8] The LXX translation *paradeisos tēs truphēs* ('a paradise of luxury') confirms this understanding of the author's intent.

The idea of a mythical, paradisal garden of Eden or garden of God seems to have been familiar in Israel, at least in the post-monarchic period, to judge by the fairly frequent allusion to it in biblical texts from the neo-Babylonian period or later. In texts where 'Eden' and 'the garden of God' stand in parallelism it is clear that these terms are interchangeable (Ezek. 28:13; 31:9, 16, 18). We are also told that in the last days both the land of Israel and the city Jerusalem will be transformed into a *gan-ʿēden*, a garden of God (Ezek. 36:35; Isa. 51:3). Other prophetic and poetic descriptions of a golden age and a golden place that existed once in the distant past and could exist again in the future belong to the same garden of Eden theme. There will then once again be harmony and peaceful co-existence between humans and animals. Thus, the well-known Isaianic text about wolf and lamb, leopard and goat, calf and lion living together in peace in the messianic age is also part of the picture (Isa. 11:6-9), though this prophet, or a later scribe, felt obliged to add that the curse on the snake will not be revoked (Isa. 65:25). He will still be eating dirt.

Among these allusions to a garden in Eden the closest to Genesis 2–3 is, without a doubt, the poem in Ezek. 28:11-19 in which the king of Tyre is represented as resident in the garden of God on God's holy mountain. Time and space do not permit detailed discussion of the many textual, linguistic and interpretative problems with which this difficult poem confronts the reader,

---

8   Kedar-Kopfstein 1999; Westermann 1984: 208–10; Millard 1984.

but it cannot be passed over without comment. The poem may be translated as follows:

You were the very seal of perfection,
full of wisdom, perfect in beauty;
you were in Eden, the garden of God
adorned with precious stones of every kind –
ruby, chrysolite, jade;
topaz, onyx, jasper;
lapis, garnet and emerald;
their settings were woven in gold,
made for you on the day you were created.
I assigned you a guardian cherub with outstretched wings,
you were on God's holy mountain,
you walked among the stones of fire.
From the day you were created you were perfect in your ways
until iniquity was found in you.
Because of your abundant commerce
violence filled your heart, and you sinned.
So I cast you down, disgraced, from the mountain of God,
the guardian cherub banished you from the midst of the stones of fire;
your heart was proud on account of your beauty,
you corrupted your wisdom on account of your splendour.
I cast you to the ground, I exposed you to the gaze of kings.
By your much sinning in dishonest trading
you profaned my sanctuary,[9]
so I brought forth fire from your midst which consumed you,
I turned you to ashes on the ground for all to see.
All who knew you among the nations were appalled at you,
you became an object of horror, and shall forever be no more.

This mock lament, addressed to the king of Tyre by the prophet speaking on behalf of Yahweh, describes his passage from exaltation to abasement. The guardian cherub (Hebrew: *kĕrûb*, Akkadian: *kāribu*) belongs to a class of sculptured deities which guard the entrance to a palace or temple, usually in the form of a formidable winged creature with a human face and the body of a large and dangerous animal; therefore quite unlike the naked infants (*putti*) who fill up background space in Renaissance and Baroque paintings. Ezekiel's cherub

9 Tentatively reading *miqdāšî* ('my sanctuary') for MT *miqdāšêkâ* ('your sanctuaries'). Several ancient versions and many modern commentators have considered it unlikely that a Judaean prophet would charge a pagan king with profaning his own sanctuaries; see e.g. Eichrodt 1970: 389. The profanation of Eden, the domain and sacred space of the deity, fits the context much better.

will bring to mind the cherubim and the flashing sword guarding the way to the tree of life in Gen. 3:24, but it is unfortunate that at this point (v. 14) we have some serious textual issues. Based on his reading of the beginning of this verse, where the Masoretic text appears to read 'You are a cherub' (*'att-kĕrûb*) addressed to this individual, James Barr argued that he is being compared to a cherub, a divine or quasi-divine being, and that therefore the situation which the poem describes is closer to Gen. 6:1-4, the 'sons of the gods, daughters of men' passage, than to Genesis 2–3. In other words, to quote Barr directly, it can be read as 'an aspect of the tremendously powerful idea, lacking in Genesis 2–3 itself except for the very limited role there of the snake, of a heavenly or angelic rebellion against God and the casting out of the rebellious heavenly forces' (1993a: 48).

The emphasis on this explanation of the origin of evil in the later stages of the tradition is one of the strongest points made by Barr in his stimulating study of Genesis 2–3 (1993a; 1988), but there are good reasons for preferring the LXX reading of Ezek. 28:14 which understands the cherub as the assigned guardian of the king on God's holy mountain. The translation of the verse offered above is reinforced by the similar language used in describing the gold or gilded cherubim whose wings formed a protective canopy over the *kapporet*, the 'mercy seat' or cover of the ark, in the inner sanctum of both the wilderness sanctuary (Exod. 25:18-22) and Solomon's temple (1 Kgs 8:6-7). We must also take account of Ezek. 28:16 in which, on a probable reading, it is the cherub who expels the man from Eden, as the cherubim and the flaming sword prevent the man from returning to Eden in Genesis (3:24). And, finally, the splendid clothing, more appropriate for a king or priest, does not make a good fit with the proposed comparison with a cherub, and engagement in commercial activity even less so. This proviso notwithstanding, many of the details in the description of the environment and its occupant have parallels in Genesis 2–3. The catalogue of precious metals, stones and gems, for example, brings to mind the gold and precious stones in the land of Havilah (Gen. 2:11-12). The fact that nine of the twelve stones or gems in the high priest's pectoral are listed here (see Exod. 28:17-20; 39:10-12) led Robert R. Wilson (1987) to speculate that the subtext of the poem is a cryptic condemnation of a contemporaneous high priest. We would want to ask, however, why anyone at that time would go to the trouble of laboriously disguising his criticism of priests and the priesthood; no one else appears to have found it necessary. The other indications in the poem cited in support of the hypothesis – the cherub, the holy mountain, the stones of fire – do, however, reinforce the idea of Eden as a holy sanctuary, a *temenos* set apart. The wisdom of the king in Eden might appear at first sight to differentiate it from Genesis 2–3, but it is a kind of ambiguous wisdom which in both cases provides the occasion for the fall from a primitive state of grace, the corruption of a primordial state of beatitude, followed by expulsion.

The religious significance of royal gardens, well-attested in ancient Mesopotamia (H. G. May 1962; Jacobs-Horning 1978; Wiseman 1983), is implied in the poem in which the royal status of the protagonist is indicated by the seal or signet ring, a familiar royal accessory (Jer. 22:24; Hag. 2:23). He is therefore the primaeval king and, as such, is endowed with wisdom and beauty. His fall from grace on account of pride (Ezek. 28:17) has a close parallel in the fate of another royal figure, an unnamed king of Babylon, in Isa. 14:12-15:

> How are you fallen from the sky,
> Star of the dawning day!

This fall from grace appears to be modelled on an incident in the Ugaritic Baal cycle in which the deity Athtar (Ashtar), corresponding to 'Day Star Son of Dawn' (*helel ben shahar*, the planet Venus), aspired to occupy Baal's throne on Mount Zaphon, the Phoenician Olympus, but ended up defeated and undone in the underworld (*ANET* 140). This raises the question whether the man in Genesis 2–3 is represented as a royal figure, as is sometimes assumed. Some of the parallel figures, Ziusudra and Gilgamesh, might point in this direction, and his naming of the animals (Gen. 2:19-20) suggests lordship and brings to mind Solomon's outstanding onomastic skills (1 Kgs 4:13). But in that case he would be monarch of all he surveyed only in the manner of Alexander Selkirk, 'lord of the fowl and the brute', in Cowper's poem. It seems, therefore, more prudent to read the Ezekiel poem as adapting a variant form of the Eden myth to a political topic, one different from that of Genesis 2–3, namely, the fall of the tyrant due to unrestrained pride and godlike aspirations.

The cultic associations of the garden theme are confirmed by the reference in the following line of the poem to 'God's holy mountain', a familiar way of referring to the temple of Jerusalem.[10] If the obscure 'stones of fire' may be identified with the six-winged seraphim (*śĕrāpîm*), fiery creatures who attend the divine throne in the great vision of Isaiah (6:1-13) and who pick up the burning coals from the brazier, we would have a further indication of the garden of Eden as the dwelling of God, a holy place, a sanctuary. Etymologically, seraphs are associated with fire and burning (from the verbal stem *śrp*, 'burn'). They are winged, serpentine creatures like those which afflicted the Israelites in the wilderness and the bronze *śārāp* set up by Moses which healed them (Num. 21:6-8). Together with the cherubim, the seraphim came early on to be recognized in both Judaism and Christianity as belonging to the angelic hierarchy, and so it has remained to the present. If, finally, the textual emendation from the Masoretic 'your sanctuaries' to 'my sanctuary' in Ezek. 28:18 is accepted, the sacred nature of Eden as a holy place would be explicitly attested.

In the literature of the Second Temple period and in rabbinic texts we often come across Eden described as the dwelling of God, a holy place, a prefiguration of Zion and its temple. According to *Jubilees*, for example, the garden of Eden is

---

10   Isa. 2:2; Jer. 31:21; Zech. 8:3; 14:10; Pss 3:5; 15:1; 24:3; 43:3; 48:3; 99:9, etc; on this theme, see Clifford 1972.

the Holy of Holies and the dwelling of the Lord. Together with Sinai and Zion, it is one of the three holy places at the centre of the earth (*Jub.* 8:19). Hence the laws of purity governing access to the sanctuary applied in Eden, with the result that the woman's entry into Eden had to be postponed 80 days in order to satisfy a complicated ritual requirement in keeping with Lev. 12:2-5.[11] A fragmentary Qumran text seems to be making the same point in alluding to ritual procedures necessary for Adam before entering the garden, 'for holy is the garden of Eden'.[12] This superimposition of the eschatological Zion on the garden of Eden is found, with variations, in such late Second Temple compositions as *1 Enoch* (25:1-5), *Psalms of Solomon* (11:5) and *4 Ezra* (8:52-53). In the Christian Apocalypse the life-giving water of the river of Eden flows through the New Jerusalem with the Tree of Life on the banks of the river (Rev. 2:7; 22:2). Variations of the same juxtaposition of Eden with sites rooted in the collective Christian imagination and memory have continued to appear. The cross on which Christ died is the Tree of Life. Golgotha, the place of the skull, is Adam's burial place and the skull is his. So, for example, John Donne in his 'Hymne to God my God in my sicknesse':

> We think that Paradise and Calvarie,
> Christs Crosse and Adams tree stood in one place

In repeating this theme, Donne is heir to a long tradition of typological exegesis of Genesis 2–3.

The presentation of the garden of Eden as a sacred enclosure, the abode of the deity, has however led some readers in a rather different direction. The thesis has been advanced that the Eden narrative, perhaps in a hypothetical earlier form, was intended as a polemic against the addiction to garden cults of a kind attributed in several biblical texts to the supposedly licentious Canaanites. The garden as a place set aside for cultic activity, a *temenos*, was certainly a familiar feature of religious practice at both the official state level and that of the kinship network, and continued to be so even after the post-monarchic period. These garden cults featured sacrifice, incense offerings, decidedly non-kosher ritual meals, sexually oriented rituals and, according to a probable interpretation of Isa. 66:17, a ritual led by a female hierophant.[13] From the denunciations of such cults in prophetic texts we can deduce a close association between sacred trees and a goddess figure. The goddess in question would be Asherah, 'mother of all the gods' in ancient Canaanite texts, as Eve is 'mother of all the living'. The association is apparent in

---

11   'When she finished these eighty days we [the Lord and angels] brought her into the garden of Eden because it is more holy than any land' (*Jub.* 3:8-14). The author ignores the fact that the woman was created in the garden.

12   4Q265 frag. 7 II lines 11–14; on this theme, see Wright 1996.

13   The case is argued in Blenkinsopp 2003; see also Isa. 1:29-30; 65:3 and, indirectly, Song 5:1 and 6:2. For the garden as a location for the *hieros gamos* in Mesopotamian texts see Nissinen 2001.

that the tree symbolic of the goddess is called an *'ăšērâ*, a cult symbol which can be planted (Deut. 16:21), cut down (Judg. 6:25-32; 2 Kgs 18:4), uprooted (Mic. 5:13) or burned (Deut. 12:3; 2 Kgs 23:15). It is also attested that these garden cults had a strong erotic content, in which respect the symbolism of the name Eden, the theme of nakedness and eating as a metaphor for sexual activity in Genesis 3 would be relevant (Hvidberg 1960; Wyatt 1981; Ackerman 1992: Stordalen 2000: 310–12). The prohibition of touching the tree, added by the woman on her own account to the prohibition of eating, is also potentially of interest since it corresponds to a taboo familiar from such rites (cf. Exod. 19:12-13).

This reading of the text or, more likely, the hypothetical *Urtext*, as anti-Canaanite might find support in the story about the drunkenness of Noah, in some respects interestingly parallel to Genesis 2–3 though much briefer (Gen. 9:20-27). As the first husbandman – literally 'man of the soil (*'ădāmā*)' – Noah planted a vineyard, drank the vine from it, got drunk and in his drunken state exposed himself in his tent. Ham, father of Canaan, or perhaps it was Canaan, saw him in this state, and summoned his two brothers who, however, covered their father with a cloak and took great pains not to look on him in his naked state. When Noah came to himself and learned what his youngest son had done to him he uttered a curse on Canaan and a blessing on Shem and Japhet. In view of the obvious inconsistencies in the story – Ham is the transgressor but Canaan is cursed; Shem and Japhet are said to be the 'brothers' not of Ham but of Canaan (9:18; 10:6) – it looks as if this paradigmatic story referred originally to Canaan but was rewritten to fit the narrative context which is about Noah, his three sons, and their descendants mentioned in 9:18-19. The structural and thematic parallelism with Genesis 2–3 is striking: Noah plants a vineyard as Yahweh Elohim planted a garden (2:8); Noah, like the first man in Genesis 2–3, is a man of the soil; the one eats, the other drinks from a plant with unfortunate or at least ambiguous consequences; the theme of nakedness is prominent in both narratives; and both Canaan and the snake are placed under a curse which determines their destiny. Whatever it was that Canaan did to his father, the story expresses repudiation of the 'abominations of the Canaanites' (Lev. 18:3; Ezra 9:1, etc.), code for sexually oriented rites as viewed by the pious Israelite looking in from the outside. The story, to which we shall return, may therefore throw further light on the symbolism of the snake and its role in the dramatic turn of events in the garden of Eden.

The Man and the Woman

The man fashioned out of wet clay and animated by the breath of God is created before the planting of the garden in Eden, and the purpose of his creation was to till the ground and serve as custodian of God's garden once it had been planted (Gen. 2:5, 15). In that limited respect he is comparable to the Igigi, the lesser deities in *Atraḫasis*, who were given the charge of tilling Enlil's earth but who, after a period of time, refused to obey (*Atraḥasis* I 27–46). In Genesis 2–3 the refusal is transferred from the world of the gods to that of humanity. The first human being in the Genesis account is made of the same material substance as the *lullu*, the first-formed lowly humans in *Enuma Elish*, namely wet clay, earth stuff. But whereas the latter were animated by the blood of an expendable deity, in the Genesis account the principle of life is the breath of God. According to the anthropology of the ancients, including Hebrews, breath and blood were the essential symptoms of life. Hence human beings and animals were alive but not plants which did not appear either to breathe or to bleed.

The man – *hāʾādām* (*ʾādām* with the article) – is not yet known and addressed by the personal name Adam, which appears for the first time in Gen. 5:1 (*ʾādām* without the article occurs in 4:25, but not in a genealogical context where the personal name can be expected, as in Gen. 5:1-5 and 1 Chron. 1:1). We do not have to wait until the creation of the woman for gender specificity to appear, as if this first human being was sexually undifferentiated. Suffice it to note that he is referred to by the same term, *hāʾādām*, 'the man', both before and after the appearance of the woman.[14]

After the man was formed, Yahweh Elohim planted the garden in Eden and made fruit trees pleasing to the sight and good for food grow from the ground. Apart from the passage about the four rivers flowing out of Eden (Gen. 2:10-14), one of only two additions to the narrative as we saw earlier, the only information about the physical appearance of the garden provided by the author is the presence of trees pleasing to the eye and good for food and, among these, two special trees destined to play a decisive part in the plot (Gen. 2:9). These trees have given the commentators a great deal of trouble, and will call for more extensive comment later on. But first we must see how the drama in Eden reached its eventual point of resolution.

The decisive event in the history of life in the garden is the passage from individual to society. This author makes it abundantly clear that, while the roots of moral deviation lie in the choices made by the individual, it is through increasing disorder in social relations at different levels of complexity that evil insinuates itself. It was therefore always an exegetical misstep, a perverse case of *chercher la femme*, to blame the woman, since the author understands the man–woman relationship as only the first of several stages of increasing complexity in social arrangements and the corresponding spread of evil. In reading the account of this first phase we have the impression that events followed each other in rapid succession, that it was all over in a matter of minutes, or maybe days, but that is simply a function of the narrative art and its requirements. In *Atraḥasis*, Enlil burdens humanity with disease and famine before bringing about the deluge, but there is an interval of 1,200 years between each of these briefly described

---

14   *Pace* Phyllis Trible (1978: 79–81), who translates *ʾādām* as 'earth creature' and understands 'it' to be sexually undifferentiated; see also Kawashima 2006.

disasters. We do not know how the biblical author envisaged the passage of time, but if we take in the entire scope of the narrative in Genesis 2–3 we see that it unfolds in four phases of indeterminate length: (1) the man is alone, mortal by virtue of his origin in the earth, but kept alive by the breath of God; (2) the man cohabits with the animals, naked as they are, but this modus vivendi proves to be unsatisfactory; (3) the man and the woman live together in the garden, this too for an unspecified period of time; (4) the man and the woman continue living, but now outside the garden, together with their offspring and descendants. Details from this last chapter are supplied in other 'Adamic writings' from the late Second Temple period to the Middle Ages, among which the *Life of Adam and Eve* (*Vita Adam et Evae*), sometimes referred to as the *Apocalypse of Moses*, provides the most detailed and most imaginative information. Several language versions of this text have come down to us, all probably dependent directly or indirectly on a Hebrew original from the first or second century of the common era. The *Life of Adam and Eve* describes the couple's search for food after the expulsion, their fasting and penance for the sin of disobedience, Eve's succumbing to a second temptation, the search for the oil of healing from the Tree of Life, Eve's retelling of the garden experience, and Adam's death and burial in Paradise (Stone 1992; Johnson 1985; Levison 1988; Callender 2000; Anderson, Stone and Tromp 2000).

In Genesis 2–3 the emergence of social life, a necessary development since 'it is not good for the man to be alone', takes place in the second and third of these four phases (2:18-24). In the first experimental stage, of indeterminate duration, the man cohabits with the animals as an integral part of their world. After all, the man and the animals have much in common. They both come from the earth, and the naming of the animals signifies not only control but the possibility that they can be addressed, that in other words they can be partners suited to a human being. Furthermore, the snake may not have been the only animal capable of speech. According to a later narrative elaboration, the animals in Eden spoke a common language (presumably Hebrew) but lost this capacity after their expulsion (*Jub.* 3:28; Josephus, *Jewish Antiquities* I 41; *Life of Adam and Eve* 37–39).

At this point we find a striking analogy in the great *Gilgamesh* poem. Enkidu, created by the goddess Aruru from the earth (*Gilgamesh* I 101–104), cohabits with the animals and sides with them against the hunter (I 109–110, 126–33, 153–60). The hunter's father proposes a solution to this problem by recruiting the prostitute Shamhat to seduce Enkidu and lead him away from the world of timeless animality into civilized life in the city. The ruse works: she seduces him, cleans him up and clothes him, a necessary preparation for the passage from animality to humanity. The outcome, unanticipated by Enkidu, is that the animals abandon him and flee his approach. They are no longer 'partners suited to him' (I 196–201), but on the other hand he is now endowed with reason and wide understanding, so that Shamhat can tell him, not without a touch of irony, that he is now just like a god (I 202, 207; II 54). He will nevertheless die, and his death will set in motion the quest of the hero for the plant which confers life without end (Bailey 1970; Blenkinsopp 2004).

In spite of the man's basic commonality of origin with the animals, and his naming of them, thereby conferring on them a degree of individual identity, this first phase, of indeterminate duration, did not prove to be satisfactory. The animals turned out not to be 'helpers fit for him' or, better worded, 'suitable partners' (REB). Suitability involved being neither inferior or superior in status, but even more important was the more intimate association encapsulated in the expression 'bone of my bone, flesh of my flesh' (Gen. 2:23). Usage elsewhere in the Hebrew Bible occurs in the context of the close physical and emotional ties of kinship. When, for example, Laban meets his nephew Jacob for the first time and it emerges that he is his own 'bone and flesh', the recognition brings about instantaneously a new relationship of intimacy (Gen. 28:14). The expression provides the key to understanding the symbolic action involving actual bone and flesh by which a partner suitable for the man is given existence (Gen. 2:21-24). Yahweh Elohim put a deep sleep on the man, according to some early Jewish and Christian commentators an ecstatic state of transformed consciousness,[15] removed one of his ribs, closed up the flesh over the place, and built up the rib into the woman. There has been some debate about the nature of this operation, since the Hebrew word translated 'rib' (*sēlā'*) occurs elsewhere as an architectural or topographical rather than anatomical term (frequently in Exod. 25–27; 2 Sam. 16:13; 1 Kgs 6:15-16; 7:3). But the sense here is clearly anatomical, and no one has suggested a better alternative.

The operation was a spectacular success to judge by the man's joyful reaction:

> This one at last
> is bone of my bone, flesh of my flesh!
> She shall be called woman (*'iššâ*)
> since from a man (*'îš*) she was taken.[16]

It is important, in the first place, to set aside misleading interpretations which have converged at this point of the story, and give due weight to the logic of the narrative. Cultural assumptions about gender relations intrude here, as practically everywhere else in the Hebrew Bible, indeed in practically all texts which come to us from the broader culture in which Genesis 1–11 came into existence. It will suffice to consider the myth of Pandora, the *kalon kakon* ('beautiful evil'),

---

15 Rather than the more usual *šēnâ*, the term used here is *tardēmâ*, also used in describing Abraham's state during the vision of the 'covenant of the pieces' (Gen. 15:12) and in the reception of prophetic communications (Isa. 29:10).

16 The derivation of *'iššâ* from *'îš* is popular and symbolic but not etymologically correct.

who brought many ills upon humanity.[17] But the main point in the Genesis story is that, unlike the animals, the woman is connatural with the man in the closest way possible. She is 'bone of his bone, flesh of his flesh', which is to say that she and the man share kinship of the most intimate kind, also indicated by the folk etymology (*'îš/'iššâ*). The man has chronological priority, it is true, and it is he who gives a name (the first of two) to this new creature. On the other hand, the woman, unlike the man, was created in the garden, and it is she who, as 'the mother of all the living', will generate more life.

We are not told how long this third phase lasted, and the omission has given rise to a great deal of debate, especially as to whether the man and the woman made love in the garden. According to *Genesis Rabbah* 22:2 the answer is positive; they had sexual relations, beginning on the day they were created. On the other hand, *Jubilees* suggests that they cohabited only after the first jubilee of seven years (*Jub.* 3:34). Early Christian writers, like Ambrose and Augustine, placed the emphasis firmly on procreation when they raised the subject at all. Opinions will remain inconclusive since we are not told; and the decision will probably depend more on the reader's attitude to these matters than on exegetical acumen. James Barr summed up the situation as follows:

The acceptance of sexuality is normal in Hebrew culture, and it is only from the profound sexual hang-ups of Christianity that could have come the idea that there was no sexual activity 'before the fall'. (Barr 1993a: 67)

Of course, not all Christians have been subject to these hang-ups. To take a distinguished example, in his great epic John Milton praised marital intimacy, denounced the hypocrites who defamed sexuality, and showed us the proto-parents as they

eased the putting off
Those troublesome disguises which wee wear,
Straight side by side were laid, nor turn'd I ween
Adam from his fair spouse, nor Eve the Rites
Mysterious of connubial love refus'd.

What we can safely say is that, if they had sexual relations, no children were born. The account of the birth of Cain outside the garden, with the joyful exclamation of Eve, leaves us in no doubt that this was her firstborn (Gen. 4:1).

The final comment, which serves as an epilogue to the first part of the Eden drama, reads like an affirmation of the positive value of monogamous marriage: 'That is why a man leaves his father and mother and adheres to his wife, so that

17 Hesiod, *Theogony* 570–90 (*kalon kakon* at 585); *Works and Days* 42–105; see also Bremmer 2000.

they become "one flesh" ' (Gen. 2:24).[18] It has been added as an explanatory gloss on the creation of the woman, the lemma or trigger for the statement being 'flesh of my flesh' (*bāśār mibbĕśārî*) in the previous verse. This brief comment served different purposes in early Christian circles. In writing to the Corinthian Christians Paul cites it to discourage the frequentation of prostitutes (1 Cor. 6:15-20). It also served to justify a point of church order about the place of women, and to do so on the grounds that the first woman was created after the man and for the man (1 Cor. 11:7-12). A similar argument is used, with less subtlety, in the post-apostolic period (1 Tim. 2:11-15), and the author of the letter to the Ephesians reinforces the authority of the husband by allegorizing the text with reference to the relation between Christ and the church (Eph. 6:22-33). Finally and most importantly, speaking in a Jewish context and in response to a question from a Pharisee, Jesus cites Gen. 2:24 to stress the primordiality of male–female union in affirming that in the law of Moses divorce was a concession rather than a right (Mk 10:2-12; Mt. 19:3-12).

The Woman and the Snake

The turning point of the narrative, the *peripateia*, is the conversation between the woman and the snake. Before this crucial point the man and the woman were naked and unembarrassed and after it they clothe themselves provisionally with the proverbial fig leaf (Gen. 2:25–3:7). This thematic rather than purely linguistic inclusion is intended to draw attention to an important theme at this point of the story. The aspect of sexual awakening is certainly present, but the motif also speaks to the transition from one phase of existence, life with the animals where to be naked was appropriate and natural, to another which is about to open out to the couple. At this point a new *dramatis persona* enters the story, and the first task for the reader is to ask what the narrative explicitly reports about this newcomer.

In view of the transformations which the snake will undergo in later tradition, it is important to begin by stating the obvious: the snake is one of the animals created by Yahweh Elohim in the garden (2:19-20). It is not a superhuman being or a fallen angel or anything of that sort, witness the fact that the verdict pronounced on it deals with snakes as the author and his readers recognized them, the only difference being that they can no longer speak. We are also told that the snake is the most cunning of all the animals. The Hebrew epithet *ʿārûm* can have the negative connotation of low cunning and deceit (Job 5:12; 15:5),

18 Beeston (1986) argued that in this context *bāśār* ('flesh') is a legal term signifying clan membership and implying that the man is entering into a uxorilocal marriage with entry into membership of the wife's clan. The point is argued on the basis of Arab parallels, but this arrangement is unattested in ancient Israel.

but in its biblical usage – especially in Proverbs (12:16, 26; 13:16, etc.) – it more frequently qualifies the prudent and wise person as opposed to the fool or the simpleton. According to the sapiential and aphoristic tradition represented by the book of Proverbs, these qualities are especially in evidence in speaking or knowing when to abstain from speaking. The conversation shows that the snake is no fool and no simpleton. He knows how to make good use of speech and is adept at eliciting the desired response with the greatest economy of language. At this point the modern versions conceal a *double entendre* in the Hebrew where the 'cunning' (*ʿārûm*) snake is mentioned immediately after the naked (*ʿărûmmîm*) couple. (The chapter break at this point, introduced only in the Middle Ages, is distracting and should be ignored). That the snake, being without hide, fur or feathers, is naked in the literal sense is obvious but, beyond that, the pun is one more pointer to this central theme of transition from one stage to another, from naked to clothed, from nature to culture.

The snake may be cunningly concealing another *lusus verborum* since in the original the word *nāḥāš* ('snake') would inevitably have brought to mind the idea of magic, divination, the occult, expressed by the same lexeme (verbal stem *nḥš* and corresponding substantive; e.g. in Gen. 30:27; Deut .18:10; 2 Kgs 17:17). The snake has earned this reputation since it lives underground, like the wise Enki lord of the underworld, and, like the snake in *Gilgamesh* (XI 279–89), it has discovered a way of perpetually rejuvenating itself. It was probably also by such occult means that the snake in Eden knew about the properties of the two trees and the decision of Yahweh Elohim about which of the two was accessible and which not. It was no doubt this arcane character, reinforced by the combination of fear and fascination aroused by snakes, which contributed to its being considered a deity, by no means malevolent, in many ancient cultures, especially Egypt, Greece and Phoenicia. Among its many functions were the protection of its devotees, spiritual regeneration and healing, this last memorialized in the caduceus, emblem of the medical profession. In ancient Greece and Phoenicia the snake was 'the good daimon' (*agathos daimōn*), and it played a prominent role in the Mysteries and the Dionysian cult (Hendel 1999; Burkert 1977: 280, 414; Attridge and Oden 1981: 62–69). We can readily understand that, confronted by such a formidable interlocutor, the woman had little chance of winning the verbal duel.

At this point something more must be said about the trees. All were apparently fruit trees, and therefore the garden was really an orchard, like the garden in the Song of Songs (4:16; 6:11). They were planted after the creation of the man, which again raises the question of the time factor, the tempo of the narrative, since the reader might wish to ask how long the trees would have taken to grow to maturity. All of them were pleasant to the sight and good for food, but two were special (Gen. 2:9). The Tree of Life is in the middle of the garden, which is the proper place for a Tree of Life, and eating its fruit confers immunity from death (Gen. 3:22). Since the reason given for the expulsion – which some commentators assign unnecessarily to a different source – is to prevent the couple's access to the Tree of Life, we may deduce that they had not eaten its fruit though not forbidden to do so.

This circumstance presents yet another puzzle for the commentators and another temptation to have recourse to source division. According to one interpretation, that of Paul Humbert, they had not eaten fruit from the Tree of Life because it was hidden; he called it 'l'arbre caché de la vie' (Humbert 1940: 21–28). Its properties may well have been unknown to the couple, but Humbert failed to explain how a tree located in the middle of the garden, surely the most prominent position, could be 'caché', More plausible is the idea that, having achieved the kind of wisdom which the Tree of the Knowledge of Good and Evil offered, they now realized for the first time the potential of the Tree of Life, thus putting the promise of immunity from death held out by the snake within reach. This is what seems to be implied in Yahweh Elohim's reason for the expulsion. Having eaten the fruit from the Tree of Knowledge, the man will recognize the properties of the Tree of Life, eat its fruit and avoid death, and this must not be allowed to happen (Gen. 3:22).

An analogous situation in the *Gilgamesh* epic suggests another explanation. After the death of Enkidu, Gilgamesh, his alter ego, sets out on a journey to the boundaries of space and time on a quest for the secret of eternal life, in other words, immunity from the fate of Enkidu which he had sorrowfully witnessed. Everyone he encounters on the way assures him that his quest is doomed to failure, but he continues nevertheless and, after many trials and adventures, arrives at the place of Utnapishtim the Far-Distant. Utnapishtim tells him the story of the great deluge as a way of explaining how he, and he alone, was granted immunity from death by the gods. He nevertheless sets Gilgamesh trials all of which the hero fails but, as a parting gift, tells him of a plant which grants perpetual rejuvenation. Gilgamesh gets possession of this plant which he calls 'Old Man Grown Young', he proposes to try it out on the elders of Uruk, his city, and to partake if it himself, but while he is bathing in a pool a snake comes out of the ground and makes off with it. As it disappears with the plant, Gilgamesh sees it sloughing off its skin. Analogy between this plant and the Tree of Life, the fruit of which grants immunity from death, suggests that the proto-parents had not eaten its fruit because, being still young, they did not yet need rejuvenation. What is at issue is not immortality as that term is generally understood by Jew and Christian but immunity from physical death, and even from the inconveniences of old age. In both narratives, moreover, a snake is the agent which deprives the human or, in the case of Gilgamesh, one-third human (*Gilgamesh* I 48), protagonist of the possibility of escaping death. Immunity from death is proper to gods and snakes, but is denied to humanity.

A Mesopotamian text, somewhat similar in theme to *Gilgamesh*, can throw another sliver of light on the symbolism of the Tree of Life and its place in the story. It tells the story of Adapa, first of the seven antediluvian sages and priest of the temple of Ea/Enki in Eridu, most ancient of Mesopotamian cities. Adapa is therefore, like Adam, the primaeval man and, as such, representative of humanity. As priest of Ea, his task was to provide food for his god, in pursuit of which he went fishing in the Persian Gulf. On the occasion in question he was threatened with drowning in a storm but broke the wings of the south wind, presumably by magic. Magical skill was appropriate in a devotee of Ea, a chthonic deity adept at magical practices. Summoned to heaven to give an account of himself by Anu, ruler of the upper regions, Adapa was first instructed by Ea on no account to accept the bread and water which Anu would offer him since it would be death-dealing. Sure enough, Anu did offer and Adapa did decline the offer, only to discover that this was in fact food which confers immortality. The theme is stated clearly in the opening line of this fragmentary text: 'To him (Adapa) Ea gave wisdom; he did not give him eternal life'. Adapa's biblical counterpart also acquired god-like wisdom by eating the fruit of the Tree of the Knowledge of Good and Evil, but was prevented by the deity from acquiring the essential attribute of divinity, the immunity from death which the fruit of the Tree of Life symbolized (Dalley 1989: 182–88; Westermann 1984: 246–47; Izre²el 2001; Mettinger 2007: 100–109).

So much for the Tree of Life. The location of the Tree of the Knowledge of Good and Evil is not stated initially, but the woman places it in the middle of the garden (Gen. 3:4). Eating its fruit is forbidden and brings death to the one eating it. To repeat a point made earlier, this is not a prediction of the man's death in the distant future – almost a millennium later according to Gen. 5:5 – much less a condemnation to mortality since the man was created mortal. The man is threatened with death on the day he eats of it (2:17), but this did not happen. What happened to the woman on eating its fruit was a new perception of the tree's capacity to confer insight and wisdom, which may be taken as paraphrasing 'the knowledge of good and evil'. Where this expression occurs elsewhere in biblical texts it connotes, among other things, the wisdom that comes with age and maturity (Deut. 1:39). The wise woman of Tekoa flatters David by referring to him as 'like the angel of God, discerning good and evil' (2 Sam. 14:17). It is therefore a god-like quality, a point on which Yahweh Elohim and the snake are in agreement (Gen. 3:5, 22).

The conversation between the woman and the snake, initiated by the latter, opens with the snake's question, 'Did God really say that you may not eat from any of the trees of the garden?'[19] The woman attempts to correct him by pointing out that the only tree from which they were forbidden to eat, and which they must not even touch, was the one in the middle of the garden. The careful reader will

---

19 The initial *'ap kî* is employed typically and frequently to express an obvious truth, often in the form of an a fortiori, e.g. Prov. 11:31; 15:11; 17:7; Job 9:14, etc. It could also introduce an interrogative.

note that it is only from the woman, who was not present when the prohibition was uttered, and who represents it inaccurately in another respect by extending the prohibition to touching, that we hear that the Tree of the Knowledge of Good and Evil is in the middle of the garden. Rather than indicating editorial carelessness or the need for source division, the relative position of the trees could have been, for the woman, a matter of perspective; or perhaps the statement could be a deliberate device of the author to emphasize a preference already present in the woman's mind for the kind of wisdom this tree offers in preference to immunity from death available through the Tree of Life. It would, in any case, be incongruous to attach the threat of death to the Tree of Life.

The snake replied by confidently assuring her that she and the man would not die but that, on the contrary, their eyes would be open and they would be like gods knowing good and evil. Then, apparently at once, the woman became aware that the tree in question was good for food, pleasant to the sight and to be desired as a source of wisdom. It requires no undue psychologizing to suspect that the idea suggested by the snake was already in her mind. Paul Ricoeur made the point that the snake stands for the experience of temptation as a force that comes upon us as if from outside, or from a part of ourselves of which we are ignorant, or which we do not acknowledge; it represents what he called the externality of desire (1967: 258–59). We know that the alimentary and aesthetic qualities which attracted the woman's attention were common to all the trees in the garden (Gen. 2:9). It therefore seems that it was this tree's capacity to confer the kind of wisdom which comes with growth and maturity which was the principal object of the woman's interest. After she had eaten its fruit her eyes and those of her mate were indeed opened, but not as they had anticipated, at least not immediately (Gen. 3:6-7).

The Sequel (Genesis 3:8-24)

As the creation of the woman brought the man's intimacy with the animals to an end, so transgressing the command brought about a different relationship between the couple and the Lord God; not a complete breakdown, but an avoidance, a distancing, indicated by their hiding among the trees of the garden. In both transitions the naked–clothed antithesis is prominent. The couple had always been naked in the presence of the Lord God, but now nakedness has become problematic, indicated by the loincloths of fig leaves. From this point on, there is a false tone to the man's speech. The reason he gives for hiding is obviously disingenuous, and he proceeds to pass the blame on to the woman and, indirectly, on to the Lord God, claiming – correctly – that she is 'the woman you gave me' (Gen. 3:12). (He could have added, but did not, that it was the Lord God who made the snake more cunning than all the other animals, thus enabling him to seduce the woman.) This is the low point for the man as he engages in the familiar tactic of complicating the situation and thus sharing the blame around. The woman follows suit by passing the blame on to the snake who had deceived her, omitting what she must have known, that the issue was really one of self-deceit.

The sequel to eating fruit from this tree was unanticipated in another respect, in that what followed was not death but expulsion from the garden. The verdicts pronounced on the three protagonists in reverse order do include death – which indeed happened but only after 930 years, Eve dying six days after Adam according to the *Life of Adam and Eve* (42) – but for all three protagonists the verdicts simply correspond to the conditions of life lived in the real world in that culture and in others: the hard labour of the agriculturalist, the pains of childbearing, the inevitable pains and frustrations inseparable from man and woman living together, even the fascination and fear inspired by snakes and their peculiar and unique appearance and behaviour (Gen. 3:14-19). The sentences, therefore, do no more than describe life in the real world at that time and in that culture, and the man is simply assigned the task for which he was created in the first place, but now under less favourable circumstances (Gen. 2:5, 15). What has changed is the man's relationship to the soil (ʾădāmâ) which is placed under a curse. The snake, too, is cursed, but even here the absence of legs like those of other animals, the apparent diet of dirt, and the characteristic hostility between snakes and people, are simply the result of casual observation of these strangest of animals. That is what snakes are like, and that is what they do.

The second naming of the woman (Gen. 3:20) was necessitated by the new situation and anticipates her role as mother, in the first place of Cain and Abel. Here, too, it is unnecessary to demote this verse to the status of an editorial addendum, either on account of the double naming or because name-giving usually accompanies child-bearing. The situation here is exceptional, indeed unique, and in any case it is a mother not a newborn child who is being named.

As for the name itself: the interpretation of *ḥawwâ* (Eve) as 'mother of all the living' suggests very naturally a reference to the earth from which we come and to which we return. We recall Job's words: 'Naked I came from my mother's womb and naked I shall return there' (Job 1:21). This is also how Ben Sira understands it. He reflects that a heavy yoke has been laid on Adam's children 'from the day they come forth from their mother's womb until the day they return to the mother of all the living' (Sir. 40:1). Others, however, have noted a similarity with titles assigned to female deities, especially the Mesopotamian mother-goddess Mami and the Canaanite–Hebrew goddess Asherah, 'mother of all the gods'. The folk etymology in Gen. 3:20 links the name with Hebrew *ḥay* ('living') and therefore indirectly with the verbal stem *ḥyh*, 'live' or its derived forms meaning to give or restore life, and some scholars have accepted this as the original sense.[20] An

---

20 Layton (1997), appeals to a Phoenician–Punic verbal form *ḥwy* justifying the meaning 'life-giver'; similarly Kapelrud 1980.

alternative explanation associates the name with *hiwwyā᾿* or *hiwwâ*, Aramaic for 'snake', as in the Targum on Gen. 3:1, suggesting the idea that the biblical author had taken over an older myth featuring a serpent-goddess. This is a familiar figure in the iconographic repertoire: typically nude, associated with a sacred tree and holding snakes in her hands. The idea had even crossed the mind of a certain Rabbi Aha who informs us that she was called *ḥawwa* because she was Adam's *ḥiwwya* (serpent) by arousing his sexual instinct and thus disturbing his serenity (*Gen. R.* 20:11; 22:2). Beginning with Wellhausen and Gressmann, the serpent-goddess hypothesis has been accepted by a number of commentators with different levels of enthusiasm.[21]

Parenthetically, as we look back on the little that is said of the role of the woman Eve in the story, we cannot but feel regret at the long tradition of denigration for which Genesis 2–3 has served as a vehicle in Judaism and Christianity. To document this tradition adequately would be a tedious task requiring a separate volume, and in any case has already been adequately done. One or two examples may nevertheless be given. One of the earliest is from that certified misogynist Ben Sira who held, inter alia, that a wicked man was better than a good woman (Sir. 42:14). Ben Sira traced sin and death back to their entry into the world through Eve (Sir. 25:24), thus setting her up as the counterpart to the Greek Pandora. *The Life of Adam and Eve* filled out the biblical account with a record of what happened after the expulsion. While doing penance by standing up to her neck in the Tigris, Eve succumbed a second time to the alluring speech of the snake-demon in terminating prematurely her penitential situation, a fault which called for yet more penance. Then, in telling the story to her offspring of what happened in the garden, she confessed that it was she who admitted the snake into Paradise, sprinkled poison on the fruit before offering it to her husband, thus exonerating him from blame. She also appears to have been an at least practical atheist since she assured him that she would 'make him safe from God'. Or, again, by means of a little linguistic sleight of hand, a certain Rabbi Joshua of Siknin tells us that God did not create the woman from the man's head so she would not be vain, nor from his eye so she would not be a flirt, nor from his mouth so she would not be a gossip – and so on (*Gen. R.* 18:2). We saw earlier how *Jubilees* (3:4-7) insinuated the rules governing female impurity into the garden of Eden. A rabbinic opinion took this a step further by speculating, on the basis of 'this one *at last* is bone of my bone, flesh of my flesh' (Gen. 2:23), that on the first attempt the woman was created while in her period but that, on the second attempt, it came out right (*Gen. R.* 18:4). A related midrashic tradition which mentions 'the first Eve' (*Gen. R.* 22:7) may, finally, have suggested the curious idea, first recorded in the mediaeval *Alphabet of Ben Sira*, that the demon goddess Lilith was Adam's first wife who abandoned him after their first and only love-making.

---

21   Westermann (1984: 268–69) discusses the hypothesis without endorsing it. See also Wallace 1985: 157–58; 1992.

This unfortunate tradition of denigration, in which male fear of the female played, and continues to play, a significant part, was perpetuated in early Christianity. The role of the woman in Eden served as scriptural warranty for the subordinate role of women in church ministries (1 Cor. 11:7-12; 2 Cor. 11:3; 1 Tim. 2:11-15), and the same prejudicial reading of the text appears frequently in patristic homiletic and exegetical writings. A well-known example is Augustine's interpretation of the phrase *adiutorium simile illi* in the Vulgate of Gen. 2:18:

> If woman is not made for man as a help in bearing children, what sort of a help is she? If it was to work with him in tilling the land, there wasn't enough work for one, let alone two. And even if he had needed help, surely a man would have been a lot better for that! The same for consolation when loneliness is a burden. How much more pleasant for life and conversation when two male friends (*amici*) dwell together than when man and woman dwell together![22]

Augustine resisted the arguments of earlier ecclesiastical writers, Origen in particular, which excluded procreation in the garden, but his contention that children were conceived without carnal pleasure was hardly an improvement (*On Genesis Literally Interpreted* IX 7, 10).

Returning to our text: the ambiguity of the prohibition is further emphasized by the solicitous care the Lord God demonstrates for the transgressive couple in clothing them with animal skins and thus fitting them out for life in the more challenging environment which awaits them (Gen. 3:21). Together with the Lord God planting a garden, this is the most anthropomorphic detail in the story: God as gardener and God as tailor is in line with the attributes of those Mesopotamian deities who provided the basic resources for human life such as bricks, tools and weapons. An instructive parallel is the affectionate gesture of Jacob who made his son Joseph a long-sleeved robe (less picturesque but more precise than 'a coat of many colours') because he loved him more than the others (Gen. 37:3). We see that the relationship has not been broken. God does not abandon them even while acknowledging that they had chosen to go their own way in striving to cross the divide between the human and the divine (Gen. 3:21). Since by eating the fruit of ambiguous wisdom they now realize that immunity from death is within their grasp, they must be denied access to the Tree of Life, guarded by the formidable *kĕrûbîm* and the flashing sword after their expulsion from the garden (Hendel 1985). The interdiction was therefore dictated by the need for a limit in created beings which orients and protects their freedom rather than serving as a constraint, the latter being the snake's view of the matter. Perhaps here too the author had the conclusion to *Gilgamesh* in mind. After losing the

---

22 *On Genesis Literally Interpreted* VIII 4; see further Louth and Conti 2001; Bouteneff 2008. Heither and Reemts (2007) treat the subject according to themes in the biblical narrative.

plant of rejuvenation to the snake, the hero, though already two-thirds divine, accepts his mortality and returns to the tasks that await him in his city. This is not an unhappy, tragic ending since it is no small thing to return to one's finite destiny, to pass from denial to acceptance. We may therefore see in these actions of Yahweh Elohim at the end of the story the character of a deity who does not give up on his creation and, rather than simply condemning these first hapless humans out of hand, nudges them away from the fantasy of immortal ego consciousness in the direction of 'the real world'.

Summary

The same question posed by the first creation account confronts us in reading the second. To put it simply: how did things go wrong in a world created by a God acknowledged to be good and benevolent towards humanity? The question is especially urgent in view of the fact that throughout Christianity the story of the man, the woman and the snake has provided, in the doctrine of original sin, the classic explanation for the universality and primordiality of moral evil. By transforming the snake into a malevolent pre-human and superhuman agent of evil, along an exegetical trajectory already established in early Judaism,[23] the doctrine in effect reinstates the idea, amply in evidence in Mesopotamian and Greek myth as we have seen, that at its creation humanity entered into, and becomes involuntarily part of, a history and a drama involving malevolent forces and agencies antecedent to it. There is therefore here something of a parallel with the primaeval chaos of Genesis 1 and its persistent but covert presence within the created order. The snake is therefore given a role comparable to that of the denizens of the abyss, the threat of whose blind malevolence can be contained but never completely eliminated. But in the context of the Yahwist account of origins as a whole, and in keeping with the narrative logic of Genesis 2–3, the emphasis in the story of the man, the woman and the snake is more about the flowering of evil within the humanity of the man and woman, their decisions and the 'devices and desires' of their hearts, than on forces external to them.

This emphasis, more accessible for our modern sensitivities, is compatible with the biblical account of creation as a whole. One of the constraints inherent in the idea of creation emerges when the man, newly created, receives a command from the Lord God; for the giving of a command implies the capacity to disobey it. In other words, the man was created with the capacity for moral deviation. Since the woman was made of the same substance as the man (flesh, bone,

---

23   Perhaps the most influential text is Wis. 2:23-24 where the entry of death into the world is due to the envy of the *diabolos*, the slanderer, the devil. From the context, John R. Levison's identification of this *diabolos* with Cain (1988: 51–52) does not seem probable. Would Cain be held responsible for the loss of immortality?

indirectly earth) she too has this capacity. The point is confirmed when, soon afterwards, we find them passing on the blame to each other and, indirectly, to their Creator. The snake is also an animal created by the Lord God, yet in its actions and discourse it reveals itself to be disingenuous, malicious and possibly envious. God could have created automata, whether animal or human, but since he chose to create beings who can be addressed with a commandment, they must be capable of trusting or mistrusting God's intentions, of obeying or disobeying God's commandments, therefore of moral deviation.

At a later point of the history the Lord God will reflect ruefully on what has happened since the beginning, and will brood over the inclinations of the human heart which turn readily to evil (Gen. 6:5), and this assessment will remain in place even after the annihilating judgement of the deluge (Gen. 8:21). These remarkable statements will form the basis for the rabbinic teaching on the evil inclination (*yēṣer hārā'*) which will claim our attention in a later chapter.

CHAPTER 4

Cain and Abel: A Murder Mystery

Adam's Three Sons

Genealogies form the exoskeletal structure of the entire book of Genesis covering a period, according to biblical chronology, of 2,236 years from Adam to Jacob's twelve sons (Gen. 49:9). Like most genealogies of families or tribes in traditional societies, the individual segments of this many-branched structure, while ostensibly the products of collective memory, contain much that is symbolic and fictitious, especially with personal names assigned to remote ancestors. There is generally, in addition, a good deal of fluidity and filling-in especially in the middle section of the family tree. A genealogy serves the purpose of expressing and promoting the unity and cohesion of the group and its links with the past through descent from a common ancestor. It can also be useful in verifying who belongs to the group and who may lay claim to superior rank and status within it. We would expect this function to be particularly in evidence in times of transition, crisis and general disorientation. We find a good example in the insistence on genealogical validation of membership in Israel in the years following the Babylonian conquest in the early sixth century BC. Anxiety on this score is palpable in Ezra–Nehemiah and Chronicles. Those Judaeo-Babylonian priests who immigrated to Judah but were unable to verify their Israelite descent by genealogical reference, namely, those whose names did not appear in 'the book of the genealogy of the first to return' were, so to speak, left in limbo until a decision could be reached by recourse to approved, traditional oracular media. We are not told if that point was ever reached (Neh. 7:5, 61-65).[1]

Genealogies which, at first sight, and even later, may well appear tedious and uninformative, have one saving capacity, that of eliciting and generating narrative. At the beginning of the books of Chronicles, the ten-generational line from Adam to the three sons of Noah, progenitors of the new humanity, consists

---

1   On genealogy in general see Andriolo 1973; Wilson 1977, 1992; Johnson 1988. With respect to the Genesis genealogies see Robinson 1986; Bryan 1987.

of a mere list of names occupying no more than four verses (1 Chron. 1:1-4). The same list appears in a more expanded form in Genesis 5, with minimal narrative development at the beginning (Gen. 5:1-2), the end (5:29), and in the critical seventh place, the famous saying about Enoch who was not because God took him (5:24). The narrative element in Genesis 4, our concern in the present chapter, is much more expansive. Before proceeding further, it may be helpful to lay out the genealogical schema within which the narrative is located. (Hebrew form of the principal names in parentheses):

	Adam (*hāʾādām*)[2] = Eve (*hawwâ*)		
Cain (*qayin*)	Abel (*hevel*)		Seth (*šēt*)
Enoch (*hănôk*)			Enosh (*ʾĕnôš*)
Irad			
Mehujael			
Methushael			
Lamech (*lemech*) = (1) Adah		= (2) Zillah	
Jabal	Jubal	Tubal-Cain	Naamah

This genealogical table is a composite of three originally distinct elements. The first is the birth of the two sons to Adam and Eve (Gen. 4:1-2a). It is not stated explicitly that they were twins, as is the case with Esau and Jacob (Gen 25:24), but it may be intimated by the fact that with the second child we are not told of Eve conceiving. In traditional societies, moreover, the birth of twins is generally taken to be ominous. The second element is the six-member Cainite line which attains the significant number seven when attached to Adam and Eve, the proto-parents (Gen. 4:17-24; Sasson 1978). The third is the two-generational line of Seth, the third son (Gen. 4:25-26).

The first of these three components (vv. 1-2a) introduces the account of the murder of Abel by Cain and its sequel (vv. 2b-16), by far the longest narrative and our principal concern in this chapter. There are, however, other fragments of narrative in all three segments which claim our attention. The first of these begins as follows:

> The man had intercourse with Eve, his wife. She conceived, gave birth to Cain, and exclaimed, 'I have created a male child [literally: 'a man'] with (the help of) Yahweh'. She then gave birth to Abel.

Whether the man and the woman had sexual relations in the garden or not, the birth cry implies that this was her firstborn. The birth narrative conforms to a familiar pattern according to which the cry indicates, generally with a play on the name of

2   Therefore he is still 'the man'. The personal name Adam appears incontrovertibly for the first time in 5:1.

the child or a folk etymology, either something remarkable about the circumstances of the birth or intimations of the child's destiny. Familiar examples are Seth (Gen. 4:25), Esau and Jacob (Gen. 25:24-26), Jacob's sons born in Mesopotamia (Gen. 30:1-24), Samuel, or perhaps originally Saul (1 Sam. 1:20), and Jesus (Mt. 1:21, 25). The wording of Eve's exclamation, expressing pride and joy at the birth of her firstborn, is somewhat mysterious. Her speaking of *creating* a child (with the Hebrew verb *qānāh*) is clearly intended as a play on the name Cain (*qayin*), but it also reinforces, and is reinforced by, the affirmation that the birth came about with the co-operation of Yahweh, the deity who created the first male as she has now been instrumental in creating the second. The choice of this verb, which more usually means 'to acquire' and less frequently 'to create', is therefore clearly purposeful.[3]

There is no cry of joy at the birth of the second son; only an ominous silence. The name of this son, probably Cain's twin as we have seen, anticipates his brief existence described in the account of the murder. The name Abel is an attempt to represent the Hebrew term *hevel*, meaning 'futility', 'emptiness'. This is the word which is repeated (30 times) like a tolling bell throughout Qoheleth: 'emptiness, emptiness, all is empty'. Only in much later Jewish and Christian exegetical traditions will Abel achieve some degree of solidity and substance.

Cain and his Descendants

The second genealogical element is the six-member line of Cain and his descendants (Gen. 4:17-24) which is vertical and linear down to the segmentation at the end with the three sons of Lamech. This triadic arrangement, which seems to have been a common feature of ancient genealogies, appears in the genealogies of Adam, and in those of Noah (Gen. 5:22) and Terah (Gen. 11:26). Further afield, it is reproduced in the myth of Deucalion, the Greek Noah, ancestor of the three branches of the Greek ethnos, and it is reflected in the Phoenician cosmogonic myth of Phōs, Pur and Phlox (Light, Fire, Flame), born of Genos, the ultimate genealogical ancestor (Attridge and Oden 1981: 40–41). Also in keeping with a common feature of genealogies is the presence of narrative elaboration only at the beginning and the end of the series (vv. 17, 20-24). Nothing is said about the three intermediate figures, Irad, Mehujael and Methushael, corresponding to what appear to be their respective variants in the ten-member list in the following chapter, namely, Jared, Mahalalel and Methushelah (Gen. 5:12-17, 21-27).

3　The verb occurs with reference to the deity as creator in biblical (Gen. 14:19, 22; Deut. 32:6; Ps. 139:13; Prov. 8:22) as well as non-biblical texts: a ninth-century BC Phoenician inscription from Karatepe in Cilicia refers to *'l qn 'rs* ('El Creator of the earth') and in Ugaritic mythological texts Asherah is *qnyt ilm* ('Creatrix of the gods'). On the meanings of the verb, see Westermann 1984: 290–91 and on the unusual expression *'et-yhwh* ('with yhwh'), see Kikawada 1972. Kikawada finds a convincing parallel in *Atraḥasis* I 200–201 where the mother-goddess Mami proposes to create human beings *itti Enkīma*, 'with (the help of) Enki'.

In the way it is formulated, the first member of the Cain genealogy is close enough to the account of Eve's childbearing (Gen. 4:1) to suggest that, at one time, it followed immediately after it, before the insertion of the fratricide narrative. Since the name Abel/*hevel* presupposes the account of his murder, as we have seen, this would be a stage at which there were only two contrasting lines of descent from the proto-parents, namely, Cainites and Sethites. But, granted this, our task is to deal with the text as we have it. The Cain genealogy begins as follows:

> Cain had intercourse with his wife. She conceived and gave birth to Enoch. He was the builder of a city, and he gave the city the name of his son Enoch.

All commentators agree that the wording is awkward, perhaps as a result of suppressing, together with the name of the mother herself, an exclamation referring to the name of the child. As it stands, the one building the 'city' ('settlement' would be a less misleading term) is certainly the father, even though the literary sous-genre of the birth narrative usually assigns this activity to the son. Hence, various technological innovations are assigned at the end of the genealogy to the sons of Lamech rather than to Lamech himself. This genre problem led Karl Budde, a prominent nineteenth-century Old Testament scholar, to suggest emending 'the name of his son' to 'his own name', and some commentators have followed his lead (Budde 1883: 83). Another proposal is to elide the second occurrence of 'Enoch' as a gloss, resulting in the reading, 'He was a builder of a city, and he gave the city the name of his son.' On this reading, the one doing the building and naming would be Enoch and the son would be Irad (*'îrād*) whose name is said to make a play on the word 'city' (Hebrew: *'îr*). There may also, it is claimed, be an allusion by assonance to Eridu, according to the Sumerian king list the most ancient of Mesopotamian cities, but this is quite uncertain.

The genealogy therefore presents Cain as the pioneer in sedentarization and urbanization, certainly a decisive stage in progress towards civilized life as generally understood. We recall how, in *Gilgamesh*, the city (Uruk) is the human centre which for Enkidu marks the transition from animality to humanity and to which Gilgamesh returns from the boundaries of space and time. The question then arises whether this role can be reconciled with the Cain who started out as a farmer, a worker of the soil (Gen. 4:2), before being condemned to live the life of a nomad, a Bedu, in the land of Nod, meaning the Land of Wandering, under deadly threat from the blood feud. It is agreed that the personal name Cain (*qayin*) stands for the Kenites, that in fact Cain functions as the eponymous ancestor of this North-West Arabian nomadic or semi-nomadic lineage. The Kenites lived in close contact with proto-Israelite clans in the Araba on both sides of the Rift Valley and in the extreme south of Palestine. They played an important part in the origins of Judah and Israelite origins in general. Kenite settlements are mentioned at 1 Sam. 30:29, and we hear of a 'city' called Cain (*qayin*) located near what later became the southern boundary of Judah (Josh. 15:57), but no city with the name of Enoch is attested. Based on such indications as these, some commentators are prepared to concede that the building of the 'city' as a stage towards sedentarization is not necessarily inconsistent with Cain the nomadic tribesman of the murder narrative. This may be the case, but conflating the two passages in this way ignores a fundamental difference between them with regard to tendency and purpose. In the murder narrative, Abel the pasturalist and Cain the farmer represent two contrasting and stable avocations, uncomplicated by ideas of cultural development. Cain's transition after the murder from farming to nomadic pasturing cannot be interpreted as a further stage in social and cultural development, and the blood feud which threatened him is a characteristic of tribal not urban society. The Cain genealogy, on the other hand, is concerned primarily with ideas about the origin and early development of the technologies on which civilized life, as generally understood, depended. This purpose will come more clearly into view as we take a closer look at Lamech and his immediate descendants with whom the genealogy concludes.[4]

Lamech, bearing a name of unknown, possibly non-Hebrew origin, has two wives, Ada and Zillah, meaning perhaps Dawn and Dusk, who serve to divide the offspring into two groups. In the LXX version (at this point MT is defective) the first of Ada's two sons, Jabal (*yābāl*), is the ancestor of cattle-raising tent-dwellers, in other words, of pastoralists who tend herds of domesticated animals and move with them in search of grazing. The other son, Jubal (*yûbāl*), is the proto-musician, ancestor of all those who play the harp and the pipe. He is therefore the counterpart to the Arcadian Pan, the shepherd-god with his syrinx, or to Orpheus son of Apollo whose music had therapeutic and oracular power and could summon the dead back to life. The comparison may remind us that in that kind of society music served for much more than entertainment. It had the power to heal and to drive away evil forces, as David the harp-player did for Saul (1 Sam. 16:16, 23). It could induce a state of ecstatic, mind-altering consciousness, as the music of harp, pipe and drum of the early Israelite prophetic conventicles (1 Sam. 10:5). The author of one of the Psalms prepares to reveal a parable and a mysterious saying which came to him with the music of the harp (Ps. 49:5), which will remind us that both music and poetry originated in incantation. The music of the harp and pipe or fife, together with other instruments, was also, of course, an essential accompaniment to ritual acts and to worship in general. On numerous occasions the psalms speak of praising God with stringed and wind instruments and percussion. The last of the canonical psalms brings together in a grand climax of praise an entire orchestra of eight instruments (Ps. 150:3-5).

---

4   By exploiting the analogy of Romulus and Remus involving fratricide, human sacrifice, and the foundation of Rome, Armin Ehrenzweig (1915) proposed an original but highly speculative way of reconciling the fratricidal Cain with the Cain who founds a city.

Zillah's children are Tubal-Cain and Naamah. The daughter's name means 'lovely' or 'pleasant', but there are biblical texts which suggest that it may also be connected with music by means of a homophonic lexeme.[5] This seems to have been the opinion of Targum Pseudo-Jonathan (on Gen. 4:22) and *Genesis Rabbah* (23:3) according to both of which she was a *chanteuse*, a professional singer. Tubal-Cain was the ancestor of coppersmiths and blacksmiths. The importance of these technologies for the development of early societies can hardly be exaggerated, and is acknowledged by the fact that bronze (copper strengthened with tin) and iron give their names to archaeological epochs covering many centuries. The first part of the hyphenated name occurs as a place name in biblical texts, always with Meshech (Gen. 10:2; Isa. 66:19; Ezek. 27:13), and it is identified with a place which traded in bronze implements. The inhabitants of this Tubal would be the *Tabali* mentioned in Assyrian annals and the *Tibarēnoi* of Herodotus (*Histories* 3:94; 7:78) who eventually settled to the south-east of the Black Sea. The second element in the name brings the family line back to the founder, but also emphasizes further the technology for which this branch of the family could claim renown. To judge by a cognate to *qayin* in Arabic, Nabataean and Syriac, this word, attested in Hebrew only with the meaning 'spear' or 'lance' (2 Sam. 21:16), can also mean 'smith' (Sawyer 1986).

The Cainite line therefore tracks a story of technological progress from its origins, a matter of great interest in many mythological systems. Its principal members are culture heroes comparable to the *prōtoi heurētai* (first inventors) of ancient Greece. In similar fashion, the *Phoenician History* of Philo of Byblos records that the ancestors considered as the greatest deities 'those who had made discoveries valuable for life's necessities', including those who had learned to work iron and were skilled in verbal arts including spells and prophecies (Attridge and Oden 1981: 32–33, 42–47). In ancient Mesopotamia this function was assigned to the *apkallu*, the antediluvian sages, also seven in number, who gave humanity, at first living like animals, the technological information necessary for survival and for progress towards civilized living, in the first place by founding cities (Reiner 1961; Burstein 1978: 13–14).

Taking the Cain genealogy as a distinct literary unit, there is nothing up to this point which would lead the reader to withhold praise for these achievements at the dawn of civilized life. However, the addition of Lamech's brutal boasting in the presence of his wives, and no doubt others, puts a different complexion on the passage as a whole (Gen. 4:23-24). The poem is brief, to the point, and makes use of much rhyming and rhythm. After the initial call to Ada and Zillah to serve as audience, Lamech declaims as follows:

5   2 Sam. 23:1; Pss 81:3; 135:3; 147:1; and compare Middle Hebrew *ně'îmâ*, 'melody', 'tune'; see Sarna 1989: 8, 355 n.23.

> I have killed a man for wounding me,
> a young man[6] for bruising me.
> If Cain is avenged sevenfold,
> Lamech will be seventy-sevenfold.

Taking 'a man' and 'a young man' as parallel terms, and therefore as referring to one and the same person, the sense seems to be that he too has killed a man like his ancestor Cain, that he has done so for even less adequate and unjustifiable reasons, and that he is proud of it. He would nevertheless merit being avenging on a much greater scale than his ancestor. Hyperbole is characteristic of this kind of martial bluster, as with Samson's claim to have killed a thousand with the jawbone of an ass (Judg. 15:16). But, more to the point, it illustrates one aspect of a process of moral deterioration in the course of the seven generations between Cain and Lamech. The law of talion (Exod. 21:25) was originally designed as an attempt to apply the principle of equity to the blood feud and the primitive urge for revenge, as if to say: 'Only an eye for an eye, only a wound for a wound', but there is nothing of that here. Killing has become more common, even casual, and the blood feud, characteristic of tribal lineages such as the Kenites and their neighbours, more prevalent and more demanding of blood, including the blood of the innocent (Robertson Smith 1894: 72, 272, and *passim*).

Adam, Seth, Enosh

The last segment of this genealogical montage is the three-member, two-generation line of Seth and Enosh (Gen. 4:25-26):

> Adam had intercourse with his wife again; she gave birth to a son and called him Seth, because (she said) 'God has granted me another child in place of Abel, since Cain killed him'. A son was also born to Seth whom he called Enosh. Then it was that people began to invoke the name of Yahweh.

This is a separate and independent genealogical fragment, perhaps adapted to the murder narrative by the addition of 'again' and 'another'. If so, the adaptation has produced some confusion since the exclamation does not explain the name Seth (Hebrew: *šēt*) linked with a verb (*šît*) which means to appoint, put in place or something of the sort but cannot mean 'substitute'. The birth account follows the same pattern of naming, exclaiming and explaining as with Eve's previous *accouchement* (Gen. 4:1). The name Seth, which much later will bear a heavy

---

6   The term *yeled*, usually translated 'boy', can be used of a man in the prime of life as opposed to an old man no longer physically active. Rehoboam, already in his forties (1 Kgs 14:21), for example, confers with his *yĕlādîm* who had grown up with him (1 Kgs 12:8-15).

weight of theological and esoteric doctrine in the Gnostic sects, occurs only here, in Gen. 5:1-8 and 1 Chron. 1:1, and is of unknown origin. The name Enosh (*'ĕnôš*), borne by the son of Seth, occurs in the Hebrew Bible more than forty times, mostly in poetic texts, with the same meaning as *'ādām*, namely, an adult male. Since its use as a personal name seems to call for some explanation, it has been suggested from time to time that it was borne by the primaeval ancestor of the human race, an alternative to Adam, in a genealogical myth no longer extant. The genealogical status of Seth is complicated even further by the ten-member list in Genesis 5 where Enosh is the father of Kenan (*qênān*), a name generally taken to be a variant of Cain (*qayin*). The difficult question of the relation of this genealogical fragment to the list in Genesis 5 must, however, be postponed to the following chapter.

Attached to the mention of Enosh is the fascinating piece of information that it was at that time that people began to invoke the name of Yahweh. To invoke or call on the name of a deity means to offer worship by external acts of cult including sacrifice. This is what Abraham did on entering the land of promise: he invoked the name of Yahweh in places where it had previously not been heard (Gen. 12:7-8; 13:4). The invocation during the generation of Enosh, however, leaves the reader somewhat perplexed. In the first place, Eve had already invoked Yahweh at the birth of her firstborn, sacrifice had been offered to Yahweh by the farmer and the pastoralist, and the same deity had dealings with Cain before and after the fratricide. According to another tradition, the name Yahweh was revealed to Moses for the first time at the burning thornbush in the wilderness (the great I AM of Exod. 3:13-15), and yet another tradition, attributed to the priest–scribe, states explicitly that the name was unknown before being revealed in Egypt during Israel's sojourn there: 'I appeared to Abraham, Isaac and Jacob as El Shaddai, but by my name Yahweh I did not make myself known to them' (Exod. 6:2-3). On the basis of these statements, the Yahweh cult, though traceable to a time before the rise of the Israelite kingdoms, belongs essentially to the origins of Israel rather than to human origins.

While this would not be the only case of the juxtaposition in the Hebrew Bible of different and conflicting accounts of origins, it may be suggested that what is being referred to here is the origin of divine worship in general; in effect, the origin of the practice of religion. If this is so, it may provide the key to understanding the theological point behind the final assembly of the narrative as a whole. The three originally separate fragments of family history combined by the author do nothing in themselves except provide genealogical information. But then the first of the three (Gen. 4:1-2a) serves to introduce the account of the first murder and intimates what is to follow by the ominous silence at the birth of the second son. The Cain genealogy (4:17-24), likewise, traces the history of this line through six generations while documenting, by examples, the early stages of progress towards civilized life. But then, right at the end, the boastful cry of Lamech casts a dark shadow back across the entire family history with its claim that Lamech outdid Cain in violence and brutality. While taking us back to the primordial murder, the third and last segment (4:25-26) sets the beginning of the worship of God, in other words, of religion, over against the development of skills and technologies which, in the Cain line, feed into what is generally recognized as civilization and progress. Unlike the account of Phoenician origins, in which the beginnings of technology and the worship of deities are mentioned together as part of an account of origins (Attridge and Oden 1981: 42–43), this narrative contrasts the two and, by doing so, raises serious questions about cultural and technological advances divorced from morality, indeed, about the idea of progress itself.

The Murder and its Sequel

The sense of foreboding we feel at the mother's silence after the birth of Abel is carried over into the description of the occupations of the two brothers:

> Abel tended the flock, while Cain was a tiller of the soil. (Gen. 4:2b)

The reader knows that the same occupation, tilling the soil, and soil on which a curse has been laid, was assigned to Adam about to be expelled from Eden (Gen. 3:23). Adam will be able to sustain himself by farming, but at a cost. It is not that there is a fundamental opposition to farming, since the reason for the creation of a human being in the first place was to work the land (Gen. 2:15). Rabbinic comment on the text at this point which disparages agriculture is no doubt a function of the social location of the commentators at the time of writing (*Gen. R.* 22:3). But living off what nature offers without human effort is a familiar feature of golden-age scenarios, and the laborious tilling of the ground is characteristic of life outside the garden, that is, in the imperfect, damaged world into which the proto-parents were thrust.

Quite different are accounts of origins – of a nation, ethnic group or city – involving brothers, often twins, to whom contrasting occupations are assigned. At the origins of Israel we have Esau the hunter, the wild man, and Jacob the quiet man, the tent-dweller (Gen. 25:27), a close parallel to Cain and Abel. Another parallel can be found in Philo of Byblos according to whom Phoenician origins go back to the brothers Hypsouranios and Ousōos. After they quarrelled, the former, who discovered how to make shelters out of reeds and rushes, founded Tyre while the latter, a hunter like Esau, went his own way (Cheyne 1897). This type of foundation myth featuring two brothers, often twins, is widespread. It is attested for the origins of Crete (Sarpedon and Minos), Troy (Dardanus and Iasius), Mycenae (Atreus and Thyestes), Athens (Lycus and Aegeus) and of course Rome (Romulus and Remus). The same pattern, with this prominent feature, is the main reason for supposing that, at an earlier stage, the Cain and

Abel story served as an origins myth in its own right. A similar argument has been made for the 'sons of God, daughters of men' episode in Gen. 6:1-4. Details consistent with a reading of the Cain and Abel story as, originally, an alternative account of human origins, are easily detected. Cain is concerned that anyone who encounters him is likely to kill him, but in the context of Genesis 1–11 the only other people who could have killed him are his parents. In addition, the story may have in mind the origins of sacrifice, the blood feud, and tribal organization in which the blood feud functions. Most importantly, Gen 4:1-16 presents a more explicit account of the origins of moral evil than the story of 'man's first disobedience', introducing for the first time, as it does, the language and the paradigmatic example of sin, the taking of an innocent human life (Gen. 4:7).

This may be conceded, but it does not absolve us from attending to the larger narrative context of the passage, therefore from reading the Cain and Abel story as one incident in a continuous history recorded in Genesis 1–11 and a sequel to what happened in the garden. It reproduces the same plot as the previous episode, entailing transgression, punishment involving expulsion and exile, followed by a mitigation of the punishment – suitable clothing on the one hand, the protective mark on the other. Similar emotions are exhibited and much of the same language and vocabulary is reproduced.[7] Yahweh exhibits the same characteristics and deals with the human actors in the same way. The style, elliptical yet direct, is also similar, featuring lively dialogue ('Where are you?' 'Where is your brother?'), and at one point even taking up a sentence from the previous narrative using the same terms:

Its desire is for you, but you can rule over it. (Gen. 4:7)

Your desire will be for your husband, but he shall rule over you. (Gen. 3:16)

After the birth of the sons, the narrative proceeds at once to the event which occasioned the crime:

In the course of time, Cain brought some of the produce of the soil as a gift to Yahweh, while Abel brought the choicest of the firstlings of his flock. Yahweh looked with favour on Abel and his gift, but on Cain and his gift he did not look with favour. (Gen. 4:3-5a)

The initial temporal phrase ('in the course of time') introduces the same compression of the time factor as we saw in the account of what happened in the

---

7 e.g. *'ădāmâ*, 'soil' (frequently throughout both narratives); Cain as *'ōbēd 'ădāmâ* (Gen. 2:5, 15; 4:2); *grš*, 'expel' (3:24; 4:14); Adam and Cain both reside east of Eden (3:24; 4:14); the rare word *těšûqâ*, 'desire', 'longing' (3:16; 4:7).

garden. How much time the brothers had spent in their respective occupations up to this point, or how old they were, we are not told. It is generally assumed that the brothers were offering sacrifice; perhaps so, but the gifts are not described as sacrificial material, not explicitly at any rate. The wording might suggest the offering of firstfruits and firstlings at harvest time as prescribed in ritual legislation (e.g. Exod. 23:19; 34:26; Deut. 18:4). This is an important point which bears on what has always been seen as the most baffling question which this story presents the reader: why did Yahweh favour one brother over the other?

It would be too lengthy and onerous a task to catalogue all the attempts to answer this question, but one or two examples may be given. In the section of his *Church Dogmatics* with the title 'The Elect and the Rejected', Karl Barth took the story of Cain and Abel as the first biblical illustration of the doctrine of divine election and rejection: 'When we read in Genesis 4:4 that God looked favourably upon Abel and his sacrifice, we may well ask, "Why Abel?" ' (*Church Dogmatics* II/2, 340–41). We cannot answer Barth's question with the suggestion that the choice of Abel, as the younger of the two in status, even if a twin, fits a common pattern in biblical narrative exemplified by the election of Jacob over Esau, and Joseph and David over their older brothers. The question is displaced but not answered. Attempts at an answer have nevertheless been forthcoming from ancient times to the present. Some commentators have proposed that the decision could have been due to Cain's evil conduct previous to the offering; or that his intentions in making the offering were suspect in contrast to the faith and moral probity of Abel – a point made by the author of the Letter to the Hebrews (11:4). Unfortunately, we have no information on either of these two possibilities which therefore remain no more than guesses. A proposal which at least has some grounding in the text is suggested by the respective offerings of the brothers. Following the prescriptions for the offering to be made at the Feast of Weeks (Shavuot, Num. 28:27; Deut. 16:9-12) and the dedication of the firstborn, a practice by no means confined to Israel, Abel's gift consists in the firstborn of the best of his flock. Cain, on the contrary, seems decidedly laconic in offering only 'some of the produce of the soil'. At the offering of produce at Shavuot, the gift of 'the best of the first fruits of your soil' (Exod. 23:19; 34:26) or 'some of the first of all the fruit of the soil' (Deut. 26:2, 10) is prescribed. Cain neglected to make this offering, a particularly offensive omission in view of his status as the first born. And since the offering served to acknowledge the lordship of Yahweh as Creator and benefactor of the earth and its inhabitants, the omission could also be interpreted as implying a refusal to accept the relationship with Yahweh, both dependent and co-operative, proclaimed by Eve at the moment of Cain's birth.

Cain's reaction to the rejection of his offering and Yahweh's admonition that follows are at any rate consistent with this suggestion:

Cain was very angry and he scowled. Yahweh said to him:

Why are you angry? Why are you scowling?
If you do well, you can hold your head high;
If you do not do well, Sin is a demon crouching at the entrance,
Its desire is for you, but you can rule over it. (Gen. 5b-7)

The language of this brief admonition is notoriously difficult. Writing a century ago, John Skinner concluded that the obscurity of 4:7 was due to 'deep-seated textual corruption' and a half-century later Gerhard von Rad suspected that 'the meaning of the passage was once quite different' (Skinner 1910: 107; von Rad 1961: 101). This is not encouraging, but we have to make the best of the textual situation as we find it. The reaction to the rejection, literally translated, was that 'Cain was very angry and his face fell'. In other words, the anger, no doubt mixed with envy and resentment, was betrayed in his facial expression. Yahweh's admonition is mildly worded. It warns him against the consequences of uncontrolled anger and presents the alternatives open to him. The wording at this point is obscure and no solution can claim more than a probability. The first alternative offered by Yahweh, if literally translated, would be 'If you do well – a lifting up'. Depending on the context, the corresponding Hebrew verb (*nāśā'*) can mean 'carry', 'raise up', 'accept', 'lift up', 'take away', 'pardon'. Some commentators have taken it to refer to the offerings, in the sense that if you perform the offering well Yahweh will 'life up your face', that is, he will accept the gift. Jacob, for example, sends a gift to placate his brother Esau and wonders whether he will, in consequence, 'lift up my face', in other words, accept him and forgive past injustices (Gen. 32:21). This language of acceptance by face-to-face encounter, we would say eye contact, goes back to the court protocol of the Near-Eastern empires. In one of the Amarna letters from the early fourteenth century BC, for example, a vassal king of Tyre asks the Pharaoh 'when shall I see the face of the king, my lord?' (*ANET* 484). Similar appeals have influenced the language of prayer and are encountered often in Psalms.

The problem with this solution is that the admonition seeks to warn Cain about the destructive consequences of uncontrolled anger, therefore about the future. He is not being given another chance to make the offering and get it right the second time. The 'lifting up' is therefore more properly taken to refer to Cain's face, and therefore his disposition and what it might lead to. We might compare the admonition of Zophar to Job:

If you are contemplating wrongdoing put it far from you;
do not let iniquity take up residence in your tents;
then you can hold your head high (literally: lift up your face)
without fault. (Job 11:14-15)

The wording of the alternative, here translated 'If you do not do well, Sin is a demon crouching at the entrance', is even more obscure, almost impenetrably so and, to judge by the ancient versions, has been obscure since antiquity. Many commentators have attempted to wrest a meaning from the three Hebrew words *lappetaḥ ḥaṭṭāʾt rōbēṣ*, literally translated, 'at the entrance sin is crouching', by dint of textual emendation or by assigning unusual meanings to one or other of the words, sometimes with surprising results.[8] A solution first proposed more than a century ago and accepted by many since, and one which does not require textual emendation, understands *rōbēṣ* to be a loan word from Akkadian *rābiṣum*, a term which has a fairly broad range of meaning but in some contexts refers to a demon. The *rābiṣum* of ancient Mesopotamian lore guarded entrances to buildings, but also lay in wait for and ambushed its victims, often at the entrance of a house or tent (Speiser 1964: 33; Barré 1999). If this is accepted, *rōbēṣ* (masculine participle) would be in apposition to *ḥaṭṭāʾt*, 'Sin' (feminine substantive), the personification of a dangerous and malevolent demon waiting to take over the disturbed soul of Cain. There may also be a connection with the threshold demons familiar from the folklore of many countries, a reminder of which is the practice of leaping over the threshold to avoid contact with the demon (1 Sam. 5:5; Zeph. 1:9). Read in this way, the demon Sin crouching at the entrance of Cain's tent would be the counterpart to the snake in relation to the woman in the garden. Its urge is to take him over, but he has the power to resist.[9]

The murder and its immediate discovery are narrated with the greatest brevity and economy:

> Cain said to his brother Abel, 'Let us go out into the country'. When they were out in the country Cain rose up against his brother Abel and killed him. Yahweh said to Cain: 'Where is your brother Abel?' To which Cain replied: 'I don't know. Am I my brother's keeper?'
>
> 'Whatever have you done?' Yahweh said, 'The voice of your brother's blood is crying out to me from the earth. Now you are cursed from the soil which has opened wide its mouth to receive your brother's blood from your hand. If you till the soil, it will no longer yield its strength to you. You will be a wanderer on the earth.' (Gen. 4:8-12)

The invitation to go out into the country, absent from the Hebrew text but supplied from the ancient versions, was no doubt dictated by the need for secrecy. Here too, and in what follows, the narrative presupposes a social setting not confined to the brothers and their parents. Unlike other murders in the Hebrew Bible – for example of Abner (1 Sam. 3:26-30), Amnon (2 Sam. 13:23-29), Naboth (1

---

8   Taking his cue from the LXX, Enslin (1967) concludes that Cain carved the image of the sacrificial animal on the doorpost; Ben Yashar (1982) translates: 'If you do not do well, sin crouches for the first-born'; Westermann (1984: 300) has the interesting suggestion that Cain is being warned that he will be haunted by the ghost of the murdered man.

9   Castellino (1960) read this last phrase as an interrogative: 'Sin will be lying in wait for you, and are you sure you will be able to master it?'

Kgs 21:8-14), Jezebel (2 Kgs 9:30-37) – this one is described starkly, without elaboration. We are told nothing about the manner of the killing, the weapon, the circumstances leading to the act or the disposal of the body. Abel is silent throughout. Only after his death his blood is heard crying out from the earth. A primaeval fratricide recurs as a theme in many cultures, often as an element in a myth of foundations. The murder of Abel has, for example, features in common with the murder by Romulus of his twin brother Remus as recorded by the historian Livy: there is an inherited curse, a dispute about which of the two is more favoured by the gods, and there is much uncertainty about how the deed was done (*History of Rome* 1 vi 3–vii 3). By its stress on Abel as Cain's brother – repeated six times in this brief passage – the biblical narrative emphasizes the categorical demands of blood kinship and the appalling nature of this violation of the social and moral order.

The cry of Abel's blood from the ground is an appeal for justice, for the setting right of the disturbed natural order. Blood is the life principle (cf. Lev. 17:11). There is something primitive and at the same time compelling about the demand that blood shed by an act of violence, especially the blood of the innocent, is a serious disturbance of the natural and social order which sets in motion an imperative demand for redress, a cleansing of the pollution of bloodshed. We recall Macbeth brooding over his crime – 'It will have blood, they say: blood will have blood' (III iv 122). Hence the reader would expect the application to the perpetrator of the judicial norm encapsulated in the traditional axiom (translated literally):

The one who sheds the blood of a man
by a man his blood shall be shed. (Gen. 9:6)

However, Cain is not put to death, just as the man in the garden did not undergo the death threatened for eating the fruit of the forbidden tree. He is declared to be cursed from the soil which has opened wide its mouth to receive his brother's blood. Being 'cursed from the soil' is a strange and unique formula which can best be explained in connection with the sentence passed on the man in the garden (Gen. 3:17-19). In that case the ground is cursed on account of the man and his act of disobedience; here the process is reversed in that the curse on the ground, now polluted by the shedding of innocent blood, is somehow transferred to the perpetrator. It is, we might say, a derivative curse. Official and judicial recourse to the curse is a way of expressing dissociation from the object of the curse. The soil, rendered polluted and unproductive, will oblige Cain to abandon it, to be a nomad, a wanderer on the face of the earth. He has nevertheless not completely forfeited a relationship with his God. There is no absolute dissociation no more than there was for the man in the garden.

The sequel to the murder, its discovery, and the verdict on the guilty party is in the form of a brief exchange between Cain and Yahweh. This is in itself significant since it confirms the impression that the relationship has not been severed. Cain and his God are still on speaking terms:

> Cain said to Yahweh: 'My punishment[10] is too great to bear. You are cursing me by driving me off the land this day, and I must remain hidden from your presence. I must be a wanderer over the earth, and anyone who encounters me may kill me.' But Yahweh replied, 'Not so. Whoever kills Cain will incur sevenfold vengeance.' Then Yahweh put a mark on Cain so that whoever encountered him would not kill him. So Cain went out from the presence of Yahweh and settled in the land of Nod, east of Eden. (Gen. 4:13-16)

Cain is expelled not only from the place where he and his brother lived, the farmer alongside of the shepherd, but also from the presence of his God. For the writer as also for his first readers or hearers, this kind of language would have conveyed the idea of expulsion from the cult community. As we know from the Psalms, to see God's face or presence (the same word) is to participate in the common worship. That is where one is in the Presence, where one sees the face of God. The psalmist who, for reasons unknown, is exiled from Jerusalem and nostalgic for the joyful ceremonies in the temple, cries out from somewhere far to the north, perhaps in the Golan, 'When shall I come and see the face of God?' (Ps. 42:4). Participation in temple worship is also behind the frequent complaint that one is hidden from the face of God or that God is hiding his face.[11] The point of Cain's lament comes more sharply into focus when we recall that exclusion from access to the divine presence in worship also entailed expulsion from the community, what we would call loss of civic status. In a late Isaianic text a seer, speaking in the name of Yahweh, addresses sexually mutilated members of the community who are being threatened with exclusion on account of their condition. He reassures them of their secure status 'in my house and within my walls', in other words, as participants in the common worship (in the house of God) and members in good standing in the city (the walls) (Isa. 56:4-5). About the same time, the community of the returned exiles obliges its members to attend a plenary session under pain of excommunication, a penalty which included loss of civic status, exclusion from the common cult, and forfeiture of immovable property (Ezra 10:8).

Cain's lament that he is destined to be a fugitive, a wanderer on the earth does not exclude the nomadic or semi-nomadic way of life characteristic of the Kenites, his putative descendants. It is a way of life viewed from the perspective

10 The more common meaning of the Hebrew lexeme *ʿāwōn* is 'transgression', but it can also take in the consequences of a transgression including guilt and punishment as, for example, in Gen. 19:15 referring to the imminent punishment of the cities of the plain; see Koch 1999.
11 Pss 13:2; 22:25; 44:25; 69:18; 88:15; 102:3; 143:7. On the expression 'in the presence of Yahweh', see Fowler 1987.

of the sedentary and urbanized cultures of antiquity, for example, that of the cultured Egyptians of the New Kingdom vis-à-vis the Shasu nomads of the Arava. That the perspective is that of nomadic tribalism can be seen from Cain's not unreasonable anticipation that his life would be in constant peril. The allusion would be to the treatment of the shedder of blood characteristic of such societies among which the protection of the sanctity of blood relationships was paramount. The penalty for shedding the blood of a member of one's own tribe was the social death of banishment, which would correspond to the situation anticipated by Cain. Strictly speaking, the blood feud would apply only in an inter-tribal incident of killing, whether deliberate or accidental, but in the harsh conditions of the desert or the scrubland which the author had in mind any individual living outside the tribal structures would be hard put to survive.

The parallelism with the garden narrative is especially impressive here at the end of the story. Just as the man and the woman in Eden not only do not die as a result of their disobedience but are prepared by Yahweh for life in the real world by being provided with clothing more suitable than fig leaves, so Cain is provided for as he faces an uncertain future. In the first place Yahweh issues a judicial edict to the effect that 'whoever kills Cain will incur sevenfold vengeance'. Attempts to explain this statement in a literally numerical sense are no more helpful here than in the saying of Jesus about forgiving 70 times 7, that is, 490 (Mt. 18:22) – evidently hyperbolic and in that respect typical of the sayings of Jesus. Since the reader might be left wondering how the edict could be enforced in the wilderness into which Cain was being thrust, Yahweh made a more specific provision by placing a mark on Cain to prevent what would otherwise be his likely fate.

From antiquity down to the present, numerous suggestions about this mark (literally 'a sign', Hebrew: 'ôt) have been advanced. Among proposals listed in *Genesis Rabbah* are the following. The Lord afflicted Cain with leprosy; the Lord made a horn grow from his head; he was given a dog, presumably a large dog, for protection (*Gen. R.* 12:12). Over the years many other interpretations, some of them absurd and offensive, have been proposed (Mellinkoff 1981). If, however, we follow our plan of staying within the language and logic of the text we must begin by insisting (1) that it was something Yahweh put on Cain; (2) that it must be visible; and (3) that it was intended to protect him from the vendetta which otherwise would be his lot. According to the first requirement, therefore, it could not have been a dog, and according to the second it could not have been circumcision, another rabbinic suggestion.

The most important requirement is the third. In the vast commentary on the mark it is also the most misunderstood and abused, especially when applied to racial and physical characteristics of the despised 'other'. We may find an instructive parallel in the fictional account of the wise woman of Tekoa suborned by Joab to persuade David to forgive Absalom (2 Sam. 14:4-7). It will be recalled that Absalom had treacherously killed his brother Amnon to avenge Tamar, his sister, whom Amnon had raped. The Tekoan woman's 'story within the story' narrates that one of her sons was killed by his brother when 'out in the country' (cf. Gen. 4:8), with the result that the rest of the family demanded that the murderer be handed over to give a life for a life, which would leave her without a son and heir. The narrative stratagem worked. David heard her petition and promised to take measures to protect the murderer from the consequences of his act; 'not one hair of your son will fall to the ground' (2 Sam. 14:11). The woman's fictionalization of a real, contemporaneous situation corresponds in plot and structure exactly to the Cain and Abel narrative.

Neither here nor in the assurance given to Cain are we told precisely what form the protection would take. Since the context is that of the tribe and tribal blood vengeance, it may be suggested that the mark was some distinguishing feature, perhaps a tattoo like the *shart* of the Beduin, which identified the individual as member of a group (tribe, clan, phratry) under the protection of a deity and therefore exempt from the blood feud. So protected, Cain moved out of the presence of Yahweh and, as a *nāʿwānād* (a wanderer), settled in Nod, the Land of Wandering. Its location east of Eden, where Adam and Eve settled after their expulsion (Gen. 3:24), may simply be a way of reinforcing the note of regret and loss on which the story of the man, the woman and the snake ended.

Filling in the Gaps in the Story

Left to themselves, texts are inert. A text requires a reader in order to come alive. We might think of the interaction between text and reader as a conversation in which, as in any good conversation, both parties have something to say and some listening to do. Where this happens, what the text has to say can emerge in the form of an interpretation which could be oral but will often be written. Unless the text is to be reduced to a sounding board which can do no more than echo what its interlocutor says, which would be the equivalent of a bad conversation, it must be allowed to impose some constraints on how it is interpreted. However, it can only do this if the reader brings to the text some degree of *critical* reflection. When carried out with care, finesse and imagination, the historical-critical method, now maligned in some quarters, makes it possible for the text to hold up its end of the conversation. To pursue this analogy a little further, a good interpretation, like a good conversation, calls for a balance between text and reader. The history of interpretations of Gen. 4:1-26, some examples of which occupy us in the present section, illustrates both positively and negatively, and perhaps more the latter than the former, this more demanding approach to the reading of biblical texts.

We saw in the previous section how this story presents the reader with many puzzles and how attempts to explain them have generated much of the vast amount of narrative expansion of the story. The greatly expanded narrative which emerges from this process has its own intrinsic interest and value, but it would be a mistake to put it on the same level of significance as the text which generated it. For one thing, the text is not completely absorbed by and does not completely disappear into the interpretative process. It is still there to be re-interpreted and expanded further after it has been worked over.

In this section we will be able to consider only a few examples of this expansive, text-generated and puzzle-generated narrative. The first of these puzzles, somewhat disguised in our modern translations, is the exclamation of Eve at the birth of Cain, her firstborn (Gen. 4:1). A literal translation would read 'I have created [or acquired] a man with Yahweh'. Since 'man' (Hebrew: *'îš*) never occurs with the meaning 'a male child', this peculiar usage seems to demand an explanation. One was forthcoming from the author of the Latin *Life of Adam and Eve*, an imaginative reconstruction perhaps based on a Hebrew original from the first or second century AD. There we read (21:18-21) that in response to Adam's prayers Eve was freed from her labour pains, and in giving birth was assisted by angelic beings and consoled by the archangel Michael. The infant, we are told, was *lucidus*, surrounded or suffused with light and, even more remarkable, immediately after delivery ran off, plucked a reed and brought it to his mother. One could therefore safely conclude that, right from the start, this was no ordinary infant; more like a mature adult, a grown man, than a baby, and hence Eve's description of him. Her exclamation was therefore provoked more by astonishment than by joy. The reed-plucking incident is explained by a simple linguistic *jeu d'ésprit*: the Hebrew word for 'reed', *qāneh*, provides an explanation of the child's name *qayin* additional to the mother's cry, 'I have acquired/created [*qānîtî*] a male child with the help of Yahweh'. Josephus (*Jewish Antiquities* I 52) and Philo (*On the Sacrifices of Abel and Cain* 2) have a less flattering explanation of the name as meaning 'acquisition' (*ktēsis*), indicating Cain's grasping and acquisitive nature, based on the Old Greek translation of Eve's 'I have acquired [*ektēsamen*]' in Gen. 4:1.

A prominent feature of this midrashic tradition is the conviction that the evil deed Cain committed casts its dark shadow back on to the birth. One version of the Aramaic Palestinian tradition, which can be presumed to date from the Tannaitic period, the first or early second century AD (Targum Pseudo-Jonathan to Gen. 4:1), draws a very negative conclusion from the statement that Adam 'knew' his wife. 'To know' (Hebrew: *yāda'*) is a common euphemism for sexual relations, but for the targumist what Adam knew was something about his wife, and something not at all good. What he knew or suspected was that she had conceived by the evil angel Sammael or, according to a variant tradition, by the serpent, the same serpent which had seduced her in the garden (*Pirqe Rabbi Eliezer* 21). This reading of the text seems to have been widespread. The mother of the seven martyred brothers may be referring to it in claiming before her execution that the deceitful serpent had not defiled her virginity (*4 Macc.* 18:7-8). The first Johannine letter (1 Jn 3:11-12) inculcates love of the brethren by appeal to the antithetic example of the murder of Abel his brother by Cain who was 'from the Evil One'. The Fourth Gospel (Jn 8:31-47) takes this further where it records a particularly bitter controversy between Jesus and some other Jews who had believed in him but apparently no longer did so. Jesus shockingly counters their claim to be descendants of Abraham by describing them as descended from the devil (*diabolos*), from one who was a murderer and a liar from the beginning. The allusion is unmistakably to Cain, the spawn of the Evil One (Brown 1966: 358, 368). In the early centuries the same tradition was a familiar weapon in both orthodox and heterodox Christian circles in the service of anti-Jewish polemic, for example in the writings of Tertullian (e.g. *Patience* 5:15).

Another way of filling in perceived gaps in this first incident in the Cain and Abel story was to enlarge Eve's family with daughters as well as sons. Josephus is content with simply stating that daughters were born to them (*Jewish Antiquities* I 52), but a tradition already in circulation assigned them names. According to *Jubilees* (4:1-9) the proto-parents had 14 children including at least two females, Awan who became the wife of Cain and Azura the wife of Seth. The *Life of Adam and Eve* (23-24) mentions 30 sons and 30 daughters in addition to the three biblical sons, and adds an account of Eve's nightmare after the birth of Abel in which she sees Cain drinking his brother's blood. Other names and other numbers show up in the early sources, among which the one most closely integrated with the central event is the rabbinic statement that the proto-parents gave birth to quintuplets: Cain and a twin sister, Abel and two twin sisters. These offspring provided a motive for the murder, since the brothers fought over the additional twin (*Gen. R.* 22:2–3, 7). According to variant traditions or inventions each had a female twin, or only Cain had a twin sister (Ginzberg 1955: 138–39). A Syriac source (*The Testament of Adam* 3:5) reports an alternative version, also carried over into Islam (Qur'an sura 33), that the brothers agreed that each would marry the twin of the other, but since Cain's twin Lebuda was more beautiful than Abel's he refused and insisted on marrying his own twin sister. One way or another, this idea that a woman was behind the murder – a woman created ad hoc for the purpose – became a persistent feature of the Cain and Abel tradition.

It was suggested earlier that the Hebrew text itself, without further elaboration, provides a clue to the rejection of Cain's offering in the way it describes the material offered. In his treatise on *The Sacrifices of Abel and Cain* Philo makes a similar point by noting that Cain offered just fruits of the soil rather than the firstfruits and, what made it worse, he delayed his offering for some time instead of doing it at once (*Sacrifices of Abel and Cain* 52, 72). *Genesis Rabbah* also notes that Cain offered inferior products, but then spoiled it by adding that, in any case, God prefers the shepherd to the farmer (*Gen. R.* 22: 3, 5). The same preference is mentioned by both Philo (*Sacrifices of Abel and Cain* 50–52) and Josephus (*Jewish Antiquities* I 53–54) as a way of explaining the rejection of Cain's offering. And, of course, if Cain's moral turpitude was already in evidence, as Josephus avers (*Jewish Antiquities* I 53), further explanations would be superfluous.

Somewhat surprisingly, the midrash shows relatively little interest in the question how Cain knew that his offering had been rejected. If we make due allowance for the compression of time in the narrative, we might suppose that an eventual bad harvest would lead to that conclusion. And since the extreme brevity of the story leaves room for speculation, perhaps fire came down from heaven and consumed Abel's offering, as happened to Aaron's in the wilderness and the offerings of Gideon and Elijah (Lev. 9:24; Judg. 6:21; 1 Kgs 18:38; Ginzberg 1955: 135–36). However he made the discovery, if for the moment we confine ourselves to the biblical text, being angry, or at least passive–aggressive, does not seem to be an unreasonable reaction to rejection, and we might have expected him to answer like Jonah to whom the Lord addressed a similar question. 'Is it right for you to be angry?', asked the Lord, to which Jonah replied, 'Yes, angry enough to die' (Jon. 4:9).

The admonition which follows provides the first indication of a basic ambivalence about Cain in the midrash.. A literal translation of Gen. 4:7 – 'If you do well, you can hold your head high' – would read 'If you do well – a lifting up' or 'If you do well – a taking away'. Some rabbinic commentary understands it to refer to the taking away of sin, in other words, forgiveness. Rabbi Berekiah in the name of Rabbi Simeon cites Ps. 32:1 in illustration: 'Happy is the one whose transgression is forgiven' (*Gen. R.* 20:6) and Targum Pseudo-Jonathan paraphrases:

> If you perform your deeds well, your guilt shall be forgiven you; but if you do not perform your deeds well in this world your sin shall be retained for the day of the Great Judgement.[12]

In fact, all versions of the Palestinian Targum interpret the sentence as an offer of forgiveness. Along the same lines, some of the midrashists take the despairing cry of Cain after the crime – 'My punishment (or guilt) is too great to bear' (4:13) – as indicating a degree of repentance which explains the relative leniency of the verdict. Juridically, murder required the death penalty, but Cain was only expelled from the arable land. Targum Neofiti I paraphrases Cain's cry of distress along these lines: 'My guilt is too great to bear, but you (the Lord) are able to loose and forgive'. The same interpretation is taken up into the Vulgate: *maior est iniquitas mea quam ut veniam merear* ('my iniquity is too great to merit pardon').

What the outcome would be in the event that Cain would not do well presented no less a challenge to Jewish interpreters. In keeping with the possibility of forgiveness for righteous behaviour, the Palestinian targumic versions (Pseudo-Jonathan, Yerushalmi, Neofiti I and the Fragmentary Targum, with minor

---

12   The translation is that of Geza Vermes (1975: 95). Compare the parallel in Targum Neofiti in McNamara 1992: 65.

variations) warn that 'if you do not perform your deeds well in this world, your sins shall be retained for the day of the Great Judgement. At the gate of your heart your sin crouches. I have placed control over the evil inclination within your power, so that you may master it, whether to be righteous or to sin' (Vermes 1975: 95–96).

Rather than suggesting to the midrashic commentators a demonic presence, the strange image of sin crouching at the entrance gave rise to reflection on the psychology of sinning. For one midrashist, the apparent grammatical incongruity between *ḥaṭṭāʾt* ('sin', feminine in Hebrew) and *rōbēṣ* ('crouching', masculine participle) suggested the idea that at first sin is weak like a woman but grows strong like a man. A certain R. Isaac came up with a more telling and, for our contemporary sensitivities, a more appropriate figure suggested by the image of sin crouching outside the entrance waiting for a chance to enter. Sin, the good rabbi explained, is at first like a transient visitor, then like a guest who stays longer, then like one who takes over and becomes master of the house (*Gen. R.* 22: 6). Reflection along these lines will continue in rabbinic teaching on the evil inclination (*yēṣer hārāʿ*), with respect to how it seeks to take over the personality of the individual and how it may be resisted.

At this point (Gen. 4:8) occurs the biggest gap, the failure of the Hebrew text to tell the reader what Cain said to Abel before going out to the killing ground in the open country. This lacuna provided an irresistible opportunity for the midrash to expatiate and, at the same time, give a more adequate explanation for the murder than the biblical account supplies. The brothers must have quarrelled. Perhaps the quarrel was about how to divide up the world between them, or on whose property the temple would be built, or maybe it was just about the additional female twin of Abel (*Gen. R.* 22: 7). For the targumists, however, only a very basic theological difference of opinion could account for the murder. The Palestinian Targum provides two versions of a remarkable theological dispute between the brothers. According to the shorter and perhaps older version represented by Targum Yerushalmi, Cain affirms that the world was created and is ruled by love or mercy (*reḥmîn*), by which he insinuates not the love of God as the saints speak of it but partiality on the part of the deity who makes decisions, grants favours or withholds them, according to personal preference and whim. Cain implies that it must have been on that basis that Abel's offering was preferred and his was rejected. Abel rejects this argument. God governs the world by justice not be arbitrary rule, rewarding and punishing according to the deeds of the individual, and since his (Abel's) deeds were more righteous than those of Cain, his offering was chosen and Cain's was rejected. In the longer version represented by the Fragmentary Targum the terms of the argument are much more direct and uncompromising. Cain affirms:

> There is no Judgement and there is no Judge, nor is there another world.
> There is no good reward for the righteous and no price to be paid by the wicked.

The world was not created by love and is not governed by love.
That is why your offering was accepted with favour, and mine was not
accepted with favour.

This moral nihilism was rejected by Abel who insisted on a world in which
justice reigns, righteous deeds are rewarded and evil deeds punished. He then
repeated the claim that he was accepted because his deeds were more righteous
than those of Cain.[13] This Nietzschean point of radical denial being reached, that
God is, if not dead, then at least indifferent to the morality of our actions, the
way was clear for an act of radical evil, settling accounts by the murder of the
innocent. The deed follows at once.

The biblical text leaves unanswered a host of questions about the actual
circumstances of the crime: How did Cain kill his brother? With what weapon?
Did Abel resist? How did Cain dispose of the body? Since no one had ever killed
before, the midrash speculates that Cain could have learned from watching his
father butcher a bullock or, if he did not slit his throat, he must have used a staff
or a stone (Targum Pseudo-Jonathan on Gen 4:8; *Gen. R.* 22:8; cf. *Jub.* 4:31).
According to Josephus (*Jewish Antiquities* I 55) he then attempted to hide the
body, at which point he was confronted by Yahweh as was Adam in the garden.
The brief conversation which follows is filled out by Josephus in his customary
manner. In rabbinic commentary on the conversation there is some concern to
explain why Yahweh asked Cain the question to which he already knew the
answer, but the interest of the commentators focuses rather on the blood crying
out from the ground. Use of the plural (*dāmîm*, literally: 'bloods'), although
grammatically unexceptional, is taken to refer to all the righteous descendants
Abel would have had if he had not been murdered, thus compounding Cain's
guilt (*Gen. R.* 22:9; *m.Sanh.* 4:5). This exegetical oddity will contribute to the
tradition which presents the fratricide as the primordial and archetypal crime
with consequences reaching far into the future, in some respects more so than is
the case with 'the fall' in the garden of Eden.

The crime narrative concludes with Cain driven out into the Land of
Wandering. According to the LXX, Cain complains that he will be 'groaning and
trembling upon the earth' (Gen. 4:14), thus giving rise to the idea that he spent
the rest of his life trembling with remorse after settling in 'the Land of Trembling'
(Mellinkoff 1981: 40–57; Kugel 1998: 163–64). Josephus, on the contrary, sees
him spending the rest of a rather long life in founding a city, but also in vice
and debauchery of every kind including the invention of weights and measures,
evidently considered to be a bad thing (*Jewish Antiquities* I 60–61). More sober
assessments retain the note of ambiguity apparent, as we have seen, in his first
reaction to the discovery of his crime. The Palestinian Targum interprets the

---

13   See the synoptic arrangements of the targumic texts in Vermes 1975: 96–99; cf. Grelot 1959. On
     the (proposed) anti-Sadducee *Sitz im Leben* of the dispute, see Isenberg 1970.

sevenfold vengeance of v. 15 in the sense that the punishment due to the crime will be suspended for seven generations. An alternative and more elaborate tradition held that punishment would be staggered over a seven hundred year period beginning at his two hundredth year and concluding with his death at age nine hundred (*Testament of Benjamin* 7:3-5). An even more benign – and certainly more inventive – outcome occurred to a certain R. Hanina ben Isaac. As Cain goes out rejoicing from the presence of the divine Judge, as if leaving the courtroom after the passing of sentence, Adam is waiting outside and asks him, 'How did your case go?' Cain replies, 'I repented and am reconciled'. Adam begins beating his face and crying, 'So great is the power of repentance, and I didn't know it!' (*Gen. R.* 23:13).

The Evil that Would Not Die

How did it all end? We have seen the tradition, if that is what it was, that Cain lived on for 900 years, an opinion no doubt dependent on the age assigned to his counterpart Kenan in the antediluvian genealogy (Gen. 5:14, actually 910 years). On the basis of Lamech's claim to have killed a man, some speculated that he died at the hands of this descendant of his (Kugel 1998: 167). *Jubilees* (4:31-32) records that he died the year after Adam when his house collapsed on him so that, in keeping with the *lex talionis* (Exod. 21:24), or just poetic justice, he who killed his brother with a stone was crushed by a stone. According to another opinion, recorded in *Genesis Rabbah* (22:12; 30:5), and less directly in Wisdom (10:3-4), he perished in the great flood. A more ominous note is struck by Philo who concluded from the Lord's prohibition of killing Cain, and the absence of any reference to his death in the biblical text, that Cain is the one 'ever dying and never dead'. He is the *athanaton kakon*, the 'deathless evil', of Homer's *Odyssey* (12:118). All the evil in the world, throughout all history, stems from the depravity whose name is Cain, and this evil, this taint, will always be present (Philo, *The Worst Attacks the Better* 177; *On the Confusion of Tongues* 122; *On Flight and Finding* 60–61, 64).

Cain, therefore, who could have become the model of the repentant sinner, became instead the embodiment of malevolence, of spontaneously generated evil, just as Abel became the first of the righteous and the proto-martyr. The blood that cries out from the ground is the blood of Abel, but it is also the cry of those righteous descendants of Abel who were denied life by Cain's evil deed. For the same reason the righteous sufferers and martyrs can claim spiritual descent from Abel. Biblical examples of the latter are Naboth murdered by the wicked Ahab (2 Kgs 9:26) and Zechariah son of the priest Jehoiada killed by Joash between the sanctuary and the altar (2 Chron. 24:22; *Gen. R.* 22:9; Palestinian Targum on Gen 4:10). This Zechariah is also seen as spiritual heir of Abel in the gospel saying about the innocent blood of the martyred prophets and sages of whom Abel was the first (Mt. 23:34-35; Lk. 11:49-51). Along the same interpretative trajectory, Abel inevitably came to be seen as a type of Jesus whose blood speaks more eloquently that the blood of Abel (Heb. 12:24). Emphasis on the righteousness of Abel and those who imitated him served to intensify the concentration of malignancy and horror on Cain's primordial crime. When taken over by early Christianity it also, tragically, provided another expression for the theological denigration of the Jewish people, a subject on which much has been written.[14]

The biblical text leaves the reader in no doubt that the murder of Abel was the act of a free agent. Cain ignored the Lord's warning and allowed the demon Sin to cross the threshold and take over the dwelling. But for many of the later interpreters, and perhaps also for the biblical author, free will was not inconsistent with the belief in a supernatural agency at work in the commission of the crime. According to one strand of tradition, noted earlier, Eve was impregnated by Satan (Sammael) under the guise of the serpent who had seduced her in the garden.[15] The same tradition is well represented in Gnostic circles,[16] and was familiar in the intellectual environment in which the Johannine writings came into existence (Jn 8:31-47; 1 Jn 3:12). Throughout the history of commentary on Genesis 4 Cain will never be free of the shadow of Satan.

---

14 Examples from early Christian theologians perpetuated through the *catenae*: Ambrose, *Cain and Abel* (who represent synagogue and church respectively); Augustine, *Against Faustus the Manichaean* 25.6; *City of God* 15:15, 17; Isidore of Seville, *Questions on the Old Testament* (circumcision as the mark of Cain); Bede *Homilies on the Gospels* 1:14 (the killing of Abel prefigures the death of Jesus).

15 Targum Pseudo-Jonathan on Gen 4:1; *Pirqe Rabbi Eliezer* 21, on which see Goldberg 1969; Hayward 1991. The statement in Wis. 2:24 that death entered the world through the devil's envy more probably alludes to Gen. 3:19 and the snake than to Cain's crime, *pace* Levison 1988: 51–52.

16 *Gospel of Philip* 61:5-10; see further Kugel 1998: 169.

CHAPTER 5

Enoch and his Times

The Antediluvians

The biblical story begins, in Genesis 1–11, with an account of the origins of the universe and the human race, followed by a brief sketch of the history of humanity during a first period of 1,656 years, and concluding with a mass extinction and a new beginning. Contemporary science assures us that the earth, in the course of its more than 4.5 billion years of existence, has experienced several catastrophic events and mass extinctions of life forms. Of these the best-known is probably the most recent, the event which resulted in the extinction of the dinosaurs about 65 million years ago and led eventually to the emergence of mammals, including humans. Most informed people today realize that humanity is now in a position to contribute to the occurrence of such catastrophic events in a perhaps not too distant future. The account of the deluge in this first segment of the human story makes the same point in a different way. Human actions have consequences which can bring into play forces which lie beyond the control and the immediate environment of the agent. History is not a closed system. There are discontinuities and intrusions from beyond the calculable linking of act and consequence. In theological terms, there is judgement and the possibility of salvation.

This first segment of the history of early humanity (Genesis 5:1–6:8) consists of the following:

1 A ten-member linear genealogy of Adam's descendants segmented at the end with the three sons of Noah (5:1-32).
2 The notoriously obscure account of the mating of supernatural males ('sons of the gods') with human females ('daughters of men'), one of the strangest incidents in the Hebrew Bible (6:1-4).
3 An explanation for the annihilating judgement of the great deluge (6:5-8).

We learn from the heading, 'These are the generations (*toledot*) of Adam's descendants' (Gen. 5:1), that this segment forms the second unit in the first *toledot* pentad. Most critical scholars assign the genealogy to the priest–author (P) and Gen. 6:1-8 to the Yahwist author (J), but we must insist once again that this section is part of the larger narrative in chapters 1–11, the work of an author in his own right, one who built different kinds of source-material into his work. We will also allow for the possibility that the genealogy from Adam to Noah is a distinct source incorporated into the work at some point. Furthermore, it is not always easy to distinguish between what is source material and what is the author's own contribution in incorporating and editing the sources. At all events, the current consensus about the extent and literary function of the two primary sources should not be taken for granted, as we shall have occasion to see.

We shall deal with these three components of the section in turn, beginning with the ten-member Adam genealogy (Gen. 5:1-32).

The list of ten names covers the period from Adam to Noah, that is, from the beginnings of the human race to the catastrophe of the deluge, an event which, according to the biblical chronological system, took place in the year 1,656 AM (*Anno Mundi*, calculated from creation). The basic formula on which the genealogy is constructed is apparent:

PN^1 was X years old when he begot PN^2;
PN^1 lived X years after begetting PN^2 and had (other) sons and daughters;
The entire lifetime of PN^1 was X years, then he died.

The regularity of this schema is disturbed at the beginning with the reference back to the creation account (Gen. 5:1b-3), at the end with the explanation of Noah's name and mention of his three sons (Gen. 5:28-29, 32), and, famously, in the privileged seventh place with Enoch who walked with God and was not (Gen. 5:22, 24). The feature which stands out here, and in the parallel ten-member genealogy of the postdiluvians (Gen. 11:10-26), is the age of the patriarch at the birth of a son. There is no secret about the purpose of this unusual feature. It enables the construction of an unbroken chronological sequence for human history from the beginnings to the deluge, then – in 11:10-26 – from there without a break to the birth of Abraham, a period according to biblical reckoning of 1,946 years. At that point we enter what in that context was considered historical time. This emphasis on the chronistic element in the genealogy gives rise to an interesting and not unimportant issue which calls for closer examination at this point.

The Search for the Structure of Time

It seems unlikely that these chronological notices in the Pentateuch, most of them in Genesis, are purely arbitrary, and much more likely that they are components of a comprehensive system of some kind. Such systems are dictated by a conviction about the meaning of the history of humanity as a whole, its initial impetus, its duration and its direction towards a terminus. In their different ways, they are attempts to invest the apparently purposeless ebb and flow of time with some semblance of meaning. Such attempts often take the form of a 'world year' or 'great year' of a kind attested in several civilizations ancient and modern, often associated with astronomical speculations. The schema will be computed either calculating forwards from an absolute beginning or backwards from the end of an epoch or the end of history full stop. Such schemata are by no means confined to the biblical world and the ancient Near Eastern, Levantine and Greek cultures of which the biblical world was, in different measures, a part. At this writing (early 2010), for example, there is considerable interest in the Mayan Long Count calendar. Based on astronomical calculations, the beginning of the present historical cycle, lasting 5126 years, is computed at a date corresponding to 3114 BC. If the calculations are correct, It should therefore end in the year AD 2012. It remains unclear whether, according to Mayan theology, this date will mark the end of history or merely the end of one epoch and the beginning of another.

The best-known of such calculations by a Christian author is that of Archbishop James Ussher's *Annales Veteris Testamenti* ('Annals of the Old Testament') published in 1650. Though apparently uninterested in apocalyptic speculations, Ussher used biblical and calendric data to calculate backwards from the birth of Christ in 4 BC, concluding that creation took place on 23 October 4004 BC. Obviously, much more than the chronological notices in the Bible entered into the archbishop's calculations. At all events, the results were widely acclaimed on account of Ussher's prestige as a scholar and ecclesiastical statesman, and his date for creation was given canonical status by its insertion in the margins of several editions of the King James Bible. The archbishop took over the idea of a 4000-year cycle or 'great year', adding four years for the interval between the birth of Jesus and the Christian era as it was then calculated. Others adopted the same base figure adding 2,000 years for the Christian era. The resulting total of 6,000 years was based on the six days of creation interpreted in the light of Ps. 90:4 (89:4, LXX): 'A thousand years in your sight is like the passing of one day' combined with 2 Pet. 3:8: 'One day with the Lord is like one thousand years'. The idea of a 6,000-year duration of the history of humanity is attested in early Christianity, for example in *The Epistle of Barnabas* which asserts that 'in 6,000 years God will bring everything to an end' (15:4-5). The belief persisted. In Shakespeare's *As You Like It* (IV i 97–98), Rosalind consoles Orlando with the thought that the end is nigh: 'the poor world is almost six thousand years old'.

Calculations based exclusively on biblical data are complicated by the different figures in the LXX and the Samaritan Pentateuch. If, however, we limit ourselves to the standard Hebrew Masoretic text, accepting as a hypothesis a 4,000-year cycle, we come up with the following results which can easily be verified. We have just seen that the pre- and post-deluge lists are designed to allow for the construction of an uninterrupted chronological sequence. Calculating forward from creation in year one, the life-spans of the ten antediluvians and ten postdiluvians (Gen. 5:1-32; 11:10-26), added together, place the birth of Abraham at 1946 AM. This is the point at which, in the biblical author's view, we pass from prehistory to history. Adding Abraham's hundred years at the birth of Isaac (Gen. 21:5), Isaac's sixty years at the birth of Jacob (25:26), and the information that Jacob was 130 years old at the beginning of the sojourn in Egypt (47:9), we arrive at 2,236 years from creation to the descent into Egypt. The addition of the 430 years the Israelites spent in Egypt (Exod. 12:40-41)[1] brings us to 2666 AM for the Exodus or 2667 AM for the setting up of the wilderness sanctuary in the following year (Exod. 40:1-2, 17). It may not be coincidence that these last dates mark approximately two-thirds of a 4000-year cycle or world epoch.

For our next chronological marker we leave the Pentateuch behind to take in the beginning of the construction of Solomon's temple in the fourth year of his reign, 480 years after the Exodus, therefore 3146 AM (1 Kgs 6:1). The solemn way in which this date is intoned is unparalleled elsewhere in the history of the kingdoms; furthermore, this is the only attempt in the historical books to link history with prehistory:

> In the four hundred and eightieth year after the Israelites came out from the land of Egypt, in the fourth year of Solomon's reign over Israel, in the second month of that year, the month of Ziv, he began to build the house of Yahweh. (1 Kgs 6:1)

Calculating from that year on the basis of the MT without adjustments or overlaps, the reigns of Judaean rulers in Former Prophets (Samuel–Kings) amount to 430 years, interestingly the same length as the sojourn in Egypt. If, finally, we take the biblical calculation of 50 years (a jubilee) for the exile or, more precisely, for the period from the destruction of Solomon's temple to the decision to replace it announced in the edict of Cyrus issued in 538 BC (Ezra 1:2-4),[2] we arrive at 3626 AM. This is 374 years short of the 4,000-year epoch and 374 years added to 538 BC (passing now into absolute chronology) brings us to 164 BC, the date of the rededication of the temple desecrated by the Seleucids (1 Macc. 4:52-59). Consistent with the priest–author's history, therefore, the periodization focuses on the place of worship: the cosmic temple of the creation account, the setting up of the wilderness sanctuary, Solomon's temple, the rebuilt temple, the

---

1   To be preferred to the alternative, 400 years (Gen. 15:13), since 430 is clearly Priestly in origin, and we shall see that it recurs later in the chronology.

2   For the exile as the sabbatical rest of the land see 2 Chron. 36:21 and Lev. 26:34-35. The temple was destroyed by the Babylonians in 587 or 586 BC. A jubilee is actually forty-nine years ('seven times seven years', Lev. 25:8), but the proclamation of liberty is to take place in the fiftieth year.

rededicated temple. To facilitate checking these calculations, we can lay out the main lines of the sequence as follows:

Gen. 1:26-27; 5:1-5	Creation of Adam	1 AM
Gen. 5:28	Birth of Noah	1056
Gen. 5:32	Birth of Shem	1556
Gen. 7:6, 11	Beginning of deluge	1656
Gen. 11:26	Birth of Abraham	1946
Gen. 21:5	Birth of Isaac	2046
Gen. 25:26	Birth of Jacob	2106
Gen. 47:9	Jacob and sons in Egypt	2236
Exod. 12:40-41	Exodus from Egypt after 430 years	2666
Exod. 40:1-2, 17	Setting up of the sanctuary	2667
1 Kgs 6:1	Solomon's temple	3146
1 Kgs 6:1 to 2 Kgs 25	Judaean monarchy	3576
Ezra 1:2-4	Decision to rebuild temple	3626
1 Macc. 4:52-59	Rededication of temple	4000[3]

If this is accepted, the chronology must have been calculated backwards from some time in the Maccabaean period. Since it is difficult (though perhaps not impossible) to accept that the genealogies in Genesis 5 and 11 could have been composed at so late a date, the conclusion suggests itself that the chronological indications in these lists were revised at that time to fit the overall system with its terminus in 164 BC. In that case, the sequence may have been originally designed to terminate with the temple of Jeshua and Zerubbabel after the return from the Babylonian exile, as reported in Ezra–Nehemiah and the prophets Haggai and Zechariah. At any rate, this type of chronography was not an oddity, the product of a mind obsessed with numerological arcana. On the contrary, it is a way of expressing the conviction that the historical process is not a closed system but has both meaning and direction under the guidance and providence of God, Creator of the world and of time.

In addition, an eschatological perspective is implicit in the chronology as set out which in some respects coincides with, or at least is not inconsistent with, the eschatology of the visions in the book of Daniel. Both calculate the final phase of the history from the same point of departure, the edict of Cyrus issued in 538 BC ('From the time that the decree went forth that Jerusalem should be restored and rebuilt', Dan. 9:25), and both have the same terminus, the rededication of the temple in 164 BC. The visions in Daniel also use a sabbatarian or jubilee type of

3   The 4,000-year schema was hinted at by Wellhausen (1885: 308–309) and expounded briefly by Kuhl (1953: 69); more recently in Johnson 1988: 31–33 and Blenkinsopp 1992: 47–51. A Zoroastrian origin has been suspected, though parallels seem on the whole remote. On Zoroastrian eschatology, see Boyce 1979: 42–43, 74–75. On the Hellenistic context of chronography of this kind see Wacholder 1968.

periodization ('seventy times seven years', Dan. 9:24), one which, as far as we know, was confined to the last or post-exilic phase of the history (Montgomery 1926: 372–404; Collins 1993: 352–58).

The Masoretic chronology, therefore, takes its place with the Danielic visions and other attempts to decrypt the course of historical events in the light of the convulsive events precipitated in the middle decades of the second century BC by the agenda of Seleucid rulers and their philhellene Jewish supporters. To examine these in detail would take us too far away from our principal theme, but texts which contain comparable examples of theological chronology may be mentioned. They include the Enochian 'Apocalypse of Weeks' (*1 En.* 93:1-10 + 91:11-17) consisting in a series of ten heptads or 'weeks' counting from Enoch, recipient of the revelation, to the end of history. Somewhat similar is the dream-vision in *1 Enoch* 85–90 in which the *dramatis personae* are represented allegorically as lambs, sheep and other domesticated and wild animals. Here, too, history is periodized in successive segments from Enoch and the descent of the 'sons of God' to the final judgement. *Jubilees* has the same strongly predestinarian view of the course of history from creation to eschaton, since everything was recorded in advance on heavenly tablets (*Jub.* 1:29). The retrospective of the *Testament of Levi* is similarly segmented in jubilees and weeks, periods of 49 and 7 years respectively (16:1; 17:1-11). Several other texts preserved in the Qumran archive, mostly fragmentary and therefore difficult to decipher, manifest a lively interest in 'the division of the times'.[4] What is common to all these historical retrospectives, whether covering the entire course of the past or the post-exilic period only, is an overwhelming conviction of sin and impending judgement (Koch 1983). In the Genesis version, this same impression is retrojected into the mythic past of the human race, with reference to the judgement of the great deluge.

Literary Characteristics of the Genealogies

It will be obvious that the antediluvian and postdiluvian lists (Gen. 5:1-32; 11:10-26) have an important role to play in the chronographic system since they cover the crucial prehistoric period from the creation of humanity to the catastrophe and beyond it to the new dispensation and the new humanity. Both lists are conventionally assigned to the basic P narrative dated by most scholars to the sixth or fifth century BC. We may accept this conclusion as a working hypothesis, if without any great enthusiasm since there is nothing specifically 'Priestly' about

---

4   4Q 180–81 (4Q Ages of Creation or Pesher on the Periods); 4Q 243–45 (4 Q Pseudo-Daniel); 4Q 390 (Apocryphon of Jeremiah, formerly 4Q Pseudo-Moses); Damascus Document (CD 1:1-12; 2:16-3:21). Berner 2006 is a recent and very substantial contribution to the study of these and similar 'heptadic' texts.

Gen. 5:1-32 in ideology, theme or vocabulary. The reference at the beginning
of the list to the creation of humanity (Gen. 5:1b-2, cf. 1:26-28), certainly P,
is clearly an insertion. It disturbs the formulaic language of the genealogy and
refers to *ʾādām* not as a personal name, as is appropriate in a genealogy, but as a
collective ('humanity') with plural suffixes. The same is the case with the phrase
'in his image, after his likeness' with reference to Adam's son (Gen. 5:3). The
explanation of the name Noah towards the end also disturbs the pattern (Gen.
5:29), though in this case the borrowing is evidently from a source attributed
to the Yahwist author: the curse on the soil links with the verdict on the man in
Eden (Gen. 3:17), and the rare term for 'toil' (*ʿiṣṣābôn*) occurs only here and in
the Eden narrative (Gen. 3:16, 17). Since these expansions are from different
sources, they were probably inserted at a late period, after the P and J sources
had already been combined.

Attention should also be paid to the fact that the ten-member genealogy from
Adam to Noah is presented under the title 'This is the book of the genealogy
of Adam' (*zeh sēper tôlĕdôt ʾādām*, Gen. 5:1). This rubric complicates the
conventional and straightforward division of Genesis 1–11 into Priestly and
Yahwistic since it suggests the strong possibility that a distinct archival document
was incorporated into the narrative at some point, no doubt a late point, in the
formation of the Pentateuch.

Something should also be said about the relation between the antediluvian
list in Genesis 5 and the genealogical material in the preceding chapter. The
similarities are obvious. Five of the names are identical (Adam, Seth, Enosh,
Enoch, Lamech) and four are close enough to be considered variants (Kenan/Cain,
Mahalalel/Mehujahel, Jared/Irad, Methuselah/Methushael). The differences are
nevertheless more significant than the similarities. In Genesis 4 Lamech's three
sons are the originators of technologies necessary for civilized life, while in
Genesis 5 Lamech has only one son, Noah, whose name portends the imminent
judgement of the flood, and the names of Lamech's three grandsons announce in
advance the new world after the flood. In addition, the antediluvian list reverses
the order of Adam's two surviving sons. It begins with Seth and his son Enosh and
continues with what appear to be variants of names in the tainted Cain line. This
reversal may by a way of intimating the message, familiar from Mesopotamian
and Greek accounts of origins, about progressive moral corruption, the downward
spiral of history. In the Gen. 4:17-24 genealogy, finally, Enoch is the son of Cain
whereas in the following chapter he occupies the significant seventh position.
His removal from the scene, well before the deluge, seems to imply a negative
judgement on his generation. Appeals to genealogical fluidity go some way to
explaining the differences between the genealogies in chapters four and five
(Bryan 1987), but it appears likely that a shared fund of genealogical material
has been used for quite different purposes by the authors of these two chapters.

The Near-Eastern Horizon of the Antediluvian Genealogy

We turn now to the question of the literary context and environment of the antediluvian list in Genesis 5. The commentators usually begin by comparing it with the lists of dynasties and kings ruling in the earliest Sumerian city-states in southern Mesopotamia, of which about twenty copies, complete or partial, have survived. One of these, which served as a preface to lists of historical rulers, contains a sequence of eight antediluvian kings whose reigns, averaging 34,650 years, greatly exceed the biblical figures (Jacobsen 1939; *ANET* 265–66). This list bears comparison with its biblical counterpart in the obvious sense that both lead up to the deluge. In addition, Enmeduranki, like Enoch seventh in the biblical list, ruled in Sippar, a city dedicated to the cult of the sun-god Shamash, which will recall Enoch's 'solar' life span of 365 years. Enmeduranki also resembles Enoch in that he is said to have been transported to the council of the gods where he was taught divinatory techniques. By virtue of this revealed learning, he founded a guild of *baru*-priests expert in divination, a crucial aspect of Babylonian religion (Lambert 1967). While the parallels would suggest an ultimately Babylonian origin for Enoch, the differences between the lists are, on the whole, more impressive than the similarities. The Mesopotamian list differs in genre, purpose, names and numbers, it deals with kings not patriarchs and sages, and it has eight not ten rulers before the deluge (Lambert 1965; Hartman 1972; Hess 1989).

The biblical author may have been familiar with one or another version of the list, but the version which is closest to Genesis 5 is the list of antediluvian kings in the *Babyloniaca* of Berossus. This work, preserved only in fragments by the first-century compiler Polyhistor and transmitted in fragments by Josephus and Eusebius of Caesarea, was composed about 280 BC and dedicated to the Seleucid ruler Antiochus I. It lists ten kings before the flood, ending with Xisouthros (the Sumerian Ziusudra), the counterpart to Utnapishtim and Noah. After burying the writings containing the accumulated knowledge and wisdom of the antediluvian age, this ancient worthy built a boat in which he survived the annihilating catastrophe, offered a sacrifice of thanksgiving, and was summoned to live with the gods. The significant seventh place in the list is occupied by Evedorachos corresponding to the Mesopotamian Enmeduranki, seventh in the Sumerian king list, and ruler in Sippar on the lower Euphrates, sacred to the sun god Shamash. Enmeduranki/Evedorachos is therefore a close parallel to Enoch who, in addition to the solar significance of his age, is closely associated in post-biblical tradition with astrological and calendric lore.[5] While the hypothesis of a

---

5   See Burstein 1978: 18–19. On the relation of Berossus to the Babylonian chronicles, see Drew 1975. Russell E. Gwirkin's contention for the dependence of Genesis 11 on Berossus is vitiated by his highly speculative arguments for the composition of the Pentateuch at Alexandria in 273–272 BC (see Gwirkin 2006).

direct dependence of the biblical list on Berossus or of Berossus on the biblical list would be difficult to sustain, the chronographic and genealogical character of Genesis 5 is an early example of the same cultural impulses which produced the *Babyloniaca* of Berossus, the *Aegyptiaca* of Manetho and similar writings from the mid to late Hellenistic period.

If it is imprudent to maintain that Berossus marks the *terminus post quem* for the Genesis 5 list, we can at least say that *Jubilees*, a composition from the mid decades of the second century BC, marks the *terminus ante quem*. In the course of a considerably expanded retelling of the Genesis story, the author presents a list of Adam's descendants by combining the genealogies in Genesis 4 and 5 and rearranging the order but with no attempt at harmonization – for example, with respect to the two quite different Enoch figures in Gen 4:17-18 and 5:18-24. He also provides these primaeval patriarchs with wives who were either their sisters or cousins. The name Jared, which he relates to the Hebrew verb *yārad* ('go down'), suggested to the author the idea that it was then that the Watchers ('the sons of the gods/the sons of God') came down, initially with the purpose of inculcating righteousness by instruction and example. Then, at the end, between the birth of Noah and that of his three sons, the author interposes an account of the death and burial of Adam and the death of his firstborn Cain (*Jub.* 4:29-32). This part of the work, together with similar perspectives on the past in *1 Enoch*, represents an aspect of the intense interest in national, ethnic, and cosmic origins in evidence during the Hellenistic period, both stimulated by and in reaction to the dominant Hellenic culture (Horst 2002: 139–58).

The Seventh Generation

When we compare the antediluvian list in Genesis 5 with the genealogies in the preceding chapter, we see that in Genesis 5 the line of Adam's third-born son Seth (Gen. 4:25-26) takes precedence over the descendants of Cain the first-born (4:17-24), and that Enoch has been moved from a position in direct sequence to Cain (Kenan) to the significant seventh position. He is also assigned a completely different function. This genealogical material is evidently constructed to convey a message, and in the case of the Adam to Noah list, read in the narrative context of Genesis 1–11, the message is about the origin and spread of moral contagion. Humanity began well with the Sethites, the first to invoke the name of Yahweh, that is, to practise religion (Gen. 4:26). Within six or seven generations, however, moral corruption had set in and the decline had begun. According to *1 Enoch*, the point of entry of true evil into humanity was the descent of the rebellious angels and their union with human women in the generation of Enoch's father Jared (*1 En.* 106:13-14, the account of Noah's miraculous birth). *Jubilees* makes the same point with reference to the name Jared (Hebrew: *yered*) by associating it with the verbal stem *yārad* ('descend'). The linguistic association explains both the genealogical link between Jared and Enoch and the link between the message of the genealogy as a whole and the myth about the superhuman-human marriages in the passage immediately following (Gen. 6:1-4). The same theme, the spread of evil, may also be deduced from Enoch's removal from the scene after 'walking with God', construed as an implicit judgement on his contemporaries.

The seventh antediluvian generation reads as follows:

> When Enoch had lived sixty-five years he begot Methuselah.
> Enoch walked with God for 300 years after begetting Methuselah and he had (other) sons and daughters.
> Enoch's entire life span was 365 years.
> Enoch walked with God and was no longer there, for God had taken him away. (Gen. 5:21-24)

In this instance the genealogical formula is disturbed in two places. First, after the birth of his son, Enoch did not just *live* like the others but walked with God for 300 years. Then, in place of the death notice common to all the others, this more religiously intense form of living called 'walking with God' is followed by the notice of Enoch's removal from the scene. An extraordinary life, therefore, and an extraordinary end to it.

The other exceptional feature is the life span, anomalously brief when set over against antediluvian longevity as a whole and, specifically, in contrast to that of his father who would outlive him by 435 years and his son by 669 years. 'Walking with God', understood by the Septuagint translator as living a life pleasing to God, is also said of Noah (Gen. 6:9), and is identical with living in the presence of God, characteristic of Abraham and the other great ancestors and, in the Psalms, of the religiously faithful in general.[6] The wording would permit the conclusion that Enoch's walking with God began only after the birth of his son, and one might then speculate that, up to that time, he had been under the baleful influence of the rebellious angels. It was no doubt this reading of the passage which gave rise to the idea of Enoch as penitent, a characterization first encountered in ben Sira (44:16) and taken up by Philo.[7] However, the phrase 'after begetting Methuselah' simply reproduces the formulaic language throughout the genealogy and need have no further significance.

---

6   Gen. 17:1; 24:40; 48:15; Pss 26:3; 56:14; 101:2; 116:9. The verbal form *hithallēk* (hithpaʿel) in these expressions connotes both duration and movement, cf. Yahweh 'walking about' in the garden (Gen. 3:8), David walking about on the roof of his palace (2 Sam. 11:2) and the Satan walking to and fro on the earth (Job 2:2).

7   In Sir. 44:16 Enoch is 'an example of repentance' (*hupodeigma metanoias*), cf. Philo, *On Abraham* 17–18; *Questions and Answers on Genesis* 1:82; see Kugel 1989: 178–79. Somewhat different is the perspective in Wis. 4:10-14 according to which Enoch was taken away to preserve him from the corruption of his generation.

Commentators frequently observe that this information about Enoch, a figure otherwise absent from the Hebrew Bible with the exception of 1 Chron. 1:3, which is dependent on Genesis 4–5 anyway, is so succinct and so loaded with unanswered questions as to be practically unintelligible. Some commentators have therefore suspected that the notice about Enoch in Genesis 5 is an abridged version of a more ample and informative tradition about this great sage and transmitter of wisdom from primaeval times, a tradition already in circulation in some form at the time of the composition of the biblical text. This raises once again the question of the relation of the Enoch books, especially the 'Book of the Watchers' and the 'Astronomical Book' (or 'The Book of the Heavenly Luminaries'), to the list in Genesis 5, the *toledot* book to which the title of the genealogy assigns it, and the additions to it dealing with Enoch in 5:21-24. Certainty is beyond our reach, but the chronological priority of the brief biblical tradition about Enoch in relation to traditions of the kind which eventuated in the Enochian 'Book of the Watchers' (*1 En*. 6–36) can no longer be taken for granted. *1 Enoch* 6–36, dated by most specialists no later than the early to mid-third century BC, is admitted to be composite; for example, there are two leaders of the rebellious angels, Semyaza and Azaz'el, who teach humanity different things. The sources must therefore be older than the text as we have it, and the traditions on which these sources draw would presumably be older still.[8] There is also the possibility, raised earlier, of dating the antediluvian and postdiluvian lists independently of the classical Pentateuchal sources. In short, Gen. 5:21-24 looks much like a summary of a more extensive and complex tradition about this great sage of the archaic period, of the kind preserved in the Ethiopic Enoch cycle.

The Enoch Profile

The task of putting together a profile of Enoch as the dominant figure of the archaic period begins with the remarkable information about him provided in the genealogy. We learn there that he lived on earth for 365 years, that he walked with God, and that instead of dying he was taken away by God and was no longer to be seen. We shall deal with these features of the profile in turn.

The obvious astronomical significance of Enoch's 365-year life span suggests that, like his Mesopotamian counterpart Enmeduranki, he occupies a special place in traditions about those antediluvian sages pre-eminent in the sciences

---

8   This is the position of Milik 1976: 30–31 on the relation between *1 En*. 6–19 and Gen. 6:1-4. On the same point Matthew Black writes as follows: 'Gen. 6.1-4 certainly does look like a hebraised excerpt from the Aramaic narrative, possibly to provide a mythological beginning (the celestial origin of evil) to the Noah saga' (Black 1985: 14, 124–25). James C. Vanderkam, is typically cautious, but concedes that it is unlikely that 'all of even the earliest writings about Enoch arose from this modest (biblical) base' (VanderKam 1995: 13–14).

of astronomy or astrology (which were indistinguishable at that time). Writing about the middle of the second century BC, the anonymous author known as Pseudo-Eupolemus asserts that Enoch rather than one or other Egyptian scholar was the founder of astronomy, which was much prized at the time of writing (Holladay 1983: 157–87). He therefore joined the ranks of the primordial sages alongside Seth, Hermes and Zoroaster (Adler 1983). Josephus also comments on the importance of 'the science of the heavenly bodies' in antediluvian times but associates it with Seth and his descendants rather than with Enoch (*Jewish Antiquities* I 69–71). Probably the oldest of the sections of *1 Enoch*, from the third century BC, maybe earlier, is the 'Astronomical Book', sometimes referred to as 'The Book of the Heavenly Luminaries' (*1 En.* 72–82). It contains instructions imparted to Enoch on astronomical matters by the angel Uriel in the course of visions during the years preceding his final 'translation'. These instructions were to be passed on to his son Methuselah (*1 En.* 76:14; 79:1; 82:1). At the end of the vision, experienced in the heavenly sphere, that is, in a state of transformed consciousness, his seven angelic escorts brought him back to earth and set him down in front of his house. Before leaving, they charged him to pass on, orally and in writing, what he had learned to his son and his posterity in general, and he was granted one year to do this before his final disappearance from among them. This mandate implies that his vision ended in his 364th year, corresponding to the length of a solar calendar year, the religious importance of which is inculcated repeatedly throughout the vision (*1 En.* 72:32; 74:12; 75:2; 82:6). The one year's grace period was therefore intended to reconcile Enoch's age with the solar calendar.

Jubilees, composed in the middle decades of the second century BC, is an expansive paraphrase of biblical history from creation to the first Passover in Egypt. In his *relecture* of Gen. 5:18-24 the author of *Jubilees*, who was familiar with the Enochic 'Astronomical Book', presents Enoch as the first sage who wrote an astronomical treatise so that his posterity could observe the festivals at the correct time according to the solar calendar (*Jub.* 4:16-26), which would in due course receive its Mosaic confirmation (*Jub.* 6:32-38). Enoch is also credited with a written account, revealed to him in vision, of the course of history from the beginning to the last judgement (*Jub.* 4:19). As was the case with Enoch in the 'Astronomical Book', who was shown the deeds and destinies of all humanity from beginning to end (*1 En.* 81:1-2), there is a connection between the adoption of the correct calendar and the ability to predict the future course of events or, in other words, between astrology and prediction, even between astrology and eschatology, a connection which remains in evidence to this day. This privileged information was revealed to him by the angels of God during the six jubilees of years (that is, 300 years) following the birth of his son (*Jub.* 4:21), but the author draws no conclusions from this about the 65 years preceding that event.

Adoption of the 364-day solar year, divisible by 7 into 52 weeks, was of the greatest importance to the sect to which the author of *1 Enoch* 72–82 belonged, and for which presumably he was writing. It was also important for the Qumran sectarians, to judge by the many fragments of *1 Enoch* discovered at Qumran. It appears there were at least four copies of the work in their library. The Psalms scroll from Cave 11 (11QPs^a 27: 4-8) also has calendric significance since it informs us that David composed by divine inspiration 364 sacred songs, which is to say one for each day of the liturgical year. We see in all of this that calendric matters were a subject of contention in the late Second Temple period as they continue to be among historians of the period and commentators to the present.[9] It should not surprise us that questions of this kind concerning liturgical practice carry so much theological weight. In the early history of the Christian church the Quartodeciman controversy – the issue being whether to celebrate Easter on the 14th of Nisan whatever the day of the week – led to excommunications and schisms, and the resolution of conflict on the date of observing Easter at the Council of Whitby in the year AD 664 decided the future of the church in England for centuries.

Enoch's Walk with God and Departure from the Earth

Coming now to the second issue, Enoch's unique relation with God. It was important for early interpreters of Gen. 5:21-24 to know why Enoch walked with God after the birth of Methuselah but, as it seemed, not before. On a critical reading, we would think it likely that the interpolator simply substituted 'Enoch walked with God' for 'Enoch lived' in a more or less mechanical manner, repeating it at the end and then, instead of 'he died', concluding with 'he was no longer there for God had taken him away'. He could well have done this without even giving a thought to the question whether Enoch walked with God before the birth of his son. This, however, was not obvious to the author of the 'Astronomical Book' for whom the visions and revelations took place after the birth of Methuselah. Nor was it clear to the author of *Jubilees* for whom everything happened during six jubilees or 300 years (*Jub.* 4:21). The same reading explains the portrait of Enoch as model penitent in Ben Sira:

Enoch pleased the Lord and was taken up,
an example of penitence to all generations. (Sir 44:16)

Likewise for Philo, Enoch changed from the worse (in the first 65 years) to the better (in the next 300 years) and thus serves as an example of repentance (*On*

---

9   See VanderKam 1992, 1995; Talmon 2000. The principal issues in dispute were stated and documented to the time of writing by Davies (1983). There are also questions about the extent and duration of changes introduced by Antiochus Epiphanes (1 Macc. 1:45; 2 Macc. 6:6; Dan. 7:25). Calendric matters played an important role in inter-sectarian disputes, e.g. CD III 14–15.

Abraham 17–18). And for those who concluded from the name of Enoch's father, Jared, that the transgressive angels came down during his (Jared's) life time, the first 65 years of Enoch's life could have been passed under their influence.

The most mysterious, the most resistant to critical enquiry and, at the same time, the most productive of imaginative comment of the three additions is the notice that – translated literally – 'Enoch was not for God had taken him'. Neither Enoch's disappearance nor the reason for it is self-explanatory. Josephus came up with a convenient solution by supposing that both Enoch and Elijah suddenly became invisible (*Jewish Antiquities* IX 28). The Old Greek (LXX) translation of Gen. 5:24, taken over by Philo (*On the Change of Names* 38), simply states that 'God transferred him', while the Palestinian Targums paraphrase 'he was not' either as 'it is not known where he is' (Neofiti) or 'he was not with the inhabitants of the earth' (Pseudo-Jonathan). The targumists may have had in mind the search for Elijah after his disappearance (2 Kgs 2:16-18). Given the extraordinary and mysterious end to the lives of both figures, it was natural that the traditions about Enoch and Elijah would come together. The same verb (*lāqah*) is used for Enoch's 'taking up' as for that of Elijah, but the account of Elijah's ascent in the fiery chariot in 2 Kings 2, one of the great masterpieces of classical Hebrew prose, is more forthcoming both in the lead-up to the final disappearance and the ascent in the chariot driven by the whirlwind. The Greek translation of the taking up of Elijah then provided a narrative structure or grid for the ascension of Jesus in the first chapter of Acts of the Apostles. The same verb, *analambanō*, is used (Acts 1:2, 11; cf. *analēmpsis*, Lk. 9:51), and there is the same link between the departure and the giving of the spirit of the master to the disciples. The disciples looking up as Jesus departed from them also recalls the promise that the spirit of Elijah will fall on Elisha if he sees him ascending (Acts 1:10-11, cf. 2 Kgs 2:10, 12).

Moses ended his life in an equally mysterious fashion: 'Then Moses the servant of Yahweh died there in the land of Moab as Yahweh had said. He buried him in the valley, in the land of Moab, opposite Beth-Peor, and to this day no one knows his burial place' (Deut. 34:5-6). The plain sense is that he was buried by Yahweh, hence there was no doubt about his death; but the fact that no one knows where he is buried left room for alternative explanations and conjectures. Josephus uses the same phrase about Moses as about Enoch, that he returned to the deity, but cannot resist the temptation to add the further detail that a cloud covered him and he disappeared in a ravine (*Jewish Antiquities* III 96; cf. I 84; IV 326), a detail also present in the account of the ascension of Jesus (Acts 1:9).

Metamorphosis by ascent into another sphere at the end of life is a familiar theme in ancient Mesopotamian and classical writings. Utuabzu, one of the antediluvian *apkallu*, is said to have ascended to heaven (Borger 1974). Etana, ruler of the city-state of Kish after the deluge, was likewise taken up riding on an eagle. (Dalley 1989: 189–202). By means of similar conveyance – Zeus in his eagle avatar – Ganymede was transported to Olympus. Aeneas and

Romulus, founders of Rome, ended their careers in the same way. But what is remarkable about Enoch is the extent to which this mythic topos expanded from the earliest traditions recoverable from Genesis 5 and *1 Enoch* to the vast, baroque accumulation represented by *2 Enoch*, the *Hebrew Apocalypse of Enoch* (*3 Enoch*) and more extensive elaborations in Islam and early Christianity. Out on the furthest reaches of this development in the identification of Enoch with Metatron in *3 Enoch* and Targum Pseudo-Jonathan to Gen. 5:24. *3 Enoch* purports to be a revelation of heavenly matters communicated to the mystic Rabbi Ishmael (early second century AD) by Enoch who is now Metatron, Prince of the Council and heavenly Scribe, the only one of the heavenly hosts who may be seated in the divine presence and may look on the face of the Enthroned One. His entire body transformed into fire after his ascent, Enoch has now taken his place at the right hand of Yahweh. He can even be referred to as 'the Lesser Yahweh' (*3 En.* 12:5; 48C:7), probably on account of identification with the angel sent to guide Israel through the wilderness who must be obeyed 'because my name is in him' (Exod. 23:21).

The danger to orthodox thinking of this kind of language is illustrated by the Tannaitic scholar and mystic Elisha ben Abuya who, after seeing Metatron in vision, remarked 'perhaps there are two powers' (*b.Hag.* 15a). The inference has been drawn that Elisha, known as *ʾaḥēr* ('the other one') or, by some, *ʾāḥôr* ('the recidivist') on account of his heretical views, had abandoned normative Torah Judaism for a form of dualism, one which may have influenced contemporary Gnostic sects.[10] These associations help to explain the negative attitude to Enoch in the opinion of many of the rabbis. We hear in *Genesis Rabbah* that the mysterious expression 'he was not' means that he was not inscribed in the roll of the righteous; that, moreover, he was a hypocrite, sometimes righteous, sometimes wicked; and that rather than being transported into heaven he died like everyone else (*Gen. R.* 25:1). But this negative verdict, a reaction to some aspects of what was made of the Enoch myth, is of minor import measured against the profile of the great sage and scribe of the old world before the catastrophe who walked with God and had access to heavenly tablets by virtue of which he revealed mysteries to humanity (*1 En.* 12:3-4; 81:1-2; *Jub.* 4:17-18; etc.).

In early Christian writings Enoch is a marginal figure. The Epistle to the Hebrews names him, together with Abel and Noah, as a model of faith from the archaic period (Heb. 11:5-6). The Epistle of Jude (14-15) cites *1 En.* 1:9 as a prophecy of the second glorious coming of Jesus in judgement on the world, and some early Christian authors – Athenagoras, Clement of Alexandria and, for a time, Origen – enrolled him among the prophets. The punishment of the rebellious angels and their confinement in Tartarus (*1 En.* 19:1) are mentioned in Jude (6) and 2 Pet. 2:4 and, since Jesus is universal judge, 1 Pet. 3:18-20 represents his

---

10 See the excellent introduction to *3 Enoch* of Philip Alexander (1983: 223–53) and, on Metatron, Scholem 1961: 67–70; 1971: 377–81.

descent into Hell and his proclamation to the spirits of the ancients. This somewhat marginal topos underwent a rich development in the *Gospel of Nicodemus*, the *Acts of Pilate*, the liturgy of the Eastern Orthodox Church and, eventually, the mediaeval mystery plays featuring the theme of the harrowing of Hell. But by then the memory of Enoch had faded from the Christian imagination with the exception of the Abyssinian Christians of Ethiopia who preserved the Enoch books as part of their scriptural canon.

Superhuman Males, Human Females, Giant Offspring (Genesis 6:1-4)

We saw earlier how *Jubilees* (5:15) places the descent of the 'sons of the gods' (superhuman males) during the lifetime of Jared, Enoch's father, based on the derivation of his name from the verb *yārad*, 'descend'. The biblical version of the descent, however, is located at the end of the genealogy and is followed by a more discursive explanation for the imminent catastrophe. It would be natural to conclude that the mating of superhuman males with human females and the birth of offspring, however it found its way into the biblical text, once in became an essential element of the explanation for the coming judgement. The episode reads as follows:

> When humankind began to increase on the face of the earth, and daughters were born to them, the sons of the gods saw how beautiful human women were, and took for themselves such as pleased them. Yahweh then said, 'My spirit shall not abide in humankind for ever seeing that they are but flesh. Their life span will be one hundred and twenty years.'
>
> The Nephilim were on the earth at that time, and even later. That was when the sons of the gods had intercourse with human women and children were born to them. These were the heroes of old, men of renown. (Gen. 6:1-4)

To many Jewish and Christian commentators from early times down to the present this passage seems out of place, extraneous, even scandalous and, withal, barely intelligible. It looks like a foreign body which has somehow found its way into the biblical text. On closer inspection, however, we see that it at least fits the narrative structure dictated by the five *toledot* units. We have seen how in each of these units a passage of P origin is followed by one traditionally assigned to the J source which supplements it or comments on it. In this instance the 'sons of the gods' episode can be read as a kind of comment on the genealogy preceding it. In the first place, the genealogy gives concrete expression to the demographic increase mandated at the first creation (Gen. 1:28) and to be repeated in the new dispensation (Gen. 9:1, 7), and the incident in 6:1-4 illustrates one effect of this increase not anticipated in the creation account. The genealogy also, and exceptionally, mentions the birth of daughters as well as sons in each generation, and these are the women referred to as 'the daughters of men' who attract the attention of 'the sons of the gods'. Following on this development, Yahweh's decision, that 'my spirit shall not abide in human beings for ever', leads to the reduction in human life span to the more credible maximum of 120 years. This new maximum longevity will be attained by Moses (Deut. 34:7) and surpassed by the three great patriarchs and the priest Aaron – which the author may either simply have overlooked or regarded as exceptions which prove the rule. In spite of what must have been a far lower average life expectancy in antiquity, 120 may have been considered an ideal. Herodotus attributes this age to a king of Tartessus in Spain (*Histories* 1:163) and reports that most Ethiopians attained that age by dint of following a diet of boiled meat and milk (*Histories* 3:23). The drastic reduction of life span not only serves as a comment on the great ages of the antediluvians, not far short of a thousand years, but erects a further barrier against the aspiration to achieve god-like immunity from death first entertained in the garden of Eden (Gen. 3:22-23). The implication is that the union between superhuman males and human females is a further step in the striving to erase the boundary between the divine and the human (Seebass 2007).

This instantiation of a myth well attested in ancient Mesopotamia and Greece about the striving to transcend the limits of humanity, to break through the boundary between the human and the divine, therefore takes its place in the unfolding narrative in Genesis 1–11. The man and the woman in Eden are expelled from the garden to prevent them from living for ever. Cain and Lamech arrogate to themselves the right to take human life and are expelled from the arable land to the wilderness. Nimrod is the first potentate and empire-builder, and the builders of the city and tower of Babel make their own attempt to reach beyond the limitations of the earthly city. We may assume thematic continuity once we are persuaded that Genesis 1–11 is a thematically well integrated narrative, the work of an author who incorporated and arranged sources in a rational way in the process of putting together a coherent and compelling story.

The broadly accepted chronological range for the dating of the Pentateuchal sources has obliged most commentators to conclude that Gen. 6:1-4 must be the point of departure for the vast amount of post-biblical narrative material dealing with Enoch, the rebellion in heaven and the descent of the Watchers. The conclusion is understandable, but not to the point of excluding alternatives. One alternative would be that Gen. 6:1-4 is a very succinct version of a narrative tradition, whether oral or written, familiar to the biblical author and his readers at the time of its insertion into the Genesis text. To repeat a point made earlier: Most specialist scholars date the Enochian 'Book of the Watchers' (*1 En.* 6–11) to the mid-third century BC.[11] Furthermore, it is agreed that these chapters represent a conflation of two versions which must be older than the finished work, and the traditions

---

11   Charles 1913: 2:170 (before the late second century BC); Isaac 1983: 7 (late pre-Maccabaean); Nickelsburg and VanderKam 2004: 3 (mid or late third century BC).

behind them older still. We can therefore no longer take for granted that the biblical version is the source and inspiration for the account of the descent of the Watchers in 1 Enoch. In this respect the Enochian version contrasts with the later account of angelic–human unions in *Jub.* 5:1-11 which, for the most part, simply paraphrases the biblical text.

The version in the Book of the Watchers corresponding to Gen. 6:1-4 may be summarized as follows:

> As humankind increased, beautiful daughters were born. The angels, sons of heaven, lusted after them and agreed among themselves to take women from among them and beget offspring. Realizing that they were about to commit a great sin, their leader Semyaza bound them with an oath not to abandon their project. The transgressive angels numbered two hundred in all, and were divided into groups of ten whose leaders are named. After descending on Mount Hermon they carried out their plan, had intercourse with the women and taught them magical arts, medicine, incantations and other arcane matters. In the alternative Azaz'el (Asa'el) version, men were taught how to make weapons and women were initiated into the cosmetic arts, alchemy and astrology. This angelic–human union brought forth monstrous hybrids, giants who devastated the earth and its wildlife and, having consumed everything in sight, began to consume each other.
>
> The afflicted earth cried out to heaven in anguish and the cry was heard by the leading angels Michael, Sariel, Raphael and Gabriel. These appealed to the enthroned Deity to intervene against Semyaza, Azaz'el and their followers who had polluted themselves with human women, revealed to them heavenly mysteries and populated the earth with giants who had filled the earth with iniquity and bloodshed. The outcome was the divine decree to bring on the deluge which would exterminate this evil brood while saving Noah as founder of a new creation and new humanity. Michael was to bind Semyaza in anticipation of the final judgement, Raphael was to do the same with Azaz'el, Gabriel was to dispose of the giants and Sariel was to warn Noah about the imminent catastrophic judgement on a corrupted humanity. The judgement was to eventuate in a purified earth and a new humanity, with all peoples united in the worship of the one, true God.

This rendering of the myth relates to the biblical version in two respects. The first is that the action of the 'sons of the gods' is considered 'a great sin' worthy of the most severe punishment. The biblical version, taken by itself, makes no explicit moral judgement on the 'sons of the gods' and certainly none on 'the daughters of men'. The punishment, if that is what it is, is simply a reduction of human life expectancy to 120 years, which can hardly be considered draconian. This declaration of Yahweh (Gen. 6:3) is sometimes reduced to the status of an insertion (e.g. Westermann 1984: 373–74), but it shares with the judgements on the man, the woman and Cain the element of leniency and even compassion, and nothing similar to the Enochian version is said of the offspring of these unions. They are simply individuals of heroic stature, men of renown.

On the other hand – and this is the second point of comparison and contrast – the emphasis in both versions is on the arbitrary nature of the act. This aspect is less clearly expressed in the biblical version, but it may be deduced from the phrase 'they took for themselves such as pleased them'. The arbitrary exercise of the sexual function and its destructive effects is a frequent theme in biblical narrative. We come across it in the 'endangered ancestress' passages in Genesis (12:10-20; 20:1-18; 26:6-11) and the struggle for the succession to David's throne (2 Sam. 11–20 + 1 Kgs 1–2) discussed earlier. Read in context, Gen. 6:1-4 relates the descent of the 'sons of the gods' to the moral degeneration which led to the judgement of the deluge, a point explicitly made in the Enochian version. This incident, all-too briefly described in the biblical version, cannot be dissociated from the sombre lucubrations of Yahweh which follow, the regret at having created humanity and the decision to destroy (6:5-8). There is, finally, the reduction of life expectancy, another counter to the attempt to erase the line between humanity and divinity, this time by generation.

Much has been written on the broader horizon of this myth of rebellion on heaven and divine–human mating. Some have found a parallel in *Atraḫasis*, in the rebellion of the Igigi against Enlil, lord of Middle Earth. But the Igigi, the lesser gods, weary of digging ditches to irrigate Enlil's realm, engage in a strike rather than a rebellion, and their dispute is resolved without violence by the decision to create an inferior race of beings – the human race – who will take over their task of serving the high gods. A closer parallel is Gilgamesh, a divine–human hybrid having two-thirds of his substance from the goddess Ninsun and one-third from Lugulbanda ruler of Uruk. At the outset he is free with the women of the city, taking for himself such as pleased him, but his heroic struggle to avoid death and transcend humanity is doomed to failure.

Other commentators have looked to a Canaanite or Phoenician background on account of the North-West Semitic origin of the expression 'sons of the gods' (*bny ʾilm*). This expression occurs in the Ugaritic texts with reference to the 70 members of the Canaanite–Ugaritic pantheon, offspring of El and Asherah. But there is no rebellion in heaven with consequences similar to those of *1 Enoch* and Gen. 6:1-4 and, as far as we can tell, no union with human women. The *Phoenician History* of Philo of Byblos has it that the primordial human trinity, Light, Fire and Flame, brought forth children larger than themselves, which is not such an unusual mythic topos, or actual situation for that matter. It adds that at that time women consorted freely with anyone who took their fancy, which is not at all the same as the situation described in Gen. 6:1-4 (Attridge and Oden 1981: 40–43).

We may find a closer parallel following the lead of Josephus who, in commenting on Gen. 6:1-4, observes that 'the deeds that tradition ascribes to them [the lustful angels] resemble the audacious exploits told by the Greeks of the Giants' (*Jewish Antiquities* I 73). According to Hesiod and Apollodorus, our principal sources, the Titans were begotten of Ouranos and Gaia, Heaven and Earth, and were therefore of divine and human parentage like the biblical giants. Under the leadership of Kronos they rebelled against the high gods, dethroned Ouranos, but were in their turn defeated by Zeus and confined in Tartarus, the lowest region of the underworld. They thus become the 'old gods', the predecessors of the Olympians, in that respect not unlike the giants (ʿănāqîm, Anakim) who walked the land in early Israelite lore. As the biblical Nephilim were presumed to have perished in the flood, so the union of gods with human women ended with the catastrophic Trojan War, the great divide in most Greek mythic traditions as the deluge is in Mesopotamian and Hebrew lore, and the point at which Zeus decided to put an end to matings between gods and human women (Bremmer 2004).

Both the mythic dimensions of the incident and its cultural and religious indigenization are in evidence in the biblical version. 'Sons of the gods' (běnê hāʾĕlōhîm) means simply individuals belonging to the category of (lesser) divinities, in the same way that 'sons of the prophets' (běnê hannĕbîʾîm) means simply 'prophets'. We met these divine beings earlier taking part in the joyful dedication of the cosmic temple (Job 38:7). They serve as messengers and retainers at the court of the heavenly monarch. A frankly mythological passage in the Deuteronomic 'Song of Moses' represents the deity, here designated Elyon, assigning members of the pantheon, the běnê ʾĕlōhîm or běnê ʾēl, to the nations of the world as patron deities, in which process Israel had the good fortune of having Yahweh assigned to it as its allotted patron:

> When the Most High [Elyon] gave the nations their inheritance,
> when he divided humanity,
> he fixed the bounds of the peoples
> according to the number of the sons of God.[12]
> Yahweh's share was his own people
> Jacob his allotted inheritance. (Deut. 32:8-9)

It was perhaps inevitable that these 'sons of the gods' or 'sons of God' would be redefined as 'angels [i.e. messengers] of God', and that is how the LXX translated

12 The MT at Deut. 32:8b reads *běnê yiśrāʾēl* (Elyon assigned territory to the nations according to the number of the sons of Israel), but most commentators agree that this is a theological correction of an original *běnê ʾĕlōhîm* (or *běnê ʾēlîm* or *běnê ʾēl*). Elyon is an epithet of the supreme Canaanite–Ugaritic deity El who, together with his consort Asherah, presided over the pantheon, the seventy 'sons' of El and Asherah. It appears that Yahweh is co-opted into the Canaanite pantheon (see Coogan 1978: 104). Hence the ancient idea that the nations of the world are seventy in number.

Job 38:7 and Deut. 32:8. The mythological basis of the rebellion and fall of the
angels as we find it in the Enoch cycle (*1 En.* 6–11) and in *Jubilees* (5:1-2) was
already familiar in Israel during the biblical period. Job asks how mortals can be
righteous with God when he finds fault even with his angels (Job 4:18). The basic
pattern is reproduced in a taunting Isaianic poem addressed to a Babylonian king:

> How you have fallen from the sky,
> Star of the dawning day! (Isa. 14:12)

The Hebrew for 'Star of the dawning day', *hēlēl ben šaḥar*, corresponds to the
names of deities known from the Ugaritic texts, and the myth correlates with the
rising of the planet Venus in the morning sky and its obliteration at sunrise. The
myth lives on in the idea of the fall of Lucifer ('the light bearer'), corresponding
to the Vulgate translation of *hēlēl*. The theme of the rebellion and fall of Satan or
Lucifer and his angels is attested in Philo (*On the Giants* 2) and Josephus who
understands their rebellion by analogy with that of the Titans of Greek myth
(*Jewish Antiquities* I 73). Early Christian writers are also familiar with the idea
of sinful angels cast down into the pit awaiting the final judgement (2 Pet. 2:4;
Jude 6). They may well have been familiar with some parts of the Enoch cycle; in
fact the Epistle of Jude cites a text from *1 Enoch* (*1 En.* 1:9 in Jude 14-15). Thus,
Satan in the guise of the snake in the garden of Eden and the rebellious angels in
the guise of the 'sons of the gods' in Gen. 6:1-4 provided alternative explanations
of the supernatural origins of evil in early Christianity, though the former is more
in evidence than the latter.

Identification of the 'sons of God' with the descendants of Seth and the
'daughters of men' with females in the line of Cain was proposed by early Christian
writers for whom the idea of angels having carnal knowledge of human women
was unacceptable. This idea also seemed to go contrary to the saying of Jesus that
angels neither marry nor give in marriage (Mt. 22:30 and parallels). The reverse
identification – Cainite 'sons of God' and Sethite 'daughters of men' – is somewhat
more to the point since daughters are mentioned in the Seth genealogy and the
Cainites are the transgressive and violent ones (Eslinger 1979). But the wording
of 6:1-4 implies human women in general not a specific group, and the evident
mythic contours of the narrative point unmistakably to the non-human nature of
the 'sons of the gods'. The same objection applies to the rabbinic identification of
the 'sons of God' with rulers and aristocrats (Alexander 1972).

The statement that the Nephilim, the 'Old Ones' (Gen. 6:4), were on the earth
at that time looks like an ethnological comment, not entirely different from learned
notes about the aboriginal inhabitants of the land in the book of Deuteronomy.[13]
Different and sometimes conflicting traditions about these peoples circulated,

---

13 Deut. 2:10-12 (Emim, Horim, Anakim, Rephaim); 2:20-23 (Rephaim, Zamzummin, Anakim,
    Horim, Avvim); 3:11 (King Og and his famous bed); 3:13-14 (Rephaim).

nourished by curiosity about prehistorical ruins, imposing megalithic structures and strange formations like Og's bed of gigantic size, probably a fallen megalith which seems to have been something of a tourist attraction (Deut. 3:11). Such curiosity is a common feature of folklore, often expressed in narrative form and in place names; for example, Wayland's Smithy in England and the Giant's Causeway in Northern Ireland. The Nephilim who peopled the earth in the antediluvian period could not have been entirely annihilated in the flood since the party sent to reconnoitre the land by Moses reported having seen them – hence the added phrase 'and even later' in Gen. 6:4. They were of huge size, like the closely related Anakim (Num. 13:32-33). The natural assumption would be that these Nephilim are the ones referred to as heroes and men of renown, a characterization which, at first sight, would seem to be commendatory or at least not pejorative. But the first of these terms, Hebrew *gibbôr* (here translated 'hero'), connotes strength in the first instance, and the reference to Nimrod as 'the first of the *gibbôrîm*' (Gen 10:8-12), to be discussed at a later point of our study, puts the use of the term in a less positive light. The same for the second designation, 'men of renown', literally 'men of name' (*'anšê haššēm*), which puts the Nephilim in the same category as the builders of the tower of Babel who went about making a name for themselves in the wrong way (Gen 11:4; Hess 1992; Coxon 1999; Hendel 2004).

The Septuagint, followed by the Vulgate, translates Nephilim as *gigantes* ('giants') and uses the same designation for Nimrod the *gibbōr* (Gen. 10:8-9). This usage is consistent with the frequent identification of the aboriginal peoples as gigantic, a not uncommon feature in the folklore of ethnic groups.[14] But more than ethnic folklore is at issue here. In *1 Enoch* 6–11 the offspring of the Watchers are the blindly malignant giants who lay waste the earth and its people and on whom a terrible judgement is passed. The giant myth seems to have been widely known. In *Jubilees* (5:1-5) the corrupt behaviour of the giants is responsible for the deluge. Sirach refers to the revolt of the ancient giants (Sir. 16:7), and both Wisdom (14:6) and *3 Maccabees* (2:4), perhaps roughly contemporary, are sure that the giants perished in the deluge in spite of the fact that, according to the biblical record, quite a number of them seem to have survived. The Enochic 'Book of the Watchers' solved the problem by supposing that their bodies perished in the deluge, but by virtue of their hybrid nature their spirits survived, and will survive until the final judgement, as agents and instigators of evil in the human race (*1 En.* 15:8–16:1). The giants therefore are transformed into evil spirits, active agents and instigators in the spiritual realm of the evils experienced and perpetrated by human beings throughout history (Stuckenbruck 1997, 2004).

---

14 Num. 13:28; Deut. 1:28; 2:10-12, 20; 9:2; Amos 2:9. These 'giants' seem to be concentrated in the northern part of the Transjordanian region, the Hebron region, the Shephelah and the Mediterranean coastal area. The stories about Samson and Goliath (also a *gibbōr*, 1 Sam. 17:51) may belong to the same tradition.

The Decree Bringing the Old World to an End

The strange story of angelic–human marriages and gigantic offspring is followed by something quite different but not unconnected; not another origins myth but a reflective comment of the author, a momentary insight into the mind and emotions of Yahweh leading to the decree bringing the old world to an end.

> When Yahweh saw that the wickedness of humankind had increased on the earth, and that all their inclinations and thoughts tended always towards evil, he regretted that he had made humankind on the earth, and it grieved him bitterly. Yahweh said, 'I shall blot out humankind *which I have created* from off the face of the earth, *human beings together with beasts, reptiles and birds of the sky*; I regret that I made them.' Noah, however, was acceptable in the sight of Yahweh. (Gen 6:5-8)

Unlike the passage immediately preceding, the language and syntax in this brief statement is straightforward: a decision to destroy couched in the first person preceded by the author's explanation for the decision and followed by a clarification. Many critical commentators have been at pains to point out that two insertions (printed in italics above), which betray the idiom and vocabulary of the priest–scribe, have found their way into this passage assigned to the J writer. This may be correct, and if so it simply provides another example that the final author combined his source material as he thought fit.

The sequence of verbs should be noted: Yahweh sees, he is sorry that he created humankind, he grieves bitterly, then – since verbs of speaking and saying often refer to mental articulation in Hebrew – he mentally formulates the decision to destroy. Yahweh's seeing is a retrospective on 1,656 years from Adam to Noah culminating in the infiltration of evil from the superhuman world. The retrospective parallels the rebellion of the lesser gods, the Igigi, in *Atraḥasis* and, less clearly, the theme of overpopulation, perhaps involving rebellion, in the same mythic narrative. But the Genesis story raised problems of a quite different nature. Since Yahweh's regretting could easily lead to the scandalous idea that the Creator God failed to foresee the future or, even more scandalous, that creating humankind was a mistake after all, one line of interpretation extracted a different sense from the corresponding Hebrew verb. The verb here translated 'regret' (stem: *nhm*) can, in the same theme, also mean 'take comfort', 'be consoled'. This suggested to the author of *Genesis Rabbah* (27:4), followed by Rashi, the curious idea that God consoled himself that he had made humankind on earth rather than in heaven where they could have incited the angels to rebel.

An interpretation which does less violence to the text is that of Rabbi Joshua ben Korha (mid-second century AD). In the course of a conversation with a sceptical Gentile who raised the question of divine foreknowledge apropos of this passage, the rabbi asked him, 'When your son was born what did you do?'

His interlocutor replied, 'I rejoiced'. 'But didn't you know that one day he would die?' said the rabbi, to which the Gentile replied, quoting Qoheleth, 'There is a time to be glad and a time to mourn'. The rabbi answered, 'Even so is it with the Holy One, blessed be He'.

In speaking of God, more so in looking into the mind of God, all language falls short, and in speaking of a god like the God of the Bible, who is in total engagement with humanity, it is impossible to avoid using the language of temporality and of changing human emotions, make of it what we will. The Hebrew Bible therefore speaks openly and often of God regretting, doing and undoing, saying and unsaying. So, for example, in spite of the prophet Samuel's statement that God is not like mortals who change their mind (1 Sam. 15:29), Yahweh regretted making Saul king (1 Sam. 15:11, 35) and brought about his downfall. We hear that the biblical God also changes his mind as a result of prophetic intercession (Exod. 32:9-14; Amos 7:1-6), or in response to repentance and the abandonment of an immoral way of life. The parade example is the imminent fate of the people of Nineveh announced to them, in contemptuously brief terms, by Jonah: 'In forty days Nineveh will be overthrown!' They repented and, in consequence, so did God: 'When God saw what they did, how they turned from their evil ways, God changed his mind about the calamity he said he would bring on them, and did not do it' (Jon. 3:10). In other words, God's response, whether communicated in *oratio recta*, or through prophetic oracle, or in some other way, fits the situation, and given that human beings are free agents and not automata, situations change in the course of time.

Rabbi Joshua ben Levi (early third century AD) compares the bitter grief of God to that of David over the death of his son Absalom (2 Sam. 19:1-3), and even represents God doing *shiva*, the seven-day ritual mourning, in anticipation of the death of his world (*Gen. R.* 27:4). At this point, the biblical author, and no doubt his readers, are wrestling with this incomprehensible decision to annihilate, and not only human beings but all living creatures listed according to the categories in the P creation account.[15] The problem certainly is about theodicy, the demand that divine justice must not only be done but must be seen to be done. The demand for *distributive* justice is met in Targum Neofiti I (on Gen. 6:8) with the statement that there was no righteous person in the world at that time except Noah. The implausibility of this explanation brings to mind the dialogue between Abraham and Yahweh concerning the fate of Sodom (Gen. 18:22-33). It opens with Abraham's rhetorical question: 'Will you sweep away the righteous with the unrighteous?' (18:23). At this point, the midrash is not content to dispose of the righteous few in the destruction of Sodom and its inhabitants as collateral

---

15 Cf. Gen. 1:24 and the same wording in 7:23, the flood narrative. Aquatic creatures go unmentioned both here and in the flood narrative for obvious reasons. No reason is given for the annihilation of non-human creatures. *Jubilees* (5:2) suggests that they too had 'corrupted their way' by engaging in cannibalism.

damage, regrettable but inevitable. The way it deals with the issue, in what must often seem to be intemperate language, reveals the enormous seriousness of sin, individual and collective, and the enormous importance of the issue of divine justice which brings into play the very existence of the providence of God. In one elaboration (*Tanhuma Bereshit*, 'Vayyera' par. 10) Abraham puts into the mouths of those not yet born a challenge to the God of traditional religious belief. If justice is not done and seen to be done future generations would say:

> This is God's *métier*, destroying the generations in the measure of cruelty. He destroyed the generation of Enosh, the generation of the deluge, and that of the dispersion of the nations. He never leaves off his trade.[16]

The outcome is that God defends himself, and his defence ends by citing Job's words to his 'friends': 'Teach me and I will be silent; show me where I have gone wrong' (Job 6:24).

The author's lucubration on the ineradicable human inclination towards evil, repeated after the deluge (Gen. 8:21), is matched by sombre reflections along the same lines in Psalms, in late didactic and sapiential writings and in late prophecy. A psalmist muses that there is no one who does good, 'no, not one' (Ps. 14:3). The great penitential Psalm 51 traces sin and guilt back to birth, indeed to conception (Ps. 51:5). Jeremiah – if it is he – concludes that the human heart is deceitful above all things and desperately sick; who can fathom it? (Jer 17:9). The Genesis text is the point of departure for the Jewish doctrine of the evil impulse (*yēṣer hārā'*) present from the moment of birth whereas the countervailing good impulse (*yēṣer tôb*) comes into play only at maturity. The evil impulse, closely associated and sometimes identified with Satan, exercizes a powerful downward force but does not take away free choice. It differs from the Christian doctrine of original sin in its more explicitly moral implications and by being paired with the impulse towards good.[17]

According to the main lines of the narrative structure of Genesis 1–11, manifested in the *toledot*, this passage (Gen. 6:5-8) concludes the antediluvian history while at the same time forming a transition to the deluge narrative which immediately follows.

16 *'ênô mēnîaḥ 'ûmānûtô*; see Blenkinsopp 1990.
17 Still very serviceable is Moore 1927: 1:479–96. The earliest occurrence of the expression *yēṣer hārā'* or *yēṣer rā'* is in the Psalms Scroll from Qumran (11QPsᵃ 19:15-16) or perhaps Sir. 15:14, as may be indicated by the Greek version (see Murphy 1958; Otzen 1990: 257–65).

CHAPTER 6

The Cataclysm

The Hebrew-Language Version of the Great Deluge

The central and structurally the most important unit in the genealogical pentad in Genesis 1–11, and the dividing line between the old world and the new, is the story of the great deluge. The story has given rise to centuries of discussion and debate, defending or calling into question the literal truth of the biblical account: how flood water could cover the highest mountains to a depth of more than 22 feet; how a vessel of the dimensions given in the biblical account could accommodate representatives of all the myriad species of insects, mammals and birds known to exist; how the biblical chronology can be reconciled with the inconceivably greater time scale of human history and so on. Beginning in the early modern period, the subject has generated, and continues to generate, an endless succession of theories including catastrophism, diluvianism, scriptural geology, close calls with comets, pre-Adamites, creation science, to name some of the better-known examples.[1]

All of this dramatically changed on 3 December 1872, when a young employee of the British Museum, George Smith, read a paper on 'The Chaldaean Account of the Great Flood' to the Society of Biblical Archaeology in the presence of the Prime Minister, the Right Honourable William Ewart Gladstone. Smith, a self-taught student of cuneiform writing, had succeeded in deciphering enough lines of the eleventh tablet of the *Gilgamesh* poem, in which Utnapishtim tells Gilgamesh the story of the great flood, to realize its close affinity with the biblical account. The lecture secured him a generous subsidy from the *Daily Telegraph* which enabled him to conduct further excavations in Ashurbanipal's library in Nineveh (Kuyunjik near Mosul in northern Iraq). In *The Chaldaean Account of Genesis* (1876), which contained the results of his labours in the field and in the British Museum, one of

---

1   The story is well told by Norman Cohn, *Noah's Flood: The Genesis Story in Western Thought* (1996).

the excerpts he presented in translation, which turned out to be from *Atraḥasis*, filled in a vital gap in the *Gilgamesh* account of the flood.

The importance of this juncture in the long history of the interpretation of the biblical account is obvious. The attempt to go directly from the biblical text to an event in real time was no longer feasible. The biblical deluge as a historical event was accessible, if at all, only by way of a textual tradition. Since the time of George Smith it has become increasingly clear that the biblical text is a relatively late Hebrew-language version of a literary mythic tradition of great antiquity. One of the earliest extant representatives of that tradition is the Sumerian flood tablet now in the University of Pennsylvania museum with six columns and about 300 lines, of which about a third is readable.[2] The story is also told on the third tablet of *Atraḥasis* and, in its most complete form, on the eleventh tablet of *Gilgamesh* where Utnapishtim tells it to Gilgamesh to explain how he was granted immunity from death by special grant of the gods. Derivative versions existed among the Hittites and Assyrians, and the tradition, if not the text, was known from early times in Syria and Palestine.[3] There is also an ancient Greek version. According to this version, Zeus decreed an annihilating flood on account of the sins of Lycaon (Wolf Man?), ruler of the Pelasgians. This aboriginal people, predecessors of the Greeks, are comparable to the Anakim, a population of giants exterminated by the Hebrews. The only survivors of the Greek deluge were Deucalion, son of Prometheus, and his wife Pyrrha who then repopulated the earth. The Roman version of the myth, transmitted by Ovid (*Metamorphoses* I 261–415), depended on the Greek, and the Greek version was to a large extent derivative from the far more ancient Mesopotamian literary tradition, perhaps mediated by the Late Bronze Age Hittites whose empire lay adjacent to the Greek-speaking peoples in Asia Minor. Even later than the biblical version is the account of the flood in the *Babyloniaca* of Berossus written in Greek and presented to the Seleucid monarch Antiochus I about 280 BC (Burstein 1978).

There are many other flood narratives from further afield – the famous folklorist Sir James Frazer counted 250 and his list is not exhaustive – but we will prudently stay within the limits of the cultural memory of the biblical author which is also ours to a considerable extent. A more pressing reason for taking seriously the literary history of the Genesis flood story is that the process of adapting and indigenizing an existing literary tradition is an important aspect of its meaning, including its theological meaning. Adaptation of a tradition is one of the filters through which the biblical text has passed before reaching us, and to neglect it is

2   First published and translated by Arno Poebel in 1914; ET by Samuel Kramer (*ANET* 42–44) and, with introduction and notes, by M. Civil in Lambert and Millar 1969: 138–72; see also Jacobsen 1981.

3   For the fragmentary Late Bronze Age flood tablet from Ras Shamra–Ugarit see Lambert and Millard 1969: 131–33. A fragment of a tablet containing a passage from *Gilgamesh*, but not dealing with the flood, was discovered in stratum VIII (15th century BC) at Megiddo.

to risk misunderstanding on a large scale. Furthermore, the biblical deluge, like the versions in *Atraḫasis* and *Gilgamesh*, has been made part of a larger narrative context, the biblical story of human origins in Genesis 1–11, which expands and modifies its meaning. It is no longer feasible to read the meaning of Genesis 6–9 off the surface of the text as if it were in the literary and cultural sense an isolated piece of writing.

A glance at a selection of the numerous commentaries on the flood narrative written over the last century and a half will confirm to what extent the emphasis has been on the identification and respective contributions of the principal sources, the Yahwist and the priestly writer. Hermann Gunkel, a major figure in the study of the Hebrew Bible in the early twentieth century, may have been justified in speaking of the distinction between J and P in what he called 'the flood legend' as 'a masterpiece of modern criticism' (1997: 138–39), but here as previously we prefer to work on the assumption that the biblical account of the deluge, in its narrative context, that is, in the context of Genesis 1–11, is the literary production of an author writing at a time when the cataclysmic events of the fall of Jerusalem, the liquidation of the Judaean state, and the deportations still cast a dark shadow. The date cannot be precisely determined, but we have seen that aspects of Genesis 1–11 suggest affinity with what is sometimes called 'late wisdom', represented by Job, Proverbs, Qoheleth and some of the more discursive psalms. Like other ancient authors, for example the incantation priest Sin-leqe-unninni whose name appears on the *Gilgamesh* colophon, the anonymous author made extensive use of sources, written and possibly also oral. In spite of occasional repetitions and discontinuities, this author has succeeded, with a minimum of editorial comment, in moulding these sources into a compelling and reasonably coherent narrative.

Among these sources the most important and the most easily identified is the priest–scribe's version. It provides the main element of narrative continuity, while the J version is more supplementary to P rather than concomitant with it, and is not nearly so continuous. For example, it has no account of the building of the ark and no explanation of its purpose, and at the end it narrates Noah's sacrifice omitting mention of his having left the ark.

A great deal has been written about the literary character of the deluge narrative which is instructive but not immediately relevant to our purpose in this study. One observation about literary structure as a guide to meaning should, however, be made. The narrative pivots on the moment when God remembered Noah, the moment when the fate of the human race hung in the balance:

God remembered Noah, and all the wild animals and all the domestic animals that were with him in the ark. (Gen. 8:1)

Leading up to that point, the water rises steadily, incrementally and inexorably, and after it the subsidence of the flood waters is measured out in precise dates. As in the creation account (Gen. 1:26-28, the creation of the first human beings), the narrator tends to adopt a kind of rhythmic *recitative* as the story approaches its climax. The narrative therefore rises and subsides with the rising and subsidence of the water. God speaks before the deluge, announcing the decision to destroy and giving specifications for the construction and provisioning of the ark. Immediately prior to the storm of water Noah is told to enter the ark (Gen. 7:1-4), and after it is over he is told to come out (8:15-17), but for the duration of the cataclysm (*kataklusmos*, the LXX translation of the Hebrew *mabbûl*, 'deluge') God is silent. We must imagine the disaster taking place in utter darkness and silence. Hence the dramatic moment of God's remembering at the point when the entire earth had been returned to the watery chaos which was there before God spoke in the first creation. The task of articulating what this means for the relationship between God and humanity, and how we are to understand why the deluge happened in the first place, is left to the reader.

Why Then Did It Happen?

This, then, is the most pressing question posed by the story of the deluge. In the earliest account, from ancient Sumeria, the decision to afflict humanity was made in the divine assembly (Lambert and Millard 1969: 142–43). In *Atraḥasis* the decision came about almost fortuitously. Enlil, on whose behalf humans were created in the first place, was disturbed by the tumult on the overpopulated earth. To remedy this problem he sent plague and famine upon humankind at intervals of 1,200 years. When these measures failed, he decreed a deluge from which only the hero Atraḥasis and his family were saved by the intervention of Enki, lord of the underworld. The decision was therefore by no means unanimous. Enlil's decree is in fact described as an evil deed (*Atraḥasis* II viii 35), and Nintu, the mother-goddess, excluded him from sharing in the sacrifice offered by the hero after the flood abated (III v 39–41). Although we are told in *Gilgamesh* that the hearts of the gods prompted them to send the flood (*Gilgamesh* XI 14), Enlil is blamed here too by the goddess since 'without reflection he brought on the deluge and consigned my people to destruction' (XI 162–69).

That the biblical author has taken over and chosen to follow this version of the myth of mass destruction in its essential structure is an exegetical fact which opens up new perspectives, provides a context for interpretation and poses its own questions. It also permits us to see more clearly what is unique in the way the biblical author has taken over and made use of his prototype. In one respect the biblical version is profoundly different. In the ancient Mesopotamian texts the reason for the cataclysm is to be sought in disputes and conflicting interests among the gods; the contribution of humanity is marginal. In the biblical version only one deity is involved, and the emphasis is on the spread of moral evil among humanity, enunciated in the first announcement of the disaster:

> When Yahweh saw that the wickedness of humankind had increased on earth, and that all their inclinations and thoughts tended always towards evil, he regretted that he had made humankind on the earth, and it grieved him bitterly. Yahweh said: 'I shall blot out humankind which I have created from off the face of the earth, human beings together with beasts, reptiles and birds of the sky. I regret that I made them.' Noah, however, found acceptance in the sight of Yahweh. (Gen. 6:5-8)

This statement, in the form of internal monologue, is surprising and even shocking since it seems to imply that over the time which had passed since the first creation Yahweh had learned something about human beings, something inseparable from their nature, which he had not known at the time of their creation and which now led him to regret having created them. The problem lies in the connection between wicked conduct, the immediate reason for the verdict, and the innate tendency to evil from which the conduct springs. The problem is mitigated if not entirely removed in the final statement about the one exception to the prevailing evil. In the following verse, which is the introduction to the central *toledot* unit, we learn that righteousness is possible in spite of the innate tendency to the evil impulse:

> These are the descendants of Noah. Noah, a righteous man, was the one blameless person of his time. Noah walked with God. (Gen. 6:9)

The negative implications for Noah's contemporaries of this emphasis on his moral uniqueness[4] are then set out in terms which clearly betray the hand of the priest–scribe:

> Now the earth was corrupt in God's sight, and it was filled with violence. When God saw that the earth was corrupt on account of the corrupt conduct of everyone on it, God said to Noah, 'I am about to make an end of all humankind, for the earth is filled with violence because of them. I will destroy them together with the earth.' (6:11-13)

What God sees when he looks at the earth recalls the first creation. The contrast in v. 12 (translated more literally) has a bitter poignancy:

> God saw the earth and, behold, it was corrupt.

> God saw all that he had made and, behold, it was really good. (Gen. 1:31)

---

4   The epithet *saddîq* (righteous, innocent) belongs to the forensic and social sphere in general, while *tāmîm* (blameless, unblemished) carries more specifically religious and cultic connotations.

Emphasis on moral corruption and violence leading to a final judgement on society reflects prophetic preaching, especially that of prophets active on the eve of the final destruction of the Judaean state. Jeremiah invites his hearers to scour Jerusalem in search of one righteous person, but assures them that they will search in vain (Jer. 5:1). The accusation of moral corruption and violence is a major theme in Ezekiel who lived to experience the final catastrophe. It is expressed with great emphasis in a sermon in verse in Ezekiel 7 in which several of the key terms in Gen. 6:11-13 appear.[5] His sermon, proclaiming repeatedly that 'the end has come upon the four corners of the earth', seems to have had for its text the words of Amos, 'the end has come for my people Israel' (Amos 8:2). It laments the prevalence of violence in its many forms, often as a by-product of prosperity, wealth and idolatry (e.g. Ezek. 7:11, 23; 8:17). These links between the P source in Genesis 1–11 and Ezekiel are understandable not only because the priest–scribe and the priest–prophet shared the same profession and culture but also because the history of early humanity is homologous with that of Israel, following a trajectory from creation to destruction and the possibility of a new beginning.

The decree of destruction which exempted only Noah and his family raises the same acute problem of the justice of God, and on a much vaster scale, as the fate of Sodom and Gomorrah taken up between Abraham and God in Gen. 18:22-33. Hence the insistence on the total depravity of that generation: only total depravity can account for the totality of destruction. It is assumed that the entire line descended from Adam and Seth had died before the deluge, presumably including Methuselah who, according to the biblical chronology, died the year in which the deluge began (1656 AM). This would have left only the descendants of Cain, whose moral depravity had already been established, and the giants, descendants of the fallen angels, analogous to the prehistoric Anakim (giants) exterminated by the Israelites or the prehistoric Pelasgians who provoked the wrath of Zeus. It was well know that these giants had perished in the flood (Sir. 16:7; 1 Macc. 2:4; Wis. 14:6). The Enoch cycle gives a detailed if somewhat overdrawn description of their misdeeds, including cannibalism, sexual promiscuity, bestiality and drinking blood. They taught men about weaponry and the arts of warfare and women cosmetics, adornment and astrology (*1 En.* 7:1-6; 8:1-4; 86:1-6; also *Jub.* 5:1). The admonitory preface to the Damascus Covenant document describes the guilt of the descendants of the Watchers in more sober terms: 'They became as if they had not been, since they did what they pleased and did not observe the precepts of their Creator' (CD 2:20-21). For Josephus, who compared the progeny of the fallen angels to the Greek Giants, the transgressors compounded their guilt by their rejection of Noah's preaching

---

5   Key words in Gen. 6:11-13: *ḥāmās*, 'violence', cf. Ezek. 7:11, 23; 8:17; 12:19; 28:16; 45:9; *šht* (verbal stem), 'corrupt', cf. Ezek. 16:47; 20:44; *qēs*, 'the end', cf. Ezek. 7:2, 3, 6, etc.; *kol-bāśār*, 'all flesh' (i.e. generally 'humankind'), cf. Ezek. 21:4, 9, 10; 37:6; on this last term, see Hulst 1958.

of repentance, a point on which the biblical text is silent (*Jewish Antiquities* I 72–75). However the situation is described, the question of the fate of the righteous caught up in the annihilating judgement on an unrighteous world is a real if tacit element of the deluge story.[6]

For the believer, the incommensurability of human thought and expression with the character of God and God's activity with respect to humanity means that a satisfactory answer to the question why God chose to destroy what God had created will always evade us. The narrative itself appears to acknowledge the problem by speaking of the irruption of evil into human history from sources beyond humanity. In the meantime, however, there remains the task of reading and interpreting the text before us, which brings us to the account of the event itself and its outcome.

Noah's Ark Sanctuary

As brief as it is, the account of the building of the ark (Gen. 6:14-16) contains too many obscure and rare technical terms for it to be fully intelligible. The term 'ark' itself (*tēbâ*), perhaps of Egyptian origin, occurs elsewhere only with reference to the papyrus-reed basket plastered with pitch in which Moses was deposited in the Nile (Exod. 2:3-5). The 'nests' (*qinnîm*) which Noah was told to incorporate in the structure are obviously not birds' nests but must have a derived technical sense, somewhat like a ship's 'crow's nest', for example. The reference would presumably be to sections, compartments, rooms or something of the sort. This is how the term is usually understood, but an attractive alternative suggested some time ago (G. R. Driver 1954) and adopted by NEB is to emend *qinnîm* to *qānnîm*, 'reeds' which in the consonantal text would have been identical in form. If this emendation is accepted, Noah would be told to cover the ark with reeds. This reading (pun unintended) would have the advantage of consistency with *Atraḥasis* and *Gilgamesh* in which the hero is told to pull down his house and build a boat, no doubt with the material from the house which, like most houses in Lower Mesopotsamia – known as 'the Sea Land' – would have been built with the huge, fibrous reeds growing abundantly in that region.

The ark is covered inside and out with *kōper*, one of several hapax legomena, but cognate with the Akkadian *kūprū*, 'pitch' which occurs at the corresponding point in the Mesopotamian versions (*Atraḥasis* III i 33; *Gilgamesh* XI 65). The wood of which the ark was constructed, Hebrew *gōper*, another hapax, is probably cypress (as in NRSV and REB), and the *sohar* is probably the roof, which could hardly

---

6   *Jub.* 5:2 interprets *kol-bāśār* ('all flesh') in Gen. 6:12 to mean that moral corruption affected animals as well as humans, presumably because, unlike animals in the first creation, they preyed on each other. But the destruction of animals, including fish not mentioned for obvious reasons, was not an issue for the author.

be omitted in a description of the ark's essential features. The instructions would therefore read as follows:

> Make for yourself an ark of planks of cypress. You are to make the ark with reeds, covering it inside and out with pitch. This is how you are to make it: the ark is to be 300 cubits in length, 50 cubits in breadth, and 30 cubits in height. Make a roof for the ark, rounding it off with an overhang of one cubit.[7] Put a door in the side of the ark, and make it with three decks: lower, middle, and upper. (Gen. 6:14-16)

As we would expect, several of these features correspond to the vessel in which Atraḥasis and Gilgamesh survived the cataclysm. Enlil urges his devotee Atraḥasis to destroy his house and build a boat covered with a roof and sealed with pitch (*Atraḥasis* III i 22–33). Gilgamesh's vessel is divided into nine sections with seven storeys, also covered in pitch and equipped with punting poles (*Gilgamesh* XI 24– 34, 56–69, 88), the only indication in any of the versions that the ark might have to move. In none of these descriptions do we detect a strong concern for realism and verisimilitude.

The same can be said for the measurements or symbolic metrics in all three versions. The base of Gilgamesh's vessel measured one *ikū*, equivalent to about 3,600 square metres, and it seems to have been conceived as an immense cube 120 cubits in length, breadth and height (*Gilgamesh* XI 29–30, 57–58). Its seven storeys suggest that it was thought of as a kind of floating ziggurat, perhaps a replica of the seven-stepped ziggurat shrine in Babylon. The measurements of both are put well in the shade by the dimensions of the vessel built by Xisoudros in Berossus which is five stadia or approximately 924 metres in length. The dimensions of Noah's ark were more modest but still impressive: 300 cubits long, 50 cubits broad and 30 cubits high. Comparison with the dimensions of the wilderness sanctuary (100 × 50 × 30 cubits) and Solomon's temple (60 × 20 × 30 cubits) suggests an underlying idea similar to the Gilgamesh vessel though, given the respective functions of the three buildings, and the fact that the wilderness sanctuary was mobile, we would not expect an exact correspondence. The height is, however, identical in all three, the wilderness sanctuary has the same breadth as the ark, it is one third its length, and Solomon's temple is one fifth as long. The measurements of Zerubbabel's temple in Ezra 6:3 and 1 Esd. 6:25 – 60 cubits (about 90 feet or 27 metres) in height and width – are not helpful. The correspondences should not be pressed, but it would be natural to represent the ark as a sanctuary, a place of refuge in the time of judgement, and it is no surprise that early Christian writers interpreted it along those lines, for example Augustine in *The City of God* 15:26 (Louth 2001: 130–50).

---

7   The translation of this last phrase, literally translated 'and to a cubit finish it off above', is
    speculative.

To this spatial symbolism corresponds symbolic representation along the temporal axis. The author seems to have simply juxtaposed two different chronological systems, though he may have had his own way of reconciling them. According to his J source, there was a 7-day prelude, perhaps as in *Gilgamesh* (XI 76) to allow for the construction of the vessel (Gen. 7:4, 10), after which the torrential rain began and lasted for 40 days and nights (Gen. 7:4, 17; 8:6). To this we must add 21 days for the dove to find her feet and the earth to dry (Gen. 8:6-12). According to this calculation, therefore the flood lasted 61 days. Conflated with this brief duration is the much longer and more complicated chronology of the priest–scribe. In the first place, it is calibrated with Noah's age and the birth of his sons (Gen. 5:32), thus fitting the deluge into the overall chronological schema discussed earlier. The deluge itself lasted exactly 150 days or five months (Gen. 7:24; 8:3), beginning on the 17th day of the 2nd month of Noah's 600th year (7:11) and ending with the ark grounded on Mount Ararat on the 17th day of the 7th month of the same year (8:4). Another 73 days would pass before the tops of the mountains would be visible (8:5), and the decisive date, marking the final retreat of the flood water, took place on New Year's Day of the following year (8:13, the first day of the first month of Noah's 601st year). This date aligns the emergence of the new world with the New Year's Day of the first creation, the cosmic temple, when the first clod of earth emerged from the watery chaos. It is also synchronized with the setting up of the wilderness sanctuary on the first day of the first month of the year following the exodus from Egypt (Exod. 40:1, 16-17). If the last date, the 27th day of the 2nd month of that year (Gen. 8:14), is a later correction, comparable to the rescheduled date at the end of the book of Daniel (Dan. 12:12), it would imply that the deluge lasted one year and eleven days (Westermann 1984: 449–50). This revised dating may represent a correction aligning the duration of the deluge with the lunar calendar of 365 days, eleven days longer than the 354-day solar calendar. In any case, the information on the structure of the ark and the chronology of the deluge, as defective and at times confusing as it is, confirms the homology with temple and worship apparent, as we have seen, in the creation account in Genesis 1.[8]

We are told very little about the interior of the vessel. It had a window, a door in the side and three decks. Rooms and compartments would have been necessary given the variety of animal inmates, some of them no doubt reserved for storage. Since no one knew in advance how long the deluge would last, provisioning was of the greatest importance. Gilgamesh took in not only 'the seed of all living creatures' but gold and silver (*Gilgamesh* XI 81–85). Noah is told to take aboard food of every kind that *may be eaten*, in keeping with the vegetarian diet mandated in the first creation and abrogated in the new dispensation after the

---

8   There is a considerable body of writing on the flood chronology, and a host of hypotheses, all of them inconclusive. Among English-language contributions I mention only McEvenue 1971: 55–59; Kselman 1973; Larsson 1977, 1985; Lemche 1980; Cryer 1985; Barré 1988.

deluge (Gen. 1:29-30; 9:2-4). This notice, drawn from the P source, contrasts with the distinction between ritually clean and unclean animals in the supplementary J source, a distinction necessary in view of the sacrifice to be offered on leaving the ark (Gen. 7:2-3; 8:20-22). The distinction between clean and unclean cannot be from the priest–scribe for whom the purity laws were first promulgated at Sinai. Sacrifice was also out of the question since there can be no sacrificing without a priesthood. Hence the P source mentions only a male and female of every living creature, the minimum necessary to repopulate the earth in the renewed creation (Gen. 6:19-20). In the same source Noah, his wife, his three sons and their wives, eight in all, are listed for the same reason. According to *Genesis Rabbah* (49:13), this number explains why, in pleading the cause of Sodom, Abraham stopped at ten righteous people in the city (Gen 18:32).

The Cataclysm Described

The coming disaster is announced once again as Noah and his family prepare to embark:

> I am about to bring a deluge of water on the earth to destroy from under heaven everything on it in which is the breath of life. Everything on the earth must perish. (Gen. 6:17)

This is the first indication of the nature of the imminent cataclysm. It is to be death by water. According to the J source the lead-up period of 7 days will be followed by forty 24-hour days of torrential rain (Gen. 7:4, 12, 17). We may detect at this point a note of bitter irony in that, at the beginning, it was the absence of rain which prevented the earth from being filled with life in its many forms (Gen. 2:5).

Leaving aside the chronological indications for the moment, the J account of the manner in which the disaster would come about is not necessarily incompatible with the more detailed version in P, the author's principal source. The preferred term in P for what happens is *mabbûl* ('deluge' 'flood'), which came to be used for the deluge in a temporal sense as event – such and such happened or so and so was born so many years after the deluge (Gen. 10:1, 32; 11:10). In the only occurrence of the term outside Genesis, in Ps. 29:10, the word may however have a more primitive and basic meaning. This is one of those psalms which praises Yahweh as lord of creation and victor over the forces of chaos and disorder:

> Yahweh sits enthroned over the flood [*mabbûl*],
> Yahweh sits enthroned as king forever.

The precise meaning of the first line is contested. In his Anchor Bible commentary on Psalms 1–50, Mitchell Dahood understood the preposition *lamed* governing *mabbûl* in a temporal sense, resulting in the reading 'Yahweh sits enthroned since the *mabbûl*', though Dahood took it to refer not to the deluge of Genesis 6–8 but to Yahweh's conflict with the forces of chaos at the first creation (Dahood 1965: 175, 180). This reading is certainly possible, but the alternative seems to be more in keeping with grammatical usage, as also with the representation in Mesopotamian myth of the victorious deity setting up his throne over the Apsū, the watery abyss.

The *mabbûl* is therefore not only the deluge as event but the source of the inundation, namely, the abyss or the deep (*tĕhôm*) of the creation account (Gen. 1:2). According to P, the inundation occurred when 'all the springs of the great abyss [*tĕhôm rabbâ*] were burst open, and the windows of the sky were opened' (Gen. 7:11). In the first creation God divided the upper from the lower waters to make a space for dry land on which human history could be played out (Gen. 1:6-10). Now, as the deluge begins, this creative act is undone. Water comes from above and below; the windows of the sky[9] are opened and the springs or fountains of the great abyss burst forth cancelling distinctions and obliterating everything in between. The deluge is an undoing of what was done in creation, a return to chaos, an obliteration of the precarious space for ordered human life. It is therefore an act of un-creation. This reading of the narrative is confirmed by the manner in which the deluge was brought to an end: the springs of the abyss and the windows of the sky were closed, and God made a wind blow over the earth, the same wind which in the beginning was swirling over the surface of the water (Gen. 1:2). Moreover, we shall see that the new world which met Noah's gaze when he was able to look out of the ark emerged from the watery chaos on New Year's Day, corresponding to the New Year's Day of the first creation (Gen. 8:13).

The brief description of the deluge itself presents in dramatic rise and fall, *arsis* and *thesis*, the inexorable surging of the flood water and its eventual subsidence:

The water kept on increasing; it bore up the ark so that it rose high above the ground;
The water kept on increasing greatly over the earth, and the ark floated on the surface of the water;
The water swelled more and more over the earth until it covered all the highest mountains everywhere under heaven;
The water kept on increasing until it covered the mountains to a depth of fifteen cubits;
Every living thing that moved on the earth perished – birds, cattle, wild animals, every creature that crawled on the ground, and all humankind.

9   Translating *ărubbâ* 'window' is traditional (e.g. *fenestra* in the Vulgate and most modern English-language versions) but a bit misleading. It refers to openings in the solid firmament, but also to smoke holes (Hos. 13:3) and dove cotes (Isa. 60:8).

Everything on dry land in whose nostrils was the breath of life died.
God blotted out everything that existed on the face of the earth – humankind,
cattle, crawling things, birds of the sky – they were all blotted out.
Only Noah and those who were with him remained alive.
The water kept increasing over the earth for one hundred and fifty days. (Gen.
7:17-24)

The pivot of the narrative, the *peripateia*, occurs at this point, with the flood water
at its highest point, almost 7 metres above the highest mountain. God remembered
Noah, the water began to recede and the vessel was grounded on Mount Ararat
in Armenia. God remembering Noah is not the reaction of an absent-minded
God who suddenly recalls what he had done. Remembering is rarely a purely
psychological process. When Joseph in prison asks the Pharaoh's cupbearer to
remember him when he is restored to favour he is asking him to act on his behalf,
which the cupbearer promptly omits to do. The same with those many requests in
the Psalms for God to remember (e.g. Pss 25:6; 74:2; 89:48; 119:49). To speak of
God remembering is a way of maintaining a meaningful linkage with significant
events in the past. God remembers at moments of crisis. The suggestion was made
earlier that the history of early humanity is, so to speak, superimposed on the
historical experience of Israel, and that the deluge is metaphorically correlative
with the destruction of the Judaean state and the deportations. In that case, God
remembering Noah will bring to mind that God also remembers his people when
in exile either in Egypt (Exod. 2:24; 6:5) or in Babylon (Lev. 26:42, 45). The
further implications of this remembering will be seen more clearly when we
consider the priest–scribe's account of the covenant which sets up and confirms
the new dispensation in the postdiluvian world.

The End in Sight

Simple narrative interest led the author, or his J source, to borrow the episode
of the reconnaissance of the birds from *Gilgamesh* (XI 131–54) and include it
at this point of the story (Gen. 8:6-12). In *Gilgamesh*, Utnapishtim first sent out
a dove and then a swallow, both of which returned. Then it was the turn of the
raven which flew about, cawed, but did not return. In the biblical version the
raven went out first and was not heard of or seen again. Since it did not return to
be debriefed, Noah sent out the dove, a more co-operative bird. The incident is
recorded in the common triadic pattern. On its first trip, the dove flew about and,
finding no resting place, returned. It was launched a second time and returned
with an olive leaf in its beak, perhaps to symbolize the re-establishment of peace
between earth and heaven and, more practically, to reassure Noah that vegetable
food would be available. Finally, it left for good, having found terra firma. These
bird missions are said to correspond to an old maritime custom of releasing birds

in order to ascertain whether land was near, and then follow their flight to landfall. They occupied four weeks, thus helping to fill out the chronological parameters of the deluge and introducing at last some feeling of uplift and euphoria. We may regret, nonetheless, that the author omitted the introductory verses to this episode in *Gilgamesh* (XI 131–37) which convey a different and, one might think, a more appropriate mood to this scene of mass death:

> The sea grew quiet, the storm abated, the flood ceased.
> I opened a window, and light fell upon my face.
> I looked upon the sea, all was silence,
> and all mankind had turned to clay ...
> I bowed, sat down, and wept,
> my tears ran down my face.

Thus, after a lapse of almost four months from the time when dry land began to appear (Gen. 8:5, 13, 14), the new creation commenced with the command to leave the ark and repopulate the earth, repeating the creation mandate to be fruitful and increase (Gen. 8:17; cf. 1:22, 28). At this point the author has inserted another narrative theme, Noah's sacrifice, also adapted from *Gilgamesh* (Gen. 8:20-22). This episode could not have been taken from the P source, since according to the priest–scribe only priests may sacrifice, and sacrifice was in any case instituted only at Sinai. Noah built an altar, the first altar of which we hear in the Hebrew Bible – since no altar is mentioned in connection with the offerings of Cain and Abel – and sacrificed as a burnt offering on it some of the ritually clean land animals and birds. On this point, J has stayed close to its own source, the great epic about the hero Gilgamesh. After the flood water had subsided, Utnapishtim offered a sacrifice and poured out a libation on the mountain peak. The sacrifice achieved its object since 'the gods smelled the savour, the gods smelled the sweet savour, the gods gathered like flies over the sacrifice' (*Gilgamesh* XI 155–71). What is of interest in the biblical version is the response of Yahweh to this first sacrifice:

> When Yahweh smelled the soothing odour he considered within himself, 'I will never again curse the ground on account of humankind, for the inclination of the human heart is evil from youth onwards. Nor will I ever again kill all living creatures as I have done. For as long as the earth endures:

> > Seed time and harvest time,
> > Time of cold and time of heat,
> > Summertime and winter time,
> > Daytime and night time
> > Shall never cease. (Gen. 8:21-22)

The 'soothing odour' (*rêaḥ hannîḥoaḥ*) is a technical term from the vocabulary of the sacrificial cult, signifying acceptance and atonement made for faults committed (e.g. Lev. 1:4; 17:11). The clear implication is that the change of heart indicated by Yahweh's reflections is the result of the sacrifice of propitiation. At the same time, the decision is prompted by the consideration that 'the inclination of the human heart is evil from youth upwards', essentially the same consideration which led to the decision to destroy in the first place (Gen. 6:5). Yahweh does not cancel the curse on the ground pronounced in Eden, in which humankind is deeply implicated (Gen. 3:17), but commits to not repeating it in the future. He also promises that there will be no more mass deaths of humankind as the result of divine decree, at least none like the deluge which had just come to an end. According to Josephus, Noah was afraid that the deluge might turn out to be an annual occurrence – he must have been following the shorter chronology – and therefore offered sacrifice to petition God to maintain the primitive order of nature necessary for the flourishing of human life on earth (*Jewish Antiquities* I 96–98). The point is well taken. Humanity cannot live for ever on the edge. The regularity of the seasons in a self-consistent and self-contained world would be a kind of guarantee of God's promise.

What are we to make theologically of this final incident in the story of the deluge? The Bible has nothing to say in the manner of philosophical theology about the divine nature in itself. But the God of the Bible is a god in continuous and ongoing relation to humanity which exists in time and in history. Viewed from our perspective, this relationship and interactivity with humanity makes it inevitable that God will have such changes of heart as are recorded in this and many other incidents recorded in the Bible. The easiest part is to admit that the theological intelligibility and interpretability of the interior monologue of Yahweh in Gen. 8:21 is restricted and to some extent predetermined by the author's choice to reproduce and adapt an incident from the version of the deluge in *Gilgamesh*. In the unfortunately defective text in *Atraḥasis*, the source of the version in *Gilgamesh*, the goddess Nintu (alias Ishtar) blames the other gods in general and Anu and Enlil in particular for the destruction of humanity, a criminal act which also affected the well being of the gods who were by it denied cultic services and sacrificial food (*Atraḥasis* III v 39–45). In *Gilgamesh*, however, she blames only Enlil who is excluded from participation in the sacrifice (*Gilgamesh* XI 166–69). In the biblical version the sacrifice is offered to Yahweh alone, and there is no other deity to question the wisdom or morality of Yahweh's decision to destroy. We will also recall that the biblical account is one version of a myth which is concerned to say something significant about human existence, in this instance about its precariousness and contingency, and the ambiguities underlying our embeddedness in our biological environment (Müller 1985). In any case, Yahweh offers no justification for his action. The repetition in somewhat different form of the assertion about the ineradicable human inclination to evil made before the flood (Gen. 6:5) is not justification for an act in the past but the reason for a change of heart in relation to humanity in the future. In the words of Gerhard von Rad, one of the most theological of modern commentators, 'the same condition which in the prologue is the basis for God's judgement, in the epilogue reveals God's grace and providence' (von Rad 1961: 119). This will not satisfy everyone, but that is perhaps as far as we can go.

The New Dispensation

The repetition of the creation blessing on humanity (Gen. 1:28; 5:2) and the command to populate, or repopulate, the earth (Gen. 1:28; 8:17) give the impression of a repetition of the first creation, and this impression is strengthened by the command to procreate with which the first of the two inaugural discourses of God begins and ends (Gen. 9:1, 7). The command is addressed to Noah's three sons who are to be the progenitors of a new humanity. This first discourse is followed by a covenant between God and all living creatures, announced solemnly at the beginning and end of the second discourse (Gen. 9:8-9, 17). The question naturally arises at this point, the inauguration of a second creation, as to what difference the catastrophe of the deluge and the mass death of early humanity has made. One difference becomes apparent at once: there is a profound shift in the relations between humankind and other animals: 'The fear and dread of you shall come on all the earth's living creatures – all the birds of the sky, everything that creeps on the ground, all the fish of the sea [at last the fish are mentioned!]; they are placed in your power' (Gen. 9:2). This goes well beyond the mandate to rule over the animal world in the first creation which, as we saw, should be given a benign interpretation (Gen. 1:28). Now, however, the key words are 'fear' and 'dread'. This abrupt alienation between humans and other animals, foreshadowed in the curse on the snake (Gen. 3:15), provides yet another parallel between the biblical story and *Gilgamesh*. It will be recalled how Enkidu, the wild man who cohabited in friendly proximity with the animals of the forest, discovered that after his initiation into 'civilized' life by the prostitute the animals fled his presence. The former intimacy had come to an end, and Enkidu even helps to hunt and kill the animals of the forest. There was to be no return to that lost world of timeless animality (*Gilgamesh* I 195–202).

The extent of the alienation becomes apparent at once: 'Every living creature that moves and lives shall be food for you. As I gave you the green plants, so now I give you everything' (Gen. 9:3). The vegetarian diet of the first creation is abrogated (Gen. 1:29-30) and, with it, the kingdom of peace and harmony comes sadly to an end. It is now acceptable to kill for food. This, too, is an ancient topos. In Hesiod's account of the golden age under the reign of Kronos (*Works and Days* 109–26), people lived from what grows of itself and had no need or inclination to hunt and kill. In a certain sense this new mandate can be seen as a kind of normalization, a realistic acceptance of life in a world which has lost its innocence. There remains nevertheless a deep and sad sense that this is not the way it was meant to be. The new order is therefore by no means a complete restoration. The deluge came about on account of the violence which had increasingly infected the antediluvian world. Now God makes concessions to violence and sanctions it within certain clearly stated limits. As in the author's J source, which acknowledges the reality of the ineradicable inclination to evil in the human heart (Gen. 8:21), it seems as if the deity had come to terms with the limitations of human moral capacity. This is now a damaged world calling for damage control.

The permission to kill for food does not distinguish between clean and unclean, understandably so since the entire narrative (Gen. 9:1-17) derives from the priest–scribe for whom this distinction came into force only at Sinai. The only reservation is the prohibition of eating meat with the blood in it. The primordiality of the blood taboo receives the greatest emphasis. It is one of those prescriptions incumbent on both Gentile and Jew, and for that reason some rabbis considered it even more basic than the Decalogue revealed to Moses at Sinai–Horeb (Milgrom 2000: 1469–1514). It survived into early Christianity, being one of the three prohibitions retained by the Jerusalem church under James (Acts 15:29). The numinous aura surrounding blood is, however, a widespread and ancient phenomenon attested far beyond Judaism and early Christianity. There is an underlying connection with the offering of blood, animal or human, as a way of communicating with the dead in chthonic cults of a kind which were certainly practised in Israel during the time of the kingdoms. According to this way of thinking, the dead can be revived and communicate only after ingesting blood. The classic case is the incident in which Odysseus conjures up the spirit of the seer Teiresias. After digging a pit with his sword, the hero poured libations, and finally (the text continues) 'I took the sheep, cut their throats, and the dark blood flowed. Then there gathered from out of Erebus the ghosts of those that are dead ... These came thronging in crowds about the pit.'[10]

In both *1 Enoch* (7:5-6) and *Jubilees* (6:7) the violation by the giants of the prohibition of ingesting blood is connected with their violent, homicidal behaviour. In Gen. 9:4-5, likewise, the blood taboo is linked with the protection of human life:

> For your life blood I shall require a reckoning:
> From every animal I shall require it,
> From human beings, each one for the blood of a fellow-human being;
> I shall require a reckoning for a human life.

---

10   *Odyssey* 11:24–26 in the translation of A. T. Murray, *LCL* 104 (2nd edn). That this is the origin of the vampire myth is fairly obvious. For another instance of the horror inspired by blood and eating bloody meat see Lévi-Strauss 1969: 152.

This solemnly enunciated statement that God is the ultimate guarantor of human life must seem strange coming after the mass death of the deluge, but we are now at the beginning of a new age, in a new dispensation. Satisfaction will be demanded not just from human beings but from animals. The idea that animals can be held judicially accountable for the death of human beings will seem strange to us, but finds expression in several ancient and some modern law codes and customs. In the so-called Covenant Code, for example, the rogue ox that gores a man or woman to death is to be put to death by stoning (Exod. 21:28-32; Finkelstein 1981: 48–85; Propp 2006: 232–36). The other noteworthy point is that the universality of the prohibition of homicide in the human community is emphasized by the statement that this is a crime involving *ʾaḥîm*, literally 'brothers', in the context meaning 'fellow-human beings'. At this point we may hear an echo of the voice of the first murderer asking, rhetorically and disingenuously, 'Am I my brother's keeper?' (Gen. 4:9).

The judicial implementation of this demand for satisfaction is stated with elegance and economy in the legal aphorism which follows:

The one who sheds the blood of a human being,
for a human being his blood shall be shed. (Gen. 9:6a)[11]

The saying is put firmly on a theological basis which connects once again with the first creation:

For in God's own image God made human beings. (Gen. 9:6b)

The aphorism reflects the well-known law of talion, which is by no means restricted to homicide (Exod. 21:23-24). This principle governing judicial proceedings (generally in the abbreviated form 'an eye for an eye, a tooth for a tooth') has not had a good press, in part due to the antithesis in the Sermon on the Mount (Mt. 5:38-39), but in fact its intent was to introduce a principle of equity into judicial proceedings. Talion was to take the place of the indiscriminate vengeance often visited by the offended party on the offender and his kin in some tribal societies and in some sub-cultures in our post-industrial world today. It is also not restricted to ancient Hebrew judicial practice. In the Hammurabi code, for example, it was applied at times quite literally: if someone knocks out your tooth you are entitled to knock out only one of the offender's teeth (#200; Huffmon 1992).

---

11 The ambiguity of the prefixed preposition in *bāʾādām* in the second line could also be translated 'by a human being' (as NRSV), and the ambiguity is exploited in other ways in the midrash, as we shall see. For the translation offered, following REB, cf. Deut. 19:21, the verdict on the false witness in which the penalty is identical with what the witness had meant to do to the accused; 'a life for a life', etc.

At this point of the biblical story, the inauguration of the new postdiluvial world, the fundamental requirement to protect human life is given a theological rationale. To cite the great Rabbi Akiva: to shed human blood, to kill a human being, is to deface the divine image (*Gen. R.* 34:14).

Duly interpreted, this gnomic saying protecting human life gave rise to the Noachide laws, laws given by God to guide the emerging new humanity and future 'sons of Noah'. In the classical Jewish sources (*t.A.Z.* 8:4; *b.Sanh.* 56a and elsewhere) these commandments number seven, but in the course of time other prescriptions (e.g. tithing, almsgiving) and prohibitions (e.g. sorcery, cross-breeding animals) accumulated. These were derived, sometimes by considerable exegetical virtuosity, from the seven original commandments. The prohibition of murder was obvious, but by parsing the saying differently and exploiting the multipurpose prefixed preposition *lamed* – 'the one who sheds the blood of a human being *by means of a human being*', proxy killing, conspiring with a third party to commit murder, taking out a contract on someone, could also be explicitly excluded. By means of another use of the versatile preposition *lamed* – 'the one who sheds the blood of a human being *in a human being*' – the statement could be cited as explicitly prohibiting killing or self-killing by strangulation (hanging) which would cause internal bleeding, and the same reading could also serve to exclude abortion (*Gen. R.* 34:14). An equally obvious corollary of the legal aphorism, which of course required interpretation in order to be implemented, was the law mandating the establishment of a judicial system and courts of law (*b.Sanh.* 56a, 59b). The basic list, therefore, reads as follows:

1   establishment of a judicial system;
2   prohibition of idolatry;
3   prohibition of blasphemy;
4   prohibition of murder;
5   prohibition of theft, including financial wrongdoing and wars of conquest;
6   prohibition of sexual promiscuity; and
7   prohibition of eating meat with the blood in it.

These statements encapsulating the foundations of moral life in society for any people at any time seem to have been known during the Second Temple period. The author of *Jubilees* was familiar with them in the form of instructions from Noah to his sons. The author does not precisely identify them, but there appear to be seven (*Jub.* 7:20-21). One of the defining moments in the development of early Christian churches was the decision of James, head of the Jerusalem cell, that converts from the Gentile world must abstain only from idolatry, sexual impurity (*porneia*) and eating meat with the blood in it or from an animal that had been strangled (Acts 15:20, 29; cf. 21:25). This too seems to imply familiarity with the Noachide tradition. Some scholars have detected an echo of the same principles in chapter 3 of the *Didache*, but these admonitions look like early Christian moral catechesis drawing on typical Jewish moral instruction, and the blood prohibition is lacking.[12]

These prescriptions are followed by the discourse in which God (still Elohim) makes a commitment by covenant never again to annihilate all living creatures on the earth by a deluge. The promise is addressed to Noah and his three sons in language which is extremely formulaic and repetitive even for the priest–author. The repetition is, however, a deliberate device for emphasizing the essential elements: the key-words 'covenant' (*běrît*) and 'all flesh' (*kol-bāśār*) occurs five times, and the sign of the covenant is repeated three times in this brief passage. As we have come to expect, the commitment is stated at the beginning and end of the discourse, indicating that this is to be read as a self-enclosed text, a *texte en soi*, intelligible in its own terms.

> God said to Noah and his sons with him: 'I now establish my covenant with you, with your descendants after you, and with every living creature that is with you, including birds and domestic and wild animals that are with you, as many as came out of the ark. I shall maintain my covenant with you, that never again will all that lives be annihilated by the flood waters; never again will there be a flood to destroy the earth.'
>
> God said: 'This is the sign of the covenant which I make for all ages to come between myself and you, together with all living creatures that are with you: I set my bow in the clouds to be a sign of the covenant between myself and the earth. When I bring clouds over the earth and the bow is seen in the clouds, I shall remember my covenant between myself and you together with all living creatures, everything that lives. Never again will waters turn into a deluge to destroy everything that lives. Whenever the bow appears in the clouds I shall see it and remember the everlasting covenant between God and every living creature, everything that lives on the earth.'
>
> God said to Noah: 'This, then, is the sign of the covenant which I have established between myself and every living creature on the earth.' (Gen. 9:8-17)

The point about the structure of the saying needs to be emphasized on account of the tendency to extrapolate by understanding the prescriptions in Gen. 9:1-7 as stipulations of the covenant, thereby normalizing the covenant idea as represented by this first instance. We find this misreading of the chapter in *Jubilees* (6:4-10) and – possibly –in Josephus (*Jewish Antiquities* I 96–103), and it is still occasionally defended on the basis of Isa. 24:5 in which the people are accused of violating the everlasting covenant (Mason 2007). The anonymous author who

---

12 On the Noachide commandments and the discussions about their relation with natural law, see Novak 1983, 1998; and more recently, Arneth 2007.

presents this apocalyptic scenario in Isa. 24:1-13 is, in all probability, referring to the covenant with Noah, together with other aspects of the primeval history – chaos (*tōhū*), the diminution of humanity, the dispersion of the peoples, perhaps Noah's drunkenness. He also seems to be adopting the same interpretation of Genesis 9 as the author of *Jubilees*. But to read Gen. 9:1-17 in this way is to underestimate the precision of the language in this passage. In the first place, there is no mention of a covenant in 9:1-7. The solemn opening of the second discourse – 'I now establish my covenant with you' – is a performative utterance, comparable to a legally binding statement redacted in due form, a reading confirmed by the concluding statement: 'This, then, is the sign of the covenant which I have (now) established between myself and every creature on the earth' (v. 17). The meaning is clear; the covenant is now, and only now, in force.

We are in a better position today than formerly to appreciate the unique features of the priest–author's understanding of covenant. Briefly, the standard biblical idea of a covenant is a bilateral agreement between two parties involving reciprocal obligations confirmed by oaths and sealed in a ceremony, usually a sacrificial meal taken together. Its classical expression can be found in Deuteronomy and the associated history (Joshua–2 Kings) where the term *běrît* occurs 96 times. Since the agreement is between a group of people and God, it has come to be accepted that the closest analogue is from the political sphere, and specifically a vassal treaty between an imperial power (e.g. Assyria) and a vassal state (e.g. the city-state of Tyre) (*ANET* 533–41). The terms of the covenant, naturally weighed heavily in favour of the hegemonic power, are subject to reconfirmation at intervals, usually on the accession of a new ruler.

In the priest–scribe's narrative, however, covenant is understood in a radically different way. If we attend to what is stated explicitly in the P history, we conclude that there are only two covenants: with Noah and his descendants, indeed with all living creatures (Gen. 9:8-17), and with Abraham and his descendants including the descendants of both Isaac and Ishmael (Gen. 17:1-22). There is no account in the P history of covenant-making at Sinai. Accepting the standard division of sources, what happened at Sinai according to P was that the Israelites arrived (Exod. 19:1), Moses went up the mountain alone, he received instructions from God for the construction of the wilderness sanctuary and the establishment of its cult (Exod. 24:15b-18a; 25–31), these instructions were carried out (Exod. 35–40), and after a stay of less than a year the Israelite tribes departed processionally from the mountain (Num. 10:11-36). Sabbath observance is inculcated as a perpetual covenant (Exod. 31:16-17), but this language is deceptive. Sabbath observance is not presented as a covenant stipulation contingent on the observance of which God will fulfil certain obligations. Sabbath is not a covenant stipulation but a sign pointing back to creation, therefore analogous to the (rain)bow in Gen. 9:8-17. In the Abrahamic covenant circumcision is also a sign (Gen. 17:13, 19) indicating a relationship already in existence (17:11) rather than a stipulation in a bilateral agreement between God and the Abrahamic people.

The priest–author, therefore, testifies to a radical shift in the understanding of covenant, a shift away from bilaterality towards the idea of a free and unconditional commitment of God, first to humanity, then to the descendants of Abraham, not confined to the people of Israel.[13] The P source has, moreover, moved the covenant out of the historical period into the prehistory of Noah and Abraham, and out of the temporality of occasional rupture and renewal to perpetuity. Now the covenant calls not for revalidation, as with the treaties, but only for God to remember. And God does that, whether the voice of a suffering people comes to him from the midst of a natural disaster, an act of God (Gen. 8:1), or from his suffering people in Egypt (Exod. 2:24; 6:4-5) or Babylon (Lev. 26:42, 45).

Many of the great commentators of the past – Wellhausen, Gunkel, von Rad and others – understood the bow in the clouds as the war bow which God was now setting aside, somewhat like burying the hatchet, an interpretation still occasionally heard (e.g. Rüterswörden 1988). This would signify the end of a period of hostility between God and creation, perhaps mixed with a sense of regret, if we may think of God looking back with regret. We find a distant parallel towards the end of the flood narrative in *Gilgamesh* where the great goddess Ishtar holds up her lapis necklace and swears by it that she will remember the deluge, implying that she will also remember the gods who brought it about (*Gilgamesh* XI 162–69). It seems more likely, however, and more consistent with God remembering towards the end of the deluge (Gen. 8:1), that the thought of the rainbow as heralding the end of a rainstorm and bringing to mind the promise is uppermost, and that is the opinion of most commentators today (e.g. Zenger 1983: 11–21, 124–31).

A New Beginning after a Bad Start

The story of the deluge ends, as it began, with Noah and his three sons, the latter now progenitors of a new humanity (Gen. 6:9-10; 9:18-19). At the same time, it points forward to the theme of the next chapter, the spread of the new humanity throughout the known world. In more direct preparation for the incident immediately following in which Canaan is cursed, we are told that Ham was the father of Canaan. Then, finally, we arrive at the inclusion rounding off this central unit of the generations (*toledot*) pentad with the death of the 950-year-old Noah (Gen. 9:28-29).

As is the case with most or all of the other incidents in the history of early humanity, in this episode about Noah the vintner, the author has taken over a mythical narrative tradition, one which probably had nothing to do with the deluge, adapting it to his own narrative context and strategy. Noah, like Adam

---

13   On the place of Ishmael in the Abrahamic covenant, see Blenkinsopp 2009: esp. 235–38.

a man of the soil, is the first to plant a vineyard, drinks a lot of the wine that comes from it, and lies inebriated and uncovered in his tent. When Ham happens to see his father naked, instead of covering him up he informs his two brothers. Contrary to his expectations, they do the right thing which could not have been easy since they walk backwards, their sight further shielded by a cloak and, with eyes averted, cover their father's prostrate form. When Noah comes to and realizes what his youngest son had done to him, he issues a curse on Canaan and a blessing on Shem and Japhet.

The problems with this not very uplifting story are at once apparent and have been endlessly discussed.[14] The most obvious is that the perpetrator is Ham, yet the one cursed is Canaan. In addition, Ham is not the youngest son, as he is said to be here. One midrashic solution – that Ham had already been blessed and blessings once uttered cannot be unspoken (*Gen. R.* 36:7) – is ingenious but unconvincing. We cannot simply accept the substitution of Canaan for Ham since the names of the three progenitors of the new humanity – Shem, Ham, Japhet – are firmly part of the tradition. But since Canaan was, from the outset, the one who must be cursed, we may suppose that the author inserted the phrase 'Ham was the father of Canaan' into the summary statement Gen. 9:18-19 and made the same addition in the narrative itself: 'When Ham [father of Canaan] saw his father naked, he told his two brothers outside' (Gen. 9:22). This seems to me to be the simplest solution to the problem. On this reading, Ham remains the perpetrator, but Canaan is assumed to have inherited the evil propensities of his father. The reputation of both Canaanites, represented by the eponymous Canaan, and Egyptians, descendants of Ham, would have made it easier to make the genealogical connection. Both shared the same unsavoury reputation in Israelite circles, as we may see from the injunction: 'You must not behave as they do in the land of Egypt where you lived, and you must not behave as they do in the land of Canaan to which I am about to bring you' (Lev. 18:3).

Speculation about what it was that Noah realized his youngest son had done to him (Gen. 9:24) has also exercised readers from antiquity to the present. The midrash presents different scenarios involving gross acts of indecency and outrage, and contemporary commentators have not been slow to follow (Ginzberg 1955: 191–92; 1961: 167–70). Perhaps Ham witnessed 'the primal scene' and took the place of his incapacitated father (Bassett 1971), or he dealt with his father as Kronos with Ouranos as reported by Hesiod (*Theogony* 173–85). If, however, we bear in mind the seriousness with which the duties of the child towards the parent were held in that culture these speculations appear unnecessary. According to a text from Bronze Age Ugarit, one of these duties is 'to hold his (the father's) hand when he is drunk, support him when he is full of wine' (Aqhat 1:32-33, trans. in Coogan 1978: 33). The same point is repeatedly made in the aphoristic

---

14   See e.g. Gunkel 1997: 79–80; von Rad 1961: 131–35; Vawter 1977: 138–39; Westermann 1984: 486–94; Wenham 1987: 197–204.

literature in the Old Testament, and how seriously it was considered to be may be seen from the following example:

> The eye that mocks a father
> and scorns to obey a mother
> will be pecked out by the ravens of the valley
> and eaten by the vultures. (Prov 30:17)

In the oracular pronouncements with which the episode concludes Canaan takes the place of Ham:

> Cursed be Canaan;
> meanest of slaves shall he be to his brothers!
> Bless, Yahweh, the tents of Shem,[15]
> let Canaan be his slave!
> May God make space for Japheth;
> may he dwell in the tents of Shem,
> and may Canaan be his slave! (Gen. 9:25-27)

The condemnation of Canaan, the first curse to be uttered in the second creation and an ominous inauguration of the new world, reflects the perception in evidence throughout the biblical texts of the moral degeneracy of the Canaanites. Accusations of moral turpitude have served at all times as a pretext for conquering and enslaving other peoples, for example during the Spanish conquests in the Americas in the sixteenth century and the first Puritan settlements in the New World a century later. To explain the condemnation of Canaan, there is no need to fix on a specific epoch, for example the Israelite conquest or the pre-conquest period, categories which, in any case, are now historically inapplicable. Suffice it to note that for the immigrant group associated with Ezra in the mid-fifth century BC the indigenous peoples are still Canaanites and still indulging in 'abominations' (Ezra 9:1).

The curse on Canaan is matched with a blessing on Shem, ancestor of the Hebrews (Gen. 10:21). The prayer for *Lebensraum* for Japhet, for some form of co-operation with the peoples of Israel, and for their mastery of the Canaanites, the common enemy, has provided the most scope for speculation. Without attempting to catalogue opinions exhaustively, Japhet has been identified with the Philistines, the Phoenician and Greek settlements in the coastal region of Palestine, the Aegean peoples in general, the bearers of Hellenic culture after the conquests of Alexander, and Greek-speaking proselytes. It has even been read by

---

15 MT reads 'Blessed be Yahweh, God of Shem', which cannot be correct since the context requires a blessing on Shem. The NRSV alternative, 'Blessed by the Lord (Yahweh) my God be Shem' is problematic since Yahweh lacks a preposition. I have followed REB which reads ʾoholê-šēm ('the tents of Shem', as in the following line) for ʾĕlōhê-šēm ('the God of Shem').

some early Christian writers as a prediction of the spread of the Christian church. We shall meet with Japhet again in the following chapter of our study.

Noah has enjoyed a mixed reputation in the Jewish exegetical tradition. On the one hand, he was favoured by God (Gen. 6:8) and righteous (6:9), and was destined to bring relief from work and toil, probably, and meritoriously, by his activities as a vintner (5:29). For Josephus, who omits the drunkenness episode, Noah preached to an obdurate generation and was persecuted for his pains (*Jewish Antiquities* I 74). His role as 'herald of righteousness' reappears in 2 Pet. 2:5, and in Heb. 11:7 he is one of those righteous by faith in the archaic period. On the debit side, however, the midrash represents him as debasing himself by planting a vine rather than a fig tree or olive tree, and since he must have known that the vine was the tree in Eden from which Adam and Eve ate, he could have anticipated the consequences. It was even believed that he succumbed to temptation and actively co-operated with Satan (or Satanel) in the planting of a vineyard (*Gen. R.* 36:3; Ginzberg 1961: 167). According to later midrashim he had three strikes against him: he was the first drunkard, the first human to utter a curse, and the first to introduce slavery (Ginzberg 1961: 167).

Perhaps the only significance of these baroque exegetical embellishments is that they replicate the ambiguities surrounding the figure of Adam in the tradition and in the biblical text itself. Like Adam, Noah is a 'man of the soil' (*'îš hā' ădāmâ*, Gen. 9:20). The environment for the one is a garden planted by Yahweh, for the other a vineyard planted by Noah. The one eats the fruit of a plant not further identified but by some taken to be a vine, the other drinks the fruit of the vine. In both cases the outcome is disastrous if unforeseen, and involves shame and nakedness. Both incidents end with a curse, on the snake in the first instance, on Canaan in the second. On this view, which is that of the author's J source, in the new creation human nature remains the same as it was before the cataclysm, as Yahweh conceded after the waters subsided and the sacrifice was accepted: 'The inclination of the human heart is evil from youth onwards' (Gen. 8:21). This will become more apparent as the story of the new race continues.

CHAPTER 7

The New Humanity

From one ancestor God caused all peoples to dwell on the entire surface of the earth, defining the established times of their existence and the boundaries of their territory. This was in order that they might seek God in the hope that, groping after him, they might find him, though he is not far from each one of us. (Acts 17:26-27)

The Descendants of Noah, the New Adam

By this stage, the reader has already been introduced more than once to Noah's three sons (Gen. 5:32; 6:10; 7:13; 9:19). While belonging to the last generation before the cataclysm, and therefore the only surviving link with the old world after the death of their father, they are destined to be the ancestors of the three branches of the new humanity (Gen. 9:19). That there are three, no more and no less, is in keeping with a familiar triadic pattern: Cain, Abel and Seth, sons of the first man and woman; Jabal, Jubal and Tubal-Cain, sons of Lemech and his two wives; Abraham, Nahor and Haran, sons of Terah; and from further afield, the three descendants of Deucalion, son of Prometheus, progenitors of the three branches of the Greek-speaking peoples, Dorians, Ionians and Aeolians, after the flood decreed by Zeus had subsided.

The list of names in Genesis 10, usually referred to as 'the Table of Nations', is the fourth unit in the five-member *toledot* arrangement of the archaic period. Within this structural framework we can detect a correspondence between the periods before and after the deluge. Whereas in the old world, the creation of the man and the woman is followed by the story of the vicissitudes of their three sons, in the postdiluvial era it is the three sons of the first man of the new creation who claim our attention. Coming now to the list itself – part catalogue, part genealogy – we see that its textual integrity is clearly indicated by closely corresponding introductory and concluding statements:

These are the descendants of Noah's sons, Shem, Ham and Japhet, descendants born to them after the deluge. (Gen. 10:1)

These are the families of Noah's sons according to their genealogies, nation by nation. From these the nations spread abroad after the deluge. (Gen 10:32)

In the list itself, the traditional order of the three sons is reversed in order to conclude with the descendants of Shem, the most significant for the author and his public and for the future. The unity of the human race is expressed symbolically in the number 70 which – omitting the Philistines (Gen. 10:14), as a later gloss – is the sum total of the names of the personified territories and peoples in the list. To this seventyfold macrocosm corresponds the microcosm of the 70 Israelites in Egypt (Gen. 46:27; Exod. 1:5; Deut. 10:22) and their 70 elders (Exod. 24:1; Num. 11:16). The symbolic resonance is strengthened by the frequent arrangement of the names in groups of seven.[1] These correspondences suggest a reading of the list in Genesis 10 as a symbolic approach to reconciling ethnic identity with a universalist perspective, implying a sense of shared moral obligation. We can then go on to read the story of the city and tower of Babel (Gen. 11:1-9) as a breakdown of this ideal of commonality and reciprocity (Crüsemann 2002).

It would be easy to miss the originality of this list in which a Judaean/Jewish author locates his own people, whose name does not occur in the list, as the invisible point from which this ethnographic catalogue is observed and recorded. Since we cannot fix the date of Genesis 1–11 without allowing for an extremely generous margin of error, it is difficult to say anything with confidence about the situation which could have generated this remarkable essay in ethnography and political geography. Herodotus is our principal witness to the interest in ethno-history which the Persian–Achaemenid empire, with its vastly improved means of travel and communication, encouraged. His highly personalized account of the origins, ecology, and customs of Egyptians (*Histories* 2:2–182) and Scythians (4:5–82) provides an excellent example. A generation before Herodotus, the logographer Hecataeus of Miletus wrote an ethnographic work entitled *Periēgēis* or *Periodos Gēs*, 'A Journey Round the Earth', of which unfortunately only fragments remain. Claiming to take in Europe, Asia and Africa, it begins at the Pillars of Hercules (the Straits of Gibraltar) and proceeds clockwise round the Mediterranean, the Black Sea, the land of the Scythians, Persia, Egypt and Nubia, ending on the North African coast (Van Seters 1983: 10–12; S. R. West

---

1   There may be a connection with the Canaanite pantheon, the 70 sons of El and Asherah (*KTU* I 4; VI 6). Deut. 32:8-9 (reading *běnê ʾēl* or *běnê ʾēlîm* for *běnê yiśrāʾēl*, v. 8b) suggests that these deities are assigned as patrons of the 70 peoples of the world, and that Yahweh has been assigned to Israel. On the significance of the numeral seven and its multiples, see Otto 2004. As an addendum to Otto's excellent article I add the mission of Jesus to the 70 disciples, signifying a mission to all humanity (Lk. 10:1).

1996). One of the many fragments of which the Hesiodic *Catalogue of Women* is composed refers to a work attributed to Hesiod with essentially the same title as Hecataeus' opus. It mentions several foreign peoples including a few named in the Genesis text – Ethiopians, Lybians, Scythians – but the disconnected fragments provide no clue to the nature and structure of the work as a whole (M. L. West 1985: 3–7, 137–38; Van Seters 1992: 177, 89–90). The biblical Table of the Nations is in broad outline not so different from the work of Hecataeus if, allowing for some imprecision on our part and that of the author, we may take Japhet, Ham and Shem as representing, respectively, Europe, Africa (i.e. Egypt) and Asia.

Intensified commercial contacts with Greek-speaking lands, mediated for the most part through Phoenician settlements on the Mediterranean coast of Palestine (Dor, Joppa, Ashkelon, etc.), must also have increased awareness of the world outside of the province of Judah even before the advent of the Persians.[2] An indication of a literary nature can be found in the ironic dirge in Ezekiel 27 over the collapse of Tyre's commercial activities following the 13-year siege of that city by the Babylonians (ca. 586–573 BC). This poem contains 42 geographical or ethnic names connected with Tyrian commerce half of which appear in the 'Table of the Nations' in Genesis 10. The expansion of the diaspora following the liquidation of the Judaean state would also have inspired reflection on relations with other peoples in the great world of which Judah formed only a very small part. An Isaian text (Isa. 11:11) lists six diaspora locations all of which appear in the Genesis list and another (Isa. 66:19) mentions eight peoples to whom Yahweh is to be made known before the final consummation, and all these too are in the list.

Close scrutiny of the structure and formulaic language of the catalogue suggests that an originally quite brief nucleus, consisting of lists of names with a formulaic introduction and conclusion, has been expanded with additional data over the course of time. In view of the nature of the material, this is no more than would be expected as knowledge and awareness of the surrounding world increased with the passing of time. The first segment, that of Japhet, is the briefest, no doubt because the territories in question, to the far north and the west, were the most distant and the least familiar.[3] This segment lists seven 'sons' of the proto-parent and seven for Gomer and Javan together, rounded off with the standard conclusion:

---

2   On the archaeology of these sites and others in the coastal region – Achzib, Akko, Abu Hawam, Shiqmona, Tel Mevorach – see Stern 1982: 9–29 and the relevant articles in *NEAEHL*. On the Greek finds in Palestine see Wenning 1990. Boardman (2000: 203) points out that the graffiti on ceramic ware of Greek origin from Palestine indicates that the Phoenicians were the principal carriers and dealers.

3   A detailed study of the names in the three lists is not directly relevant to the present study, but the reader may care to consult Westermann 1984: 495–530; Wenham 1987: 210–32; Hess 1993; Simons 1954; Oded 1986.

> Descendants of Japhet: Gomer, Magog, Madai, Javan, Tubal, Meshech, Tiras.
> Descendants of Gomer: Ashkenaz, Riphath, Togarmah. Descendants of Javan:
> Elishah, Tarshish, Kittim, Rodanim. From these the peoples of the coastlands
> and islands spread abroad. These, then, are the descendants of Japhet in their
> respective territories, each with its own language, family by family, nation by
> nation. (Gen. 10:2-5)

The name of this proto-parent, third son in the list, cannot easily be dissociated from the Iapetos of Greek myth, son of Ouranos and Gaia (Sky and Earth), father of the triad Atlas, Prometheus and Epimetheus, and brother to the crafty and violent Kronos (Hesiod, *Theogony* 134). The Greek connection is understandable since the list includes Javan, originally referring to the Greek-speaking cities of the Ionian seaboard incorporated into the Persian province of Ionia, later still to the empire of Alexander (e.g. Dan. 8:21; 10:20; 11:2) and the Greek-speaking world in general. The location of the 'sons' of Javan follows a broad ark from Cyprus and Rhodes in the eastern Mediterranean (Elishah, Kittim, Rodanim) to much-fabled Tarshish somewhere in the far west, perhaps the Phoenician settlement at Carthage (Baker 1992). Of the other names in the Japhetic list, it will be enough to say that they correspond to tribes and nations settled around the Black Sea, in the Ukraine and Armenia and, in one instance, the Medes, in western Iran. Josephus sums it up neatly by saying that the Japhetites settled in Asia as far as the river Tanais (the Don) and in Europe as far as Gadeira (Cadiz) (*Jewish Antiquities* I 122–29).

Ham, the longest of the three lists, has been the most subject to expansion resulting in the breakup of the neatly formulated shape and wording of the catalogue. Its original content may have been limited to four descendants of Ham, seven for Cush and Raamah taken together, and the conclusion. If so, it would have read more or less as follows:

> Descendants of Ham: Cush, Egypt, Put, Canaan. Descendants of Cush: Seba,
> Havilah, Sabtah, Raamah, Sabteca. Descendants of Raamah: Sheba, Dedan.
> These, then, are the descendants of Ham according to their families and
> languages, each nation in its own land. (Gen. 10:6-7, 20)

Cush stands for the vast region south of the first cataract of the Nile, now comprising Sudan, Ethiopia, Eritrea and Somalia. It is frequently named together with Egypt (*misrayim*) in biblical texts. The list of peoples attached to Egypt (Gen. 10:13-14) has almost certainly been added since Egypt is already represented in the list by Ham, as it is elsewhere (Pss 78:51; 105:23, 27; 106:22). That seven Arabian place names are categorized as Hamitic can be explained by the geographical proximity of peoples settled on both sides of the Red Sea and by commercial relations with south-west Arabia, which is rich in incense and precious metals. But knowledge of these locations and associations may not have called for much geographical or historical expertise since many of them occur elsewhere in biblical texts. Put, identified with Libya following LXX, the Vulgate and Josephus, has no 'descendants', probably because none were known.

Of more immediate significance would have been Canaan, here taken in its broadest extent including all the region west of the Jordan, Syria, the coastal region and the Phoenician cities. Its attachment to the Hamitic line may retain some memory of Canaan within the Egyptian sphere of influence during the Late Bronze Age, but the link would have been required in view of the preceding narrative involving the personifications of Ham and Canaan (Gen. 9:18, 20-27). That Sidon rather than Tyre, which is absent from the list, is the eldest 'son' of Canaan may be explained by the decline of Tyre after the siege by Nebuchadnezzar and the subsequent ascendancy of Sidon during the Achaemenid period. The same post-monarchic dating would explain the inclusion of Heth ('the Hittite'), in view of the fact that the designation *ḥēt* or *běnê-ḥēt* ('Hittites') corresponds to the description of Syria-Palestine in neo-Babylonian royal inscriptions as *māt ḥattu* ('Hatti land') (Wiseman 1961: 68–75).

The account of the empire-building activities of Nimrod, 'son' of Cush, will claim our attention in the following section of the chapter.

Modifications and additions are also responsible for the present shape of the Shem list, last of the three. Shem has given his name to the Semitic peoples by way of the Greek translation (*sēm*), though at least one of the peoples in the list, the Elamites, are non-Semitic. The list begins in the standard formulaic way in Gen. 10:22. The opening statement in the previous verse has been added to connect at once with the Hebrews and their eponymous ancestor Eber the proto-Hebrew, *ʿēber* being a secondary formation from *ʿibrî*, 'Hebrew'. According to both the genealogical detail in the present list (Gen. 10:22-24) and the ten-member Shem line in the following chapter (11:10-14), Shem is the great-grandfather not the father of Eber (Shem–Arpachshad–Shelah–Eber). We are also reminded that he is the elder brother of Japhet, a reminder which may reflect an early stage of the polemic, conducted by Josephus and other authors, claiming for Jewish culture and literature an antiquity greater than those of the Greeks. The original Shem list therefore begins in Gen. 10:22 and follows the same pattern as the previous two:

> Descendants of Shem: Elam, Asshur, Arpachshad, Lud, Aram. Descendants of Aram: Uz, Hul, Gether, Mash. Arpachshad was the father of Shelah, and Shelah was the father of Eber. These, then, are the descendants of Shem according to their families and languages, each nation in its own land. (10:22-24, 31)

This reading of the Shem list in its original form assumes that its purpose was to establish the genetic connection with Eber, eponym of the *ʿibrîm*, the Hebrews, and to locate the Hebrews among the Semitic peoples of the east, namely, Ashur (Assyrians), Arpachshad (Babylonians) and Aram (Aramaeans). As noted above, the Elamites, in what is now southern Iran, were not Semitic and their language belongs to no known language group. Lud has not been successfully identified nor have the four peoples associated with Aram. Another problem is the location of Yoqtan as descendant of Eber. Yoqtan is an Arabic name and his 13 'sons' are Arabian tribes which, to the extent that they and their territories can be identified, were settled in the Hadramaut, the Yemen, and other places in the west and south-west of the Arabian peninsula (Gen. 10:25b-30). The name Peleg means 'division' (from the verbal stem *plg*, 'divide'), with reference to the division or dispersion of the peoples of the earth – those listed in the Table of the Nations – recorded in the Babel narrative immediately following.

Together with the story of the city and tower of Babel (Gen. 11:1-9), this triadic list forms the fourth unit of the genealogical pentad which gives Genesis 1–11 its narrative structure. The three basic genealogies are generally attributed to the priestly–scribal source – though they are more likely archival material incorporated into the story with appropriate adaptations. At least the longest of the insertions, about Nimrod (Gen. 10:8-12), together with the story of the city and temple tower is accredited to J. This raises once again, and in sharper focus, the differing theological perspectives of these two sources, an issue which will occupy us later in this chapter. For the moment, it will suffice to note that the links between the list and the story about the city and temple tower are easily detected. The 'Table of the Nations' deals with the spread of the new humanity over the earth with the creation of large kinship groups and eventually nations. The force behind this new development is the creation command to increase and multiply and the blessing which accompanies the command (Gen. 9:1, 7). The perspective on this increase in population and political complexity is therefore positive. The Babel story backtracks to a point in time before this demographic expansion, and the Nimrod account indicates developments of a political and cultural nature which prove to be inseparable from self-assertion, ambition and violence. Divine blessing is absent from this scene. By the same token linguistic differentiation, taken for granted in the lists (Gen. 10:5, 20, 31), is reinterpreted by the author of the Babel story as an indication of alienation and non-communication, the antithesis of the one language in Eden which even the animals shared. This, again, is seen in the Babel story as the outcome of destructive political ambition and imperialistic hubris. These points of contact and contrast prepare the way for reading the Babel story as a commentary in narrative form on the insertion into the genealogical list about Nimrod, warrior, hunter, and builder of cities (Gen. 10:8-12). To this imposing legendary figure we now turn.

Nimrod, First Empire-Builder

Nimrod has been fitted into the genealogical framework as the son of Cush and grandson of Shem, but the account of his activities in Gen. 10:8-12 evidently derives from a source independent of the basic Hamitic list. In the first place, it comes as an afterthought since the descendants of Cush have already been listed. In the second place, the Cush from whom Nimrod is descended cannot be the same as Cush, first son of Ham mentioned earlier: the latter represents the land south of the first cataract of the Nile and is the ancestor of Arabian tribes (Seba, Havilah, Raamah and Dedan), while Nimrod clearly belongs to the land between the two rivers. His ancestry therefore designates him as of Kassite or early Mesopotamian rather than Cushite descent.[4] The proverbial saying about his hunting prowess, which contains the only mention of Yahweh, indeed of any deity, in the list, has evidently been inserted, and is generally if hypothetically attributed to the J source which we have encountered throughout the narrative to date. In that literary context Nimrod represents yet another in a series of firsts. He is the first to become a potentate on the earth, as the Sethites were the first to worship Yahweh (Gen. 4:26), the descendants of Adam were the first to increase on the earth (6:1), and Noah was the first vintner (9:20). All of these notices are conventionally assigned to J. Like Cain, Nimrod built a city (Gen. 4:17), and like the Nephilim destroyed in the deluge, he was one of the *gibbōrîm*, the 'mighty men' of old, though clearly a different kind of *gibbôr*. While the brief narrative about Nimrod is not explicitly prejudicial and negative, in the broader context of Genesis 1–11 these associations suggest a negative verdict on his political and military accomplishments and a further stage of deterioration according to the Yahwist's realistic and disenchanted view of human affairs.

Who, then, was Nimrod? From Gen. 10:8-12 we learn the following. He was a warrior and hunter, the first of the great potentates. He established a kingdom in southern Mesopotamia known as the land of Shinar, and he expanded his empire into Assyria to the north where he built cities including the great city of Nineveh. Some of the cities mentioned – four Babylonian[5] and four Assyrian – are known: Babylon (Hillah about 50 miles south of Baghdad), Erech (Uruk, now Warka, Gilgamesh's city), Nineveh (Kuyunjik, near Mosul), and Calah (Kalhu, now Nimrud, south of Nineveh). It therefore seems as if Nimrod is modelled on a historical figure rather than – as is often suggested – a Mesopotamian deity, whether Ninurta, god of warfare and hunting – two forms of the same basic activity – or Marduk, imperial deity of the Neo-Babylonian empire, an identification which has a long history going back to Wellhausen.[6] Human candidates, historical rather than mythical, have therefore been proposed, though we must add that mythological resonances are rarely absent from this kind of writing. The list of candidates includes Sargon, founder of the dynasty of Akkad in the late third millennium BC (Levin 2002); Tikulti-Ninurta I (ca. 1244–1208 BC),

---

4   The Cassites (*kaššu*), from land east of the Zagros, assumed power in Babylon after the fall of the Hammurabi dynasty and were a major power in the Amarna period. After their defeat by Elamites in the mid-twelfth century they reverted to tribalism.

5   Only three if *kalnēh* is parsed *kullānāh*, 'all of them', as NRSV, REB and some other modern versions.

6   Lipiński (1966) proposes a more *recherché* explanation: the name 'Nimrod' represents a *tiqqun soferim*, a deformation of the name Marduk.

a great builder who was also the first Assyrian ruler to conquer Babylon (Speiser 1958; 1964: 72–73); Ashurnasirpal II (878–707 BC), who made Calah (Kalhu, now Nimrud, on the east bank of the Tigris south-east of Mosul) his capital; and Sargon II (721–705 BC), whose new capital at Dur Sharrukin (Khorsabad) was abandoned after his death (Uehlinger 2003; van der Kooij 2006). To these we may add Ashurbanipal (668–627 BC), last significant ruler in the long succession of Assyrian kings, in spite of the fact that 'the beginning of his kingdom' was Assyria not Babylon. It seems that Ashurbanipal modelled himself on Gilgamesh as heroic warrior and hunter. Parts of four copies of *Gilgamesh* were recovered by Austen Henry Layard in the mid-nineteenth century after lying in the ruins of Ashurbanipal's library for two and a half millennia. During the first 30 years of his reign he fought successful campaigns in several directions and maintained control of Babylon. Equally formidable as warrior and hunter, he claimed success in both activities under the patronage of Ninurta and Nergal, gods of warfare and the hunt (Luckenbill 1927: 378–82). The wall plaques adorning Ashurbanipal's palace in Nineveh depicting the king engaged in these activities found their way into the Assyrian room in the British Museum. Since none of these proposals is definitive, it may be that Nimrod represents a composite of several of the great conquerors who ruled in Mesopotamia from the time of the Sumerians to that of the Persians.

The interpretation of the figure of Nimrod outside of the Hebrew Bible, where apart from Genesis the name only appears once, at Mic. 5:5, is overwhelmingly negative.[7] It may be summed up in the haggadic derivation of the name from the Hebrew verbal stem *mrd*, 'rebel' with the meaning 'let us rebel' (*nimrod*): Nimrod the rebel against God. In a brief retelling of the archaic period, the Wisdom of Solomon (10:1-5) sets up a parallel between the crime of Cain leading to the flood from which the righteous Noah is rescued and the confusion of tongues and dispersion of the nations out of which the blameless Abraham emerges. Nimrod is not mentioned, but the author would very likely have concluded from his city-building activity that he was involved in the building of the city and tower of Babel. 2 Esdras follows a similar pattern (3:4-13). For Josephus (*Jewish Antiquities* I 113–19), Nimrod (here Nebrodes following the LXX) was the worst of tyrants. Actively hostile to God and suspecting that there would be another flood, he vowed to defeat God's purposes by building a tower which would reach higher than the anticipated flood waters. Paraphrasing a passage from the *Sibylline Oracles* (3:97–109), Josephus concludes by recording how the tower, which was to reach to the heavens, came to an ignominious end, being blown down by the wind. Philo used philological licence to interpret the phrase 'a mighty hunter before the Lord' as 'a mighty hunter against the Lord' (*Questions and Answers on Genesis* II 82). Like the giants of old, Nimrod deserted the path

---

7   For what follows, see van der Toorn and van der Horst 1990; van der Horst 1990; Machinist 1992; Kugel 1998: 228–34; Uehlinger 1999.

of reason and the cause of God, went over to the enemy, and set up his rule in Babylon (*On The Giants* 66–67).

The disparaging note is no less clear in the targums and haggadah. For Targums Neofiti I and Pseudo-Jonathan he was a giant in sinning. According to the Fragmentary Targum, in addition to being mighty in sinning he hunted people in preference to animals, persuading them to abandon the good precepts of Shem and accept his rule. In a comment on Gen. 25:27, Pseudo-Jonathan relates how Nimrod was killed by Esau, another mighty hunter, out of jealousy. This connection with Esau is exploited in *Genesis Rabbah* (37:2). Both were godless characters and both snared people by speech, persuading them to adopt their way of life. Long before this time Edom, personified by Esau, had supplanted Babylon as the archetypal oppressive power embodied for Jews in the Roman empire. The targums and haggadah frequently redirect the fierce hostility towards Edom in biblical texts on to Rome. For example, in translating the prediction that 'the streams of Edom will be turned into pitch' in Isa. 34:1-17, the Targum replaces 'Edom' with 'Rome'. This tendency will go some way to explaining the association between Esau and Nimrod, the latter being the first of the nine world rulers between his time and the messianic age (*b.Pes.* 44b; *Pirqe Rabbi Eliezer* 11, 24).

The association in the haggadah between Nimrod and Esau and between Esau and Rome, and thus between Nimrod and Rome, provides a point of departure for a provisional recapitulation of Nimrod's place in the early history of humanity according to Genesis 1–11. We have seen that the Nimrod episode is assigned to the Yahwist strand which supplements the priest–scribe's version, thereby providing contrasting theological perspectives on events, the one in counterpoint to the other throughout. To repeat: the main thrust of the history focuses on the question how things could go so wrong in a world created by God and acknowledged by God to be really good. In the J version the first episode has to do with individuals, one male and one female, and their choosing to distance themselves from the God who created them and go their own way. In this instance the verdict is simply that they are placed in the world as we know it, and as men and women in all ages have known it, a world in which hardship and suffering are inevitable and, above all, a world bounded by death. With the birth of children and emergence of the family we have the spectacle of strife, jealousy and uncontrolled anger leading to murder. As human society reaches the more complex stage of the clan and the tribe, murder becomes more indiscriminate with the practice of the blood vendetta about which Lamech boasts to his wives. But it is only after the intrusion of forces and agencies from beyond the human sphere – the intermingling of the divine with the human – that we hear the complaint about the ineradicable nature of human evil (Gen. 6:5), a judgement which remains unchanged even after the annihilating cataclysm of the deluge (Gen. 8:21). With Nimrod the process has reached the stage of the formation of nations and empires, of nationalism, imperialism and colonialism and the endemic violence and injustice to which they give rise, summed up in the haggadic notion of the nine world empires. It is this stage which comes under critical review in the final narrative of the archaic history, the attempt to build a city and tower at Babel.

The Unfinished Tower and the Abandoned City

Now the whole world had one language with the same words.

As the people journeyed from the east, they came to a valley in the land of Shinar and settled there.

They said to one another, 'Come, let us make bricks and bake them thoroughly'. (They had bricks in place of stone and bitumen served them for mortar.)

Then said they, 'Come, let us build ourselves a city and a tower with its top reaching to the heavens, and let us make a name for ourselves; otherwise we shall be scattered over the entire face of the earth.'

Yahweh came down to see the city and the tower these people[8] had built.

He said, 'Look, they are one people with a single language, and now that they have begun to do this, nothing that they propose to do will be beyond their reach.

Come, then, let us go down and confuse their language there so that they will be unable to understand each other's speech.'

So Yahweh scattered them from there over the entire face of the earth, and they stopped building the city.

(That is why it is called Babel, since it was there that Yahweh confused the one language of the whole world, and from there Yahweh scattered them over the entire face of the earth.) (Gen. 11:1–9)

In order to achieve maximum economy and effect, the author composed this brief narrative in ring composition. At the centre (Gen. 11:5) there is the statement on which the incident pivots: 'Yahweh came down to see the city and the tower these people had built.' This is the *peripatea*, the turning point, when the project of the new humanity is viewed from a perspective independent of their own devices, desires and decisions. In the inner circle of the ring the parties engage in monologue. The human actors engage in it collectively, Yahweh's monologue is internal using the deliberative plural, but the parties do not at any time speak to each other. This is a new and ominous departure. Yahweh spoke to the man and woman in the garden and to Cain both before and after the murder of Abel, but now there is no communication. A human proposal is met with a divine disposal.

---

8   *běnê hāʾādām*, literally: 'sons of man'.

In the outer circle, the final situation cancels out the initial situation. First they settled, then they were scattered; first they spoke the one language, then they no longer understood each other's language. Linguistic differentiation is now seen as expressive of non-communication, an aspect of alienation. In the course of the narrative there are two authorial comments, indicated in parentheses: the first, about building materials, which looks like an explanation addressed to readers resident in Palestine where stone was plentiful and used for building (Gen 11:3b); the second, explaining how Babylon (Babel) got its name (Gen. 11:9).

The initial situation connects the incident with the preceding narrative. The people are travelling from the east, that is, from their original settlement east of Eden (Gen. 3:24), where the garden had been planted (Gen. 2:8).[9] There is no mention of the deluge, which might suggest that Gen. 11:1-9 began its career as a tradition about origins independent of the context of chapters 1–11. In their present narrative context, however, the travellers must be the survivors of the deluge, representatives of the new human race. As some early commentators suggested, the journey from Eden to Shinar occurred in the fourth generation after Shem, the generation of Peleg (whose name means 'division') when, as we are told, the population of the earth was divided (Gen. 10:25; 11:18-19). The one language in which they communicated would therefore be the language of Eden, though no longer shared with the animals. A shared, universal language is characteristic of golden age scenarios, and perhaps also of their end time counterparts, to judge by a prophetic text which predicts a time when all people will speak 'a pure language' (Zeph. 3:9). The language in question is no doubt Hebrew, the language God used when he spoke the twelve words of creation and the language spoken in Eden.[10]

In the course of their wanderings they came upon a valley in the land of Shinar where they settled and from which they were destined to be scattered over the surface of the earth. Whatever the earlier history of the name Shinar (*šin'ār*) may have been,[11] the Greek translators and targums were certainly justified in identifying it with Babylon. The same conclusion is suggested by biblical usage (Isa. 11:11; Zech. 5:11; Dan. 1:2), and confirmed by the reference to the valley in which they settled. This would no doubt be the valley by the Chebar canal (*nar kabari*, 'the Grand Canal') where Ezekiel had his great visions of the chariot throne and the field of desiccated bones (Ezek. 3:22-23; 8:4; 37:1-2).

It was inevitable that commentators in the modern period would find evidence of source division even in such a succinct narrative as 11:1-9. Gunkel argued that it must have resulted from a combination of a city source and a tower

---

9   This is the normal meaning of the preposition in *miqqedem*, though other possibilities exist, as in Gen. 2:8 where the garden is planted *miqqedem* ('over in the east') and Gen. 13:11 where Lot is travelling *miqqedem*, which in the context would be to the east.

10   Often attested in the haggadah, for example, *y.Meg.* 1:11; see Kugel 1998: 235–38.

11   According to Ran Zadok (1984), the name dates from the second half of the second millennium BC under Kassite rule; see also Davila 1992.

source, principally because Yahweh appears to have come down from heaven twice (Gen. 11:5, 7). But that is to be too literalistic. By being placed at the centre as the pivot of the story, Yahweh's descent to inspect the city and tower is programmatic rather than sequential. It is also unnecessary to hold that making a name for themselves and avoiding dispersion are incompatible and therefore derive from parallel versions. On the contrary, they must avoid dispersion in order to be able to make a name for themselves (Gunkel 1997: 94–95; cf. Skinner 1930: 223–24). At any rate, whatever putative early stages, oral or written, the story may have undergone, for the author the city which they proposed to build and in which they planned to settle was Babylon, the imperial Babylon which destroyed the kingdom of Judah in 586 BC and was itself conquered by Cyrus the Persian about half a century later.

This is the Babel of the author's concluding statement (Gen. 11:9) explained – not very effectively one must say – by assonance with Hebrew *bālal*, 'confuse', 'make a babble of' (REB), the builders' one language. The note of parody and irony with which this brief story is suffused can be compared with Second Isaiah's satirical view of the Babylonian cult of the deity Marduk, patron of the city and empire, together with his son Nabû, resident deity of Borsippa (Isa. 46:1-2; 47:1-15), the ruins of which, now Birs Nimrud, were at one time thought to be the remains of the Tower of Babel. These diatribes belong to the collection of post-exilic Isaian prophecies (Isa. 40–55) from the years immediately preceding the fall of Babylon in 539 BC. But since Babylon remained a byword for imperial oppression long after that time, the comparison does not necessarily establish the date of the J author of Gen 11:1-9, much less the date of the composition of which it is a part.

Denunciation of Babylon, emblematic of imperialistic hubris, injustice and oppression, entailed an equally radical critique of the Marduk cult which projected the ideology of political power and legitimated and promoted the building projects and wars of conquest of Babylonian rulers. The principal literary expression of this cult was the creation myth *Enuma Elish*, recited on the fourth day of the New Year *akitu* festival in the month of Nisannu (Nisan) in the spring. The more public part of the 12-day festival took place in the *esagila* sanctuary and its attached Etemenanki ziggurat in Babylon. The author of Gen. 11:1-9 seems to have had this structure in mind in speaking of the tower built, but perhaps not finished, by the arrivals from the east. The Etemenanki, meaning 'the house (temple), foundation of heaven and earth', was a ziggurat (*ziqqurattu*, meaning 'a building raised high'), a seven-storey pyramid, accessible by a ramp or steps, dedicated to the cult of Marduk and associated deities whose shrines occupied the top level. According to *Enuma Elish* it was constructed by the Anunnaki, deities of the earth and underworld: 'One year they made bricks for it; when the second year arrived they raised the head of Esagila on high, level with the Apsu. After they had built the lofty stage tower of the Apsu, they established an abode for Marduk, Enlil, and Ea' (*Enuma Elish* VI 59–64). This language, reminiscent of Gen. 11:1-9, intimates the god-like aspirations of these representatives of the new humanity. It may also provide some support for those early haggadic commentators who regarded the project as essentially idolatrous.

In spite of its distinguished origin, the Etemenanki temple tower was destroyed or plundered by Sennacherib – or so he claimed – but restored by his son and successor Esarhaddon. The restoration was then completed by his son Ashurbanipal, last significant Assyrian monarch, who claimed to have reintroduced the cult of Marduk into Babylon then subject to his rule (Luckenbill 1926: 370–71). After the fall of the Assyrian empire, the Etemenanki was restored once again by Nebuchadnezzar II, destroyer of Jerusalem, a name of infamy in the Hebrew Bible. About a century after the fall of Babylon, Herodotus, who may have visited the city and seen what there still was to see of the Etemenanki, described an eight-storey tower (probably one storey too many) dedicated to Zeus Belus (i.e. Marduk), with a base 220 yards in length and breadth, the upper levels accessed by a spiral stairway, with a great shrine in the uppermost tower (*Histories* 1:181–82). These Mesopotamian temple towers were not as resistant to time as the Egyptian pyramids, though the remains of the Ur ziggurat in southern Iraq are still visible after more than 4,000 years.

Familiarity with the ziggurat temple tower and what it stood for is also detectable in the familiar account of Jacob's stopover in Bethel on his way to a 20-year exile in Mesopotamia (Gen. 28:10-22). Jacob slept in 'that place'[12] following the familiar practice of passing the night in a sanctuary, a practice known as incubation. By doing so he hoped to receive a revelation that would provide guidance for an uncertain future, and so it happened. In the dream he saw a ramp,[13] presumably attached to a structure though none is mentioned, on which angels were ascending and descending. Like the Babel temple tower imagined by the travellers from the east, its top reached to the heavens (Gen. 28:12; cf. 11:4). On awakening from sleep Jacob, overcome with a feeling of numinous awe, recognized the place to be the abode of God and the gate of (to) heaven. At this point of the incident the Etemenanki comes more clearly into view since 'the gate of heaven' or, which is the same, 'the gate of the gods' (Akkadian: *bab ili*), is the real etymology of the name Babylon.

The statement that the builders aimed to make a name (Hebrew: *šēm*) for themselves or, in other words, to achieve lasting fame, may be one of several linguistic *jeux d'ésprit* of the author, in the sense that the builders aimed in this way to fulfil their genetic or genealogical destiny as descendants of Shem, the man whose name is Name. For this to happen, they had to avoid disaggregation

---

12 The word *māqôm*, 'place', repeated six times in this brief passage, is a standard synonym for 'holy place', sanctuary, as in the frequent Deuteronomic expression 'the place which he (Yahweh) will choose'.

13 'Ramp' rather than 'ladder' for the hapax legomenon *sullām*. It is difficult to imagine even angels going up and down a ladder simultaneously.

and loss of identity. They had to render themselves invulnerable to assault or interference from external sources, human or divine, which entailed maintaining linguistic identity. If we read the story in a straightforward way, leaving aside the literary context in which it is embedded, we may well conclude that there was nothing particularly reprehensible about wishing to settle down, build a city and a tower, and keep their own language. But if we read it in the context of Genesis 1–11, we see that the new arrivals are intent on building a different world from the world displayed in the Table of the Nations in which the different peoples settle in their own territories with their own languages. The city and tower are then revealed as a means of concentrating political power legitimated by potent religious symbols, and the settlers' resistance to linguistic differentiation is seen to be dictated by an awareness of language as an instrument of power, control and coercion, which it certainly is. In reacting to their project, Yahweh speaks ironically and even mimics their language ('Come, then, let us go down'), but there is no irony in the statement that 'nothing that they propose to do will be beyond their reach' (Gen. 11:6). For, as Job confesses to God in almost identical terms, this is an attribute of divinity:

> I know that you can do all things,
> and that no proposal of yours is beyond your reach. (Job 42:2)

The scattering which follows is consequently different from the spreading abroad of the peoples in the catalogue of the descendants of Noah's sons (Gen. 10:5, 25, 32), which is in response to the creation command to increase, multiply and take over guardianship of the earth, thus fulfilling their God-given destiny. It is more like the expulsion from the garden of Eden (Gen. 3:23). But there, too, the intervention of the Higher Power was not so much a punishment as a redirection of the human subject away from alluring and misleading ends, and especially from striving to take on the attributes of divinity ('Lest he reach out his hand, take from the Tree of Life, eat, and live for ever.') In that respect the message is not so different from *Gilgamesh* – 'return, return to finitude!' (Ricoeur 1967: 190). The scenery is different from the garden episode, but the theme is basically the same.

It follows that, in order to understand what is going on, or at least avoid misunderstandings, we should read the incident of the unfinished tower and the abandoned city *in context*, that is, as one episode in a series which constitutes a history of origins composed in the idiom of myth. More specifically, it is to be read in connection with the Table of the Nations immediately preceding (Gen. 10:1-31), and especially as a comment on the inserted notice about Nimrod (Gen. 10:8-12). In Gen. 11:1-9 the situation of post-deluge humanity, described in the previous chapter, with each tribe or nation settled in its own territory with its own language, is now seen as the result of a primordial event of hubris when the descendants of the first survivors of the deluge decided to go their own way, settling down in one place, retaining their own language, imitating Cain by building a city, and making a name for themselves. A link with Nimrod is suggested in the first place by the description of his achievements as ruler of Babel (Babylon) in the land of Shinar: both names occur in Gen. 11:1-9.[14] Nimrod was also a builder of cities, including Nineveh 'the great city', and the account of his exploits suggests that for him, as for the builders of the tower, nothing he proposed to do would be beyond his reach.

Later interpretations of the story of the city and temple tower in antiquity, none of which is greatly concerned with its literary context, take a decidedly negative view of the project of those who came from the east, and many of them placed the builders under the leadership of Nimrod. One of the earliest of these interpretations is that of the author of *Jubilees* (10:18-27), according to whom the building project was undertaken by Peleg who, accompanied by his wife Lomna, migrated east from Ararat to Sinar. He spent 43 years building the tower only to see it blown down by a wind sent by the Lord. Most, however, assigned the leading role to Nimrod who was, according to the LXX and other ancient authors, one of the giants who survived the deluge. Josephus (*Jewish Antiquities* I 109–21) fills in the gaps in the story in his own inimitable way. In spite of their fear of further devastating floods, the three sons of Noah came down from the mountains into the plain called Senaar (Shinar). God told them to avoid overpopulation, with all the problems associated with it, by sending out colonies (*apoikiai*). But then their leader Nebrodes (Nimrod) convinced them that God's motives in giving this advice were suspect since he was planning another flood. Thereupon Nebrodes defied the omnipotent God by proposing to build a tower higher than any flood waters could reach. At this point Josephus cites a passage from the third *Sybilline Oracle* in support (3:97-109) of his interpretation, according to which they wanted to reach up to heaven but the Immortal One sent winds to blow down the tower. There followed strife among mortals, confusion of tongues (in this case a Bad Thing) and the fragmentation of humanity.

A Jewish tradition represented by the targums (Neofiti I and Pseudo-Jonathan) views the project as an assault on God by means of an idol armed with a sword placed on top of the tower. *Genesis Rabbah* (38:8) justifies this interpretation by reading 'name' (*šēm*) in 'let us make a name for ourselves' as 'idol'. According to a variant tradition the assault was to be carried out by the builders themselves (*b.Sanh.* 109a) under the instigation and leadership of Nimrod (*Pirqe Rabbi Eliezer* 24).[15] The point is made, in a different idiom, in a prophetic denunciation of a later ruler of the same city – Babylon – and his pretensions to divinity:

14 The phrase *rēʾšît mamlaktô* (Gen. 10:10) can indicate either 'the main part or capital of his kingdom' or 'the beginning of his kingdom', this last perhaps indicating Nimrod as founder of Babylon.
15 For further details on these traditions see Ginzberg 1955: 201–206; 1961: 179–81; Kugel 1998: 227–42. For early Christian readings see Louth and Conti 2001: 166–70.

How have you fallen from the sky,
Star of the dawning day!
How felled and fallen to the ground,
you who laid low all the nations.
You thought in your heart:
'I will ascend to the sky,
I will set up my throne
higher than the highest stars ...
I will ascend on the highest clouds,
become like the Most High God!' (Isa. 14:12-14)

Without lapsing into homiletic mode, we may add that the present reality of ecological degradation, global warming, the proliferation of nuclear and biological weapons, cloning, the spread of Aids and the prospect of other pandemic diseases, could induce us to read the story of the unfinished tower and the abandoned city as a parable about the ambiguities and dangers of limitless technological progress. Our technologies are so much more advanced than those of the travellers from the east – for them it was a mere matter of using bricks instead of stone and putting up a seven-storey building – but it is to be doubted whether our wisdom, or our consciousness of the limitations of our moral capacity, is any greater. To quote a saying of Michel de Montaigne, 'Presumption is our natural and original malady ... It is by the vanity of this very imagination that man sets himself up as the equal of God.'[16]

16   I take this quote from Roger Shattuck (1996: 28).

CHAPTER 8

From Shem to Abraham, From Myth to History

Unlike the previous four units of the generational structure in Genesis 1–11, this final one which concludes the biblical story of creation has no narrative follow-up, and can therefore be dealt with more expeditiously. It serves as the epilogue to the series and, at the same time, as the transition from the archaic period narrated in the idiom of myth to historical times, though not history as we understand and practise it today. The genealogy from Shem to Terah parallels the genealogical list of antediluvians in Gen. 5:1-32 with some variations. Beginning with Shem, Noah's firstborn, linear descent is maintained down to the final descendant, Terah, at which point the genealogy is segmented horizontally with Terah's three sons, Abram, Nahor and Haran, parallel with the three sons of Noah in the antediluvian genealogy (5:32) and other triads noted earlier. A basic difference is that the scope has narrowed down from humanity as a whole to one of the three founders of the post-disaster humanity. This is Shem, Noah's firstborn who, in due course, by way of the Greek version (*sēm*), would give his name to the Semitic peoples.[1]

The list begins as follows:

These are the descendants of Shem.
Shem was a hundred years old when he became the father of Arpachshad two years after the deluge. After the birth of Arpachshad, Shem lived five hundred years and had other sons and daughters. (Gen. 11:10-11)

The pattern is straightforward: age at the birth of the first child; length of life after this point; birth of other sons of daughters. As in the antediluvian list, the crucial

---

1 The term appears for the first time in the late eighteenth century as a linguistic designation, and only later as an ethnic marker in Johann Friedrich Eichhorn's *Einleitung ins Alte Testament* (1780–1783).

point is the age of the patriarch at the birth of the first child since it allows for the construction of the continuous chronological schema discussed above. Unlike the earlier list, there is no grand total of years and no death notice, both of which, however, are supplied in the Samaritan Pentateuch. The LXX also adds the death notice and inserts Kainan (Hebrew: *qênān*) in the third place after Arpachshad to bring the number up to ten, as in the parallel genealogy. The suggestion has been made that the number nine in MT was intended to leave room for Abram as the tenth.[2] But Abram, as the first son of Terah, is structurally parallel with Shem, Noah's first son (Gen. 5:32), and he belongs by rights to the beginning of the following *toledot* series (Gen. 11:27). The addition of Kainan in the principal manuscripts of the Old Greek version (Alexandrinus and Vaticanus), together with *Jubilees* (8:1-5) and Luke's genealogy of Jesus (3:36), cannot very well be the original reading. First, Kenan/Kainan, son of Enosh, is fourth in the antediluvian list of Adam's descendants (Gen. 5:9-14), and is the only name to appear in both antediluvian and postdiluvian lists, which strongly suggests that it has been added to the Shem list. Second, the first five names in the Shem–Terah genealogy correspond to the same five names – Shem, Arpachshad, Shelah, Eber, Peleg – in the same order in the Table of the Nations (Gen. 10:22-25) – and were almost certainly taken over from there. Kainan is therefore intrusive.

An alternative explanation of the apparent disparity in number – nine instead of ten as in the antediluvian list – could be explained as follows. There may have been originally only one list of the descendants of Adam drawn up by learned theologians or mythographers and deposited in the temple archives. When this list came to be incorporated into the history of early humanity, which we have seen hinged on the mid-point of the deluge, the list was divided into antediluvians and postdiluvians. In keeping with this central arrangement, Noah would be the focal point of the list, and his name would be preceded and followed by nine others. The list would therefore read as follows:

Adam	Seth	Enosh	Kenan	Mahalel Noah	Jared	Enoch	Methuselah	Lamech
Shem	Arpachshad	Shelah	Eber	Peleg	Reu	Serug	Nahor	Terah

Having construed the lists differently, the LXX intended to align the second with the first by adding a name. Why they added Kainan/Kenan remains a matter of speculation, especially in view of the close affinity with Cain, a name of ill omen. In the Greek arrangement Kenan would be fourth in line from Noah as the other Kenan was fourth in line from Adam, but what conclusion the translators may have drawn from this parallel, if indeed they noticed it, is unclear.[3]

---

2   e.g. Westermann 1984: 560.
3   Other explanations in McEvenue 1971: 55–59. Helen Jacobus (2009) sets out an impressively detailed argument to prove, *inter alia*, that Kenan, as the thirteenth in line from Adam, and

Another puzzle follows hard on the heels of this one. The notice at the beginning of the list that Shem became the father of Arpachshad two years after the deluge (Gen. 11:10) is problematic. The mathematics is straightforward: We already know that Shem was born when Noah was 500 years old (Gen. 5:32), and that the deluge began in Noah's 600th year (Gen. 7:6, 11). If, therefore, Arpachshad was born when his father Shem was 100 years old, he must have born in the year of the deluge not two years later. The most likely explanation of the inconsistent dating is that the phrase 'two years after the deluge' is a gloss. One indication is that it is the only place at which the regular genealogical pattern is disturbed. The glossator may have been concerned about consistency of a different kind, since it is stated unambiguously that Noah's sons had children *after* the deluge (Gen. 10:1, 32). He could also have noticed that the eight human occupants of the ark (Noah, his wife, his three sons and three daughters-in-law) did not include Noah's grandchildren. The original redactor of the list may have simply rounded out Shem's age to 100 which, together with the 500-year life span after the birth of Arpachshad, reproduces, in reverse, Noah's 500 years before the birth of his sons and 100 from then to the deluge (Cryer 1985). We recall that these ages are not only fictional but designed to fit into an overall chronistic schema.

The transitional character of the list is apparent from the names themselves. We have just seen that the first five are drawn from the Table of the Nations, the list of the first expansion of population after the deluge, and are reproduced in the list in the same genealogical order. The ancestor Shem, the man whose name is Name, which is to say Fame,[4] was born one hundred years before the deluge and is therefore the last link with the first creation (Gen. 5:32). His primordiality is also apparent in his life span of 600 years. None of his descendants exceeds 500 years, and none of the last four in the genealogy attains even half that number. The decline will continue with Terah, whose name stands at the head of the following *toledot* and whose life span of 205 years none of his descendants, not even Abraham, Isaac and Jacob, would attain (Gen. 11:32).

It should be noted parenthetically that both LXX and the Samaritan Pentateuch add 100 years to the age at the birth of the first child for the names of the patriarchs from Arpachshad (second) to Serug (seventh), and 50 for Nahor (eighth). In both versions most of the other numbers also differ from MT. These discrepancies have been much discussed and different solutions have been proposed (Cassuto 1961: 255–59; Klein 1974; Westermann 1984: 559–61). The most likely explanation,

---

therefore subject to a curse, was omitted from the MT and the Samaritan Pentateuch. The association with the name Cain would not have been helpful, but it is not clear that the number 13 was considered ominous in early Judaism: on the contrary, see the 13 attributes of God, the 13 *mitzvot* of Maimonides, and 13 as the age for bar mitzvah.

4   Hebrew *šēm* = 'name'; cf. the warriors in 6:4 who were *'anšê haššēm*, 'men of renown' and the builders of the city and tower who intended to make a name for themselves (Gen. 11:4). No alternative satisfactory derivation of Shem has been proposed.

would be that both versions wished to avoid the embarrassment of Noah alive and presumably flourishing during the first 60 years of Abraham's life.

The first five names therefore form a distinct group. Since the name of the fifth, Peleg, is explained with reference to the dispersion following the failed attempt to build a city and tower – the verbal stem *plg* means 'divide' – the names belong to the period immediately subsequent to the deluge, a period which, calculating by the ages at the birth of the first child, adds up to the relatively modest length of 199 years. The derivation of none of the five names has been established with certainty. Shem we have already seen to be probably an artificial creation. Arpachshad may refer to Babylon (cf. Gen. 10:22). Eber is often taken to be the eponym of the Hebrews (*'ibrîm*) in spite of the fact that, according to the Table of the Nations, he is the ancestor of fourteen Arab tribes. Shelah (*šelah*) may be named for a Canaanite chthonic deity, but this is no more than a guess (Tsevat 1954; Wenham 1987: 210–32).

The remaining four names in the list belong to a quite different class. Though occurring elsewhere as personal or tribal names, three of the four, and possibly all four, are attested as settlements in the region of Harran (Harrānu) in Upper Mesopotamia, now in south-eastern Turkey near the Syrian border. Serug, seventh in the list, is Sarugi mentioned in neo-Assyrian records, now Serudj north-west of Harran. Nahor (Nahur, Til Nahiri), eighth, also the name of Abraham's brother, is in the same region, as also the ninth and last, Terah (Turahi), on the Balih river. Reu, sixth in the list, is unattested elsewhere as a personal name, unless it is an abbreviated form of Reuel, father-in-law of Moses (Exod. 2:18) and a son of Esau (Gen. 36:4, 10, 13). It has been identified with the Ru'ūâ, an Aramaic tribe named in an Assyrian inscription, and with Til Rahaua, a toponym, but these are no more than guesses. At all events, three at least of the names point clearly to an association with Israelite history and especially to traditions about Israelite origins. The Harran region is the location of the Northern Israelite diaspora after the Assyrian conquest of Samaria. The biblical texts, which place their settlements in the region of Gozan (Guzāna on the river Khābûr) a few miles east of Haran (2 Kgs 17:6; 18:11; 1 Chron. 5:26), have some archaeological support (Cogan and Tadmor 1988: 197; Younger 1998). It is also the homeland of the Israelite ancestors. It was here, in Aram Naharaim, the land of his birth, that Abraham sought a wife for his son Isaac (Gen. 24:1-10), and it was in Nahor that his servant finally encountered Rebekah (24:10). To escape the vengeance of Esau, Jacob fled to the protection of his uncle Laban at Harran, and there met and married his cousin Rachel (Gen. 27:43; 28:10; 29:4). And it was there that Jacob's daughter and 11 of his sons were born (Gen. 29:31–30:24).

It seems, therefore, that the genealogy has been put together with two quite different sets of names: one from the list of the descendants and settlements of Shem in the immediate post-deluge period; the other from the traditions about Israel's ancestors beginning with Terah and his three sons, and pre-eminently with Abraham. The intention was no doubt to present the list as transitional between the archaic period narrated in the language of myth and the beginnings of the history or prehistory of Israel, a function which it certainly serves. From the literary point of view, however, it is the fifth and last unit of the *toledot* pattern according to which Genesis 1:1–11:26 is structured, and therefore rounds out the primaeval history. The larger pattern of which it is a part is not unprecedented. The practice of prefacing the history of a people with an account of cosmic and human origins is exemplified by the Greek myth of Deucalion and the flood which leads into the history of the Greek-speaking peoples by way of his son Hellen and the latter's descendants. In his *Babyloniaca*, Berossus prefaced his brief history of the Assyrian, Babylonian and Persian kingdoms with an account of cosmic origins including the flood, the connecting link being the list of ten postdiluvian dynasties (Burstein 1978: 13–29). In much the same way, an originally independent account of cosmic origins was at some point, attached to the history of Israel beginning with the ancestors.

With the Terahite family history a new epoch begins framed within a new *toledot* series, and marked by events of great significance, and not only for the people of Israel.

Towards a Biblical Theology of Creation

Is There an Old Testament Theology of Creation?

To write a theology of creation would be a daunting task and one not to be undertaken lightly. This would be the case whether creation is limited to an event, the coming into existence of the physical world and humanity, or extended to include the created order, the phenomenal world in relation to God as its origin and the source of its intelligibility. A theological study of this scope, written from a Christian, Jewish, Islamic or any basically theistic perspective, would entail more than a consideration of the respective canonical and privileged texts. It might take as its starting point a dialogue with the relevant sciences on current issues – cosmological theory, evolution, creationism, ecology – bringing in the texts wherever they might be considered relevant. About two-thirds of Hans Schwarz's excellent recent study of the subject, for example, covers these issues in the physical sciences before turning to creation in the biblical texts (Schwarz 2002). In the same year, Willem B. Drees published an imaginative study of the relation between science and religion in connection with creation which deals only incidentally and briefly with the Bible (Drees 2002). It is certainly the case that the astonishing advances in recent years in understanding the nature of physical reality, deep time and the space–time continuum have contributed to bringing the subject to the public attention. Issues in social ethics of relevance to all humanity irrespective of religious affiliation or commitments – universal human rights, international law, care for the environment, globalization – would also be legitimate subject matter for such a theology.

The title of this epilogue to the commentary indicates that it was not my ambition to embark on such a theology. My idea was to follow up on the commentary by identifying some of the issues which have arisen throughout the history of the interpretation of the texts, and to add some observations on the specifically Christian understanding of creation which emerges from a reading of

New Testament texts. But since an eventual Christian theology of creation would have to incorporate a theological understanding of what the Jewish Scriptures have to say on the subject, it will be worth noting that creation had a hard time establishing itself as a distinctive theme in the study of the Hebrew Bible. Throughout the history of Old Testament theology which, as a distinctively Christian discipline, began only in the late eighteenth century, the tendency has been to regard creation as secondary, a kind of appendix to the great themes of revelation, election and salvation within history, meaning of course the history of Israel. It is as if the real beginning of the Bible is the first chapter of Exodus rather than the first chapter of Genesis.[1] A survey of Old Testament theologies will demonstrate how difficult it has proved to be to assign due importance to the creation texts and integrate them into an overall theological synthesis.[2] In some cases the problem lay with the writer's choice of an organizing principle or ruling concept which could not readily accommodate the creation theme. A well-known example is the concept of covenant which dictated the organization of Walther Eichrodt's influential theology first published in the 1930s (Eichrodt 1961, 1967). Even more influential was the central role played by the history of salvation (*Heilsgeschichte*) in the decades following the Second World War, the prime example of which was Gerhard von Rad's theology which came out in the 1950s (von Rad 1962, 1965). Von Rad brought the matter to a head with his claim that the idea of creation came to be seen as significant only when linked at a late stage with election and redemption within the history of Israel.[3] The claim would seem to imply that the relatively late articulation of creation faith implies its relatively minor importance and explains why it never achieved the status of an independent doctrine within the discipline.

On this view, creation faith is propaedeutic to and derivative from the history of salvation. In other words, it is ancillary to the religious history of Israel. James Muilenburg made the point very clearly:

> The biblical doctrine of creation is a derivative of history, the sacred history of the chosen people. The creation account in Genesis 1 is not only prologue to the history which follows it, but is also a development of the election-historical life, of the redemptive history which has the Exodus as its center. (Muilenburg 1961: 242, cited in Reventlow 1985: 141)

---

1   A claim made by Westermann (1961: 6). Since that publication, Westermann has, however, modified his position in his *Theologie des Alten Testaments in Grundzügen* (1978) and in his commentary (1984), especially his concluding remarks, pp. 600–606.

2   For an entry into these issues connected with Old Testament theology see Reventlow 1985 and, with special reference to creation, Reventlow and Hoffman 2002: 153–71; see also Knierim 1995; Barr 1999.

3   Von Rad 1962: 136–53. The point was made much earlier in his essay on 'The Theological Problem of the Old Testament Doctrine of Creation' in his *Gesammelte Studien zum Alten Testament* published in 1961, pp. 136–47.

This way of reading the texts did not encourage close attention to the issue of God's relationship to the physical world and to humanity, or provide a point of departure for reflection on the moral obligations arising out of a common humanity. Such concerns, grounded in a careful reading of the creation narratives, only began to surface as a set of issues for biblical theology in the 1970s, in part in response to the emergence of ecological concerns at that time, and they still have some headway to make. It may have been uneasiness about this neglect of the creation theme which led von Rad to publish a volume in 1970 on the biblical concept of wisdom which contains a chapter on 'The Self-Revelation of Creation' (von Rad 1972).

It is therefore only in relatively recent years that the problems inherent in the approach to a theology of the Old Testament exemplified by Eichrodt and von Rad have begun to be addressed. It may be symptomatic in this respect that one of the most recent and substantial theologies of the Old Testament, that of Rolf Rendtorff, at one time a student of von Rad at the University of Heidelberg, begins the section on the Pentateuch, exceptionally, with the first chapter of Genesis (Rendtorff 2005).

Genesis 1 and Deutero-Isaiah (Isaiah 40–55)

The biblical text, apart from Genesis 1–11, which speaks most explicitly about creation is the anonymous work known as Deutero-Isaiah (Isaiah 40–55). Read together, these two texts form the core of any biblical synthesis about creation. Historical references in Isaiah 40–55, especially the conquests of the Persian Cyrus (559–530 BC) who is named in it (Isa. 44:28; 45:1) and the anticipated collapse of the Babylonian empire, place at least the first part of Deutero-Isaiah (40–48) in the last years of the Neo-Babylonian empire, from ca. 550 to 539 BC when Babylon itself fell to Cyrus and his allies. The author[4] seeks to persuade his fellow-Judaeans in Judah and the diaspora that the political situation holds out the hope for a new beginning to be brought about by Cyrus as the agent of the God of Israel now revealed to be the Creator God still creatively active in human affairs.

Our best estimate for the date of the priest–author's work, the principal narrative strand in Genesis 1–11, falls roughly into the same period, let us say the half century between the fall of Jerusalem to the Babylonians in 586 BC and the fall of Babylon to the Persians and Medes in 539 BC or, at the latest, the first decades of Persian–Achaemenid rule. In their different idioms, both the creation narrative and Isaiah 40–55 celebrate the God of Israel as Creator of the world.

---

4 Use of the term 'author' does not preclude the possibility, indeed probability, that more than one hand contributed to the final form of Isaiah 40–55. On the formation of this section of the book, see Blenkinsopp 2000: 69–81.

Deutero-Isaiah almost certainly does not depend on Genesis 1 in the form in which we have it but, if not, those for whom it was written were presumed to be familiar with an account of cosmic and human origins in some form, written or oral. At one point the author asks his readers rhetorically, 'Do you not know? Have your not heard? Has it not been told to you from the beginning? Have you not grasped how the earth was founded?' (Isa. 40:21). Another indication of a close relationship with Genesis 1 is that the key verb for the act of creation, *bārā'*, used only with God as subject and occurring seven times in Gen. 1:1-2:4a, appears sixteen times in Isaiah 40–55, far more often than in any other biblical text. Deutero-Isaiah also speaks of the process of creation in much the same way. The similarities begin with the technomorphic details: control of the upper and lower waters from which the dry land emerges, the sky stretched out like a curtain or tent over the circle of the earth, setting in motion the heavenly luminaries, and human beings given life by the breath of God breathed through their nostrils (Isa. 40:12-17, 21-26; 42:5; 45:18). One difference is that, in Deutero-Isaiah, God creates both light and darkness:

I form light, I create darkness,
I bring about well being and create woe. (Isa. 45:7)

Some commentators have suspected that this is directed against Zoroastrian dualism, according to which light is the sphere of Ahura Mazda and darkness belongs to Angra Mainyu, an independent, uncreated evil deity. But we know too little about the spread of Iranian–Zoroastrian ideas about creation at that time to conclude that they would have spread to Jewish communities either in Judah or elsewhere.

On the other hand, the prophetic author of Isaiah 40–55 is as familiar with the theogonic, cosmogonic and anthropogonic Mesopotamian texts as the priestly author of Genesis 1. Polemic against the ideology inscribed in *Enuma Elish* and in the corresponding Mesopotamian cult practices is not difficult to detect, especially in chs 40–48. Unlike Marduk, imperial god of Babylon, who enlisted the help of the wise and cunning Enki in creating humanity and its environment, Yahweh needed no counsellor in the work of creation:

With whom did he consult to be enlightened?
Who taught him the right way to go?
Who imparted knowledge to him
or showed him the way of discernment? (Isa. 40:14)

Theogony was, of course, ruled out: 'Before me no god was formed, and there will be none after me' (Isa. 43:10). The procession of Marduk (Bel) and his son Nabū (Nebo) to the *akitu* house during the great spring festival, the central event of the Babylonian cultic calendar, is satirized:

> Bel crouches low, Nebo cowers,
> their images are loaded on animals, beasts of burden.
> These things you once bore aloft
> are a load for weary animals. (Isa. 46:1)

The author of Isaiah 40–48 is therefore directing his satire against the religious underpinning of Babylonian imperialism. Though using a different genre and idiom, the story about the city and tower of Babel (Gen. 11:1-9) is also aimed at the same target, namely, the imperial pretensions of Babylon (the city) and the cults which provided their religious legitimation (the tower). And, finally, Deutero-Isaiah, more than any other biblical text, mocks the actual manufacture of images of deities.[5] However the connection is to be explained, the rejection of these artefacts in human form brings to mind the priest–author's insistence that the human being is to be the only image and likeness of God on earth (Gen. 1:26-28).

As we read on through Isaiah 40–55, we realize that it comes from a time in which the loss of national independence and the destruction of the political, social and religious infrastructure of the Judaean state made it easier to release the deity from territorial and ethnic attachments, a development of great importance for the future. For this, however, a price had to be paid, and it came in the form of profound collective disorientation, collapse of confidence in the traditional sources of religious reassurance, and uncertainty about even the possibility of a future. This condition is in evidence in practically every text extant from the post-disaster period. Both the author of Isaiah 40–55 and the priest–author, whose work forms the basic narrative strand of the primaeval history, address this crisis in their different ways. In the period following the flood, after the water had retreated, the priest–author presents a Creator God who does not give up on his creation, who commits to a future in the form of a covenant with all living things, offers the prospect of order out of chaos, including in the first place moral order – the Noachide laws – and repeats the original creation blessing. The author of Isaiah 40–55 also writes in the aftermath of a disaster comparable to the deluge in the archaic period:

> This is to me like the days of Noah,
> as I swore an oath that Noah's flood water would never again inundate the earth,
> so now I swear no longer to be angry with you or rebuke you. (Isa 54:9)

The message is therefore not just about creation as a past event, *in illo tempore*, but about the renewal of creation as a present experience. Deutero-Isaiah is full of the language of creation, social and religious unravelling, and a new creation. It is

---

5   Isa. 40:18-20; 41:6-7; 44:9-20. Whether this satire represents a genuine understanding of the role of images in worship is, of course, another matter.

pervaded with the language of renewal. The Creator God proclaims this message repeatedly:

New things I now declare,
before they emerge I announce them to you. (Isa. 42:9)

I am about to do something new,
now it is unfolding, do you not perceive it? (Isa. 43:19a)

From now on I divulge new things to you,
hidden things of which you had no knowledge. (Isa. 48:6b)

At a later point in the evolution from visionary prophecy to apocalyptic eschatology within the Isaianic tradition, this prospect for the future is transformed into the scenario of a new creation, a new heaven and earth, a visionary image the influence of which has continued to be felt down to the present:

See, I am about to create new heavens and a new earth. The former things will no more be remembered, nor will they come to mind. (Isa 65:17)

At this stage, the promised creative act of renewal is linked with social and political transformation. Speaking of the eschatological Jerusalem, the author says:

No more will the sound of weeping be heard in her,
no more the cry of distress.
No child will ever again live but a few days,
no old man fail to live out the full span of his life ...
When they build houses they will dwell in them,
when they plant vineyards they will eat their produce;
they will not build houses for others to live in,
they will not plant for others to eat ...
They will not toil in vain
or raise children destined for disaster. (Isa. 65:19-23)

The scenario is idealistic or utopian: a return to the lost world of Eden, a *palingenesia*, literally, a being born again, a restoration of the primaeval creation.[6]

6   The term *palingenesia* occurs in Mt. 19:28 and Tit. 3:5. In Philo (*On the Life of Moses* 2:65) it applies to the new order after the deluge, and with Pythagoreans and Stoics it refers to the anticipated future renewal of the cosmos. Paradise as the eschatological Eden is mentioned in Rev. 2:7; cf. *1 En.* 32:3 and *b.Ber.* 28b according to which Johanan ben Zakkai, on his deathbed, foresees his post-mortem destiny as either the garden of Eden or Gehenna. Jesus promises this Paradise to the dying thief (Lk. 23:43), and Paul claims to have been admitted to it in a visionary experience (2 Cor. 12:4).

There will be no more distress and weeping, no infant mortality, no lives cut off by disease, no death and deprivation due to war and conquest, even a restoration of peace and harmony in the animal world:

> The wolf and the lamb will graze together,
> the lion will eat hay like the ox.
> (As for the snake, dust will be its food.)
> No longer will they hurt or destroy
> on all my holy mountain. (Isa. 65:25)

The power of this visionary theme will continue to nourish the imagination of many from that time to the present. We meet it at an early stage in the sectarian writings of the late Second Temple period. In the Enoch cycle (*1 En.* 45:4-5; 72:1; 91:16) the seer predicts the future transformation of the heavens and the earth. Towards the beginning of *Jubilees* (1:29), the Angel of the Presence consults the tablets which contain the record of all history from the first creation to the new creation when the heavens and the earth with all their inhabitants will be renewed. The Qumran community rule (*serek hayyahad*) also speaks of the end time as a new creation (1QS 4:25). The most familiar allusion to the theme, at least for Christian readers of the Bible, is the revelation of the new heavens and new earth to the seer of Patmos:

> I saw a new heaven and a new earth, for the first heaven and the first earth had passed away, and the sea was there no longer. And I saw the holy city Jerusalem, the new Jerusalem, coming down from out of heaven, from God, prepared like a bride adorned for her husband. And I heard a loud voice from the throne saying, 'The dwelling of God is now with humanity! God will dwell with them, they shall be God's people, God's self shall be with them. God will wipe every tear from their eyes. There will no longer be death, no mourning, no crying or pain, for the former things have passed away.' (Rev. 21:1-4)

This passage is one of many examples of the ubiquitous influence of the book of Isaiah on all aspects of early Christianity.[7] Accompanying the vision, the seer hears a voice from the throne, from the One Who is the Alpha and Omega, the Beginning and the End, proclaiming, 'Behold, I make all things new' (Rev. 21:5-6).

The emphasis in this apocalyptic vision is on the city as a symbol of the new people of God – also a major Isaianic theme – rather than on cosmic transformation. For the latter we turn to a Christian pseudepigraphical text from

---

7   New heavens, new earth (Isa. 65:17; 66:22); the end of the old heavens and earth (Isa. 51:6); Jerusalem as a bridegroom (Isa. 61:10; 62:5); the end of weeping, crying, pain, and death (Isa. 25:8; 65:19); see Blenkinsopp 2006: 129–221.

the late first or early second century. The author of 2 Peter (3:3-13) is responding to those contemporary Christians who were hinting broadly that there was not going to be a second coming. He reminds them that, as the first creation was destroyed by water, so the present creation will end with the heavens and the earth and everything in them consumed by fire. The time remaining should be used to repent. He concludes with a reminder of the same Isaianic prophecy of new heavens and new earth which will inaugurate a new era of righteousness:

> In keeping with his promise, we look forward to new heavens and a new earth in which justice will dwell. (2 Pet. 3:13)

Old Creation, New Creation in Paul

For the most part, the first Christian communities simply took over the Jewish Scriptures and applied them to their own situation. They took for granted the creation of the world and humanity out of nothing.[8] They prayed the same psalms, celebrating God as Creator in prayer and praise. In the first prayer session of the Jerusalem community recorded in the Acts of the Apostles, following the release of Peter and John from prison (Acts 4:24), they praised God as Creator of heaven and earth, citing and probably reciting Psalm 146 which speaks of prisoners being set free. Their appeal to the creation texts discussed in the commentary are for the most part limited to the first three chapters of Genesis, sometimes by allusion rather than citation. In matters of church order, Paul's use of these texts will often sound arbitrary or at least ad hoc. On one interpretation of 1 Cor. 11:7-15, an obscure text, he appeals to Gen. 1:27 (creation in the divine image) combined with Gen. 2:21-23 (creation of the woman) to prescribe that in the assembly men must not wear their hair long and women must bind up their hair. The point at issue may escape us, but the exegetical argument is that the male is created in the divine image and the female in the image of the male, a conclusion we trust few would accept today. Along the same lines, the Eden narrative provides warranty for the leading position of men in the eucharistic assembly (1 Cor. 11:7-12; cf. 1 Tim. 2:13-15). Less controversially, the comment in Gen. 2:24 about the two becoming one flesh is cited to discourage casual sexual encounters (1 Cor. 6:16) and to support the religious significance of matrimony (Eph. 5:31). In the Synoptic Gospels Jesus combines the same text with Gen. 1:17 ('male and female he created them') in his reply to certain Pharisees about the legal status of divorce (Mt. 19:5 = Mk 10:8).

The eschatological orientation of the sectarianism from which the early Christian movement emerged, including the regenerative movement led by John

---

8   e.g. Jn 1:3; Rom. 4:17; 11:36; 1 Cor. 8:6; Col. 1:16; Heb. 11:3. Consult the encyclopedias and Copan and Craig 2004; Schwarz 2002: 172–75.

the Baptist, is apparent in different degrees throughout the New Testament. It resulted in these first Christians being concerned more with the end than the beginning of human history, and more with their founder as the herald and agent of a regeneration or new creation than with the origins of the universe. For Paul, the correspondence between the beginning and the end, between *Urzeit* and *Endzeit*, old creation and new creation, is interiorized as a renewal or reorientation of life. In baptism, the Christian puts off the old self and puts on a new self (Eph. 4:22; Col. 3:9). Ephesians and Colossians are probably deutero-Pauline, but the authentic Paul himself speaks of the old self (*palaios anthrōpos*) being crucified (Rom. 6:6). By identification with Christ, the new Adam, the Christian becomes a 'new creation' (2 Cor. 5:17; Gal. 6:15). What is more, expressed as an intuition rather than a clearly stated conviction, the Christian renewed in Christ becomes in some mysterious way participant in the eventual renewal or rebirth of the physical universe, the entire created order:

> We know that all creation groans with birth pangs up to the present. What is more, we, too, who have the first fruits of the Spirit, groan inwardly, eagerly awaiting adoption as children, the redemption of our bodies. (Rom. 8:22-23).

Paul's distinction between the first Adam, a living being, based on a reading of Gen 2:7 (LXX), and the last Adam, a life-giving spirit (1 Cor. 15:45), is reminiscent of Philo (*Allegorical Interpretation* I 31–32; *On the Creation of the World* 134) who distinguishes between the heavenly, incorporeal Adam of Genesis 1 and his earthly counterpart of Genesis 2–3, the latter being a copy of the former (Runia 1993: 64–86). The idea of an Adamic duality, Adam as type and antitype, leads to Paul's Adam–Christ typology in Rom. 5:12-21. The passage opens as follows:

> As through one man sin entered this world, and through sin death, so death passed into all inasmuch as all have sinned. Until [the time of] the law sin was in the world, but no reckoning was kept of sin since the law was not yet in existence. Nevertheless, death reigned from Adam to Moses even in those who did not sin after the manner of Adam's transgression, who is a type [*tupos*] of the one to come. (Rom. 5:12-14)

This passage has been the object of an enormous amount of commentary (e.g. Barrett 1962; Scroggs 1966; and the commentaries), but for our present purpose only one point need be made. It has served as a proof-text for the doctrine of original sin, but it is not clear that it can bear this interpretation. What was passed on from Adam was not sin but death which is contrasted in the following verse with the gift of life available through Christ. In affirming this, Paul is reproducing – whether consciously or not we cannot say – the point of view of the author of the Wisdom of Solomon (2:23-24):

God created us for incorruption,
making us in the image of his own eternity;
but death entered the world through the envy of the devil,
those who are on his side experience it.

Paul does not say that Adam was the *cause* of all the sin that followed throughout history, certainly not in the sense of introducing sin into the gene pool as a kind of germ or bacillus passed on by heredity. As the first sinner, Adam is the prototype of sinful humanity 'inasmuch as all have sinned'. The universality of sin has already been established by Paul in the most uncompromising manner in the first three chapters of the epistle ('All alike have sinned, and are deprived of the divine glory', Rom. 3:23 REB). The originator of the doctrine of original sin is not Paul but Augustine who, unlike Paul, had to depend on a Latin translation which could more easily be construed in the sense which came to be widely accepted.

Christ, the Wisdom of God

The idea of Christ as mediator, agent or demiurge[9] in creation is not developed in the New Testament in the philosophical or discursive way characteristic of Philo. For Paul, Christ is the full expression of God's wisdom (1 Cor. 1:24, 30). In the sayings source known to modern scholarship as Q (German *Quelle* = source), recoverable from Matthew and Luke, Jesus is represented not only as wise teacher but as personified wisdom. One of these sayings, attributed to Jesus in the Matthean version (Mt. 23:34), is introduced in the Lukan parallel (Lk. 11:49) as emanating from the wisdom of God. According to the prologue to the Epistle to the Hebrews (1:1-3), God who spoke to us in the past by means of the prophets has in these latter days spoken to us by means of the Son through whom he made the world. This author's exalted description of the Son – the reflection of God's glory and the imprint of God's being – corresponds closely to what the Wisdom of Solomon says of personified Wisdom:

She is a breath of God's power,
a pure emanation of the glory of the Almighty ...
a reflection of eternal light,
a spotless mirror of the workings of God,
an image of God's goodness. (Wis. 7:25-26)

Similar claims about the transcendence and cosmic significance of Christ are expressed in the Christological hymn preserved in Col. 1:13-20 (perhaps 15-20)

---

9   Originally meaning a public worker or official, *demiourgos* was used by Plato to designate the fashioner of the world. In Gnostic sects, the demiurge was responsible for the world but subordinate to the supreme deity.

which was cited and briefly discussed in the commentary: Christ is the firstborn of creation, through him everything visible and invisible was created, and he preserves and holds the created order together. All of this is said of Wisdom in the texts in which *ḥokmâ/sophia* is celebrated as primordial and active in the creation of the world.[10] As the principle of cosmic coherence and order, Christ also embodies the divine *sophia* which the Wisdom of Solomon – taking over the Stoic idea of the *logos* as the principle of cosmic order – praises as 'reaching mightily from one end of the earth to the other, and ordering all things well' (Wis. 8:1).

The Dark Side of Creation

The question which we have heard calling for an answer throughout Genesis 1–11 is how evil could have infiltrated so quickly and established itself so firmly and ubiquitously in a creation declared by God to be good. This we have taken to be the central theme of Genesis 1–11. The commentary was based on the assumption that the initial act of creation cannot be detached from the sequence of events leading to the deluge as an act of un-creation followed by a renewal of creation under changed circumstances. To confine oneself to the initial act of creation involves leaving the post-deluge world, the world which was born out of disaster, in other words, the damaged but as yet intact world in which we live, without an adequate explanation. This is, after all, the world the author was really concerned about, as we the readers also are. The purpose of the history of the pre-deluge world, constructed as we saw from originally independent origin stories, is precisely to explore, in the idiom of myth, the mysterious onset of evil in a world created good.

If the first Christians were more concerned with the end than with the beginning of history, they were also more concerned with the negative aspects of the created order in need of salvation than with the positive and optimist view of a world declared to be very good by God at the beginning. Paul, whose correspondence is chronologically the earliest extant Christian writing, begins his great statement in Romans with the universality of sin, a condition common to Gentile and Jew alike (Rom. 1:18–3:20). Then, at a later point, he provides what we might call a historical–typological explanation of this situation by speaking of Adam as the type of sinful humanity.[11] Paul is obviously aware of the role of Satan under the guise of the snake (Rom. 16:20) and of Eve's

---

10   Prov. 3:19; 8:22-31; Sir. 24:1-22; Wis. 7:22; 9:1-3. See above pp. 43–52.

11   E. P. Sanders (1977: 442–47) insists that for Paul the solution precedes the problem, that is, Paul begins with the gift and grace of Christ, antitype of Adam, and only then considers the sinful plight of humanity. If, however, we read Romans sequentially, we see that Paul goes to great pains to establish the universality of the sinful condition before proceeding to the event

seduction by the snake (2 Cor. 11:3), but the introduction of these other actors would have distracted from the Adam–Christ, first man–last man typology, which he develops in Rom. 5:12-19. Satan is elsewhere acknowledged to be 'the god of this age' (1 Cor. 4:4), reflecting the Jewish teaching about the two ages and the contrast between them (e.g. 2 Esd. 7:10-14). In another passage in which he exhorts believers not to consort with unbelievers (2 Cor. 6:14-7:1), the authenticity of which is sometimes questioned (Betz 1973; Fitzmyer 1974: 205–17) and less often defended (Murphy-O'Connor 1987), the author asks: 'What is there in common between light and darkness? What agreement can Christ have with Beliar?' (6:15). Beliar, more commonly Belial, is a familiar figure in sectarian or quasi-sectarian writings from the late Second Temple period (*Jub.* 1:20; 15:33; *Testament of Reuben* 4:7,11; 6:3; *Testament of Levi* 3:3; 18:12; Lewis 1992; Otzen 1975). In several of the Qumran texts he is the ruler of the present age, the dark force behind the evil and corruption in the world (1QS 1:18; 2:19; 1QM 14:9). This worldview is consistent with Paul's conviction about the universality of sin, the corruption of the present generation (Phil. 2:15) and the distinction between the children of light and the children of darkness (1 Thess. 5:4-5). It is also compatible with belief in the 'principalities and powers' about which we hear especially in the deutero-Pauline writings. These supernatural forces and agencies continue even after the event of salvation to exercise their malign influence.[12] It is quite clear that Paul is presenting a worldview that goes far beyond the contemporary liberal assumption that evil can be accounted for exclusively in terms of our biological history and psychological resources.

Turning now to the Gospels, the conviction that the Christ event is a new creation is intimated in the superscript to Matthew's Gospel where he describes the genealogy of Jesus as a *biblios geneseōs* ('a book of generations') in imitation of Adam's *sēper tôlĕdôt* ('book of generations') in Gen. 5:1. The same point is made even more clearly in the opening words of John's Gospel, announcing a new *bĕrē'šît*, 'in the beginning', a new Genesis. But it is the dark side of creation which is most clearly in evidence in all four canonical Gospels. It is no exaggeration to say that the contest between Jesus and Satan is the leading theme in the Synoptic Gospels. The theme is announced in the testing of Jesus by Satan which serves as prologue to the public activity of Jesus (Mt. 4:1-11; Lk. 4:1-13). Satan shows Jesus all the kingdoms of the earth and claims that all political power has been handed over to him, a claim Jesus does not contest (Lk. 4:5-6). It seems that Satan, here described as the *diabolos* ('adversary', 'slanderer'), is seeking to co-opt Jesus and his miraculous powers for his own ends, perhaps as

---

of salvation in Christ ('But now, apart from the law, the righteousness of God has been made known', 3:21) and, eventually, to develop his Adam typology.

12   Eph. 2:2; 6:12; Col. 2:15. These or similar expressions can also refer to good as well as evil angelic beings, as in *1 En.* 61:10 and *Testament of Levi* 3:8. According to *Testament of Solomon* 18:1-2, there were 36 demonic powers (*stoicheia*), one for each ten-degree band of the 360 degrees of the celestial sphere.

his deputy and vassal on earth. The attempt failed, and Satan left Jesus until the appointed time, which was to be the time of his death (Lk. 4:13).

Satan's involvement in the death of Jesus is given full weight in the New Testament. Judas acts as his agent (Mt. 26:14-16), an aspect of the death narrative much emphasized in the Fourth Gospel (Jn 6:70-71; 13:2,27), and Simon Peter succumbs to his wiles but repents in time (Lk. 26:31). As he faces his death, Jesus seems to be acknowledging Satan's role when he says to those who arrested him, 'This is your hour, and that of the Dark Power' (Lk. 22:53).[13] Satan's triumph was, as Christians confess, illusory. Matthew's Gospel, which begins with Satan claiming all power and authority in the world, ends with the resurrected Jesus announcing that 'all authority in heaven and earth has been given to me' (Mt. 28:18).

The thesis is confirmed by the exorcisms viewed as incidents in the struggle against Satan, ruler of the present age, which the Qumran Community Rule refers to as 'the dominion of Belial' (1QS 2:19). The Jesus of the Synoptics, and even more so the Jesus of the Fourth Gospel, has no illusions about the present age, often referred to as 'this evil and adulterous generation' (Mt. 12:39; 16:14 [= Lk 11:29]; 17:17 [= Lk 9:41]; Mk 9:19). From this point of view, the defining moment of the contest between Jesus and Satan, the Dark Power, is the Beelzebul controversy in which Jesus is accused of exorcizing by Beelzebul, prince of demons.[14] The occasion was the healing of a possessed blind and mute man by Jesus. His Pharisee opponents attributed his powers to necromancy or satanism, consequent on his invocation of Beelzebul. Jesus responded with the rhetorical questions 'How can Satan cast out Satan? If Satan is divided against himself, how can his kingdom survive?' The conclusion was incontestable: 'If by the Spirit of God I cast out demons, this means that the kingdom of God has already come among you.'

No one in New Testament times addressed the issue of the origin of evil with reference to the biblical traditions of human origins in a formal, systematic way. Apart from the fact, noted earlier, that the focus was more on the end than the beginning of human history, no one would have denied the role of supernatural agencies, present in human history since the beginning, in the ubiquitous presence of evil in its many forms, including sickness and possession. This is taken for granted in the accounts of the healings and exorcisms by Jesus. It is assumed, often

---

13 The phrase *hē exousia tou skotous*, literally, 'the power of darkness', corresponds to a common genitival idiom in Hebrew and Aramaic which substitutes for an adjective, cf. 'the sword of the spirit', meaning 'the spiritual sword'. Some commentators have argued that the 'rulers of this age' who, according to 1 Cor. 2:7-8, crucified Jesus, refers to supernatural satanic powers. But Paul would not in that case have added that, if they had possessed the true wisdom, they would not have done it. The reference is more naturally to the hegemonic power of that time, i.e., the Roman empire and its local representatives.

14 Mt 9:32-34; 12:22-32 [= Mk 3:22-30]; Lk 11:14-23. Beelzebub, the alternative and more familiar form, is probably a dysphemism meaning 'lord of the flies' (*baʿal zĕbûb*), referring to a deity of the Philistine city of Ekron (2 Kgs 1:2); see Herrmann 1999.

tacitly, in prayers ('deliver us from the Evil One', Mt. 6:13), in teachings, and especially in the parables: the Evil One in the parable of the sower (Mt. 13:1-23), the enemy, who is the Devil, in the parable of the tares (Mt. 13:24-30, 36-43).

Wherever in the New Testament the origins of Satan are alluded to or hinted at, more often than not the reference is to the garden of Eden narrative (e.g. Rom. 16:20; 2 Cor. 11:3); however, an episode recorded in the Fourth Gospel represents a variant tradition. The incident in question is the particularly bitter dispute recorded in Jn 8:31-47 between Jesus and some Jews who were no longer among his disciples. Jesus claimed that these people who were opposing him as one possessed, and perhaps also illegitimate, planned to kill him. In response, Jesus rejected their claim to be children of Abraham. Their father is not Abraham but the devil who was a murderer from the beginning. The allusion is best explained with reference to the midrashic interpretation of Gen. 4:1, mentioned in the commentary on that verse, about the seduction of Eve by the serpent resulting in the birth of Cain the murderer. Cain is therefore the spawn of Satan, the first murderer, and the forerunner of all who kill, or plot to kill, the innocent. The identical or a similar tradition is behind the reference in 1 Jn 3:12 to Cain, son of the Evil One who murdered his brother, the antithesis of the fraternal love recommended by the writer. According to this variant tradition, therefore, Cain, the 'undying evil', is at the origins of violence and injustice visited by one human being on one another.

The New Testament has very little to say about 'the sons of God/the gods and the daughters of man' myth (Gen. 6:1-4). Early Christian writers were familiar with the tradition about rebellious angels cast down out of heaven and confined in the underworld to await the day of judgement.[15] Related to this tradition is the precipitous fall of Satan seen by Jesus as his disciples were exorcizing demons (Lk. 10:18), an exclamation inspired by the Isaianic text about the fall of a tyrant, whose other name is Lucifer, from his god-like eminence (Isa. 14:12-15). A similar fate awaited the descendants of the divine–human commingling, the generation of the flood, those who did not share Noah's faith in God and his word (Heb. 11:7). That fate is described by the Jesus of Luke's Gospel with reference to the original cataclysm, and in terms which are prosaic, chilling and psychologically credible in the light of the many lesser catastrophes which have been the human lot since then:

As it was in the days of Noah, so it will be in the days of the Son of Man. They were eating, drinking, marrying and giving in marriage, until the day when Noah went into the ark. Then the flood came and made an end of them all. (Lk. 17:26-27)

15   Rev. 20:1-10; 2 Pet. 2:4-5; Jude 6. In some way related to this tradition is the descent of Jesus into the underworld to preach to the spirits of those who perished in the flood (1 Pet. 3:19-20).

Here, as elsewhere in the biblical archive, our reading can provide often surprising resources for understanding our place in the world, opening up new perspectives, and suggesting fresh points of entry into a revelation and worldview that can free us to go beyond our mundane formulations and taken-for-granted assumptions.

Bibliography

Ackerman, Susan (1992), *Under Every Green Tree: Popular Religion in Sixth Century Judah*. Atlanta: Scholars Press.

Adler, William (1983), 'Berossus, Manetho, and *1 Enoch* in the World Chronicle of Panodorus'. *HTR* 76: 419–42.

Albright, William Foxwell (1938), Review of Gustav Hölscher, *Das Buch Hiob. JBL* 57: 227–28.

Alexander, Philip S. (1972), 'The Targumim and Early Exegesis of 'Sons of God' in Gen 6'. *JJS* 23: 60–71.

——— (1983), '3 (Hebrew Apocalypse of) Enoch: A New Translation and Introduction', in Charlesworth 1983: 223–315.

Alonso-Schökel, Luis (1962), 'Motivos sapienciales y de alianza en Gen 2–3'. *Bib* 43: 295–316.

Anderson, Bernhard W. (1978), 'From Analysis to Synthesis: the Interpretation of Genesis 1–11'. *JBL* 97: 23–39.

Anderson, G. A., M. E. Stone and Johannes Tromp (2000), *Literature on Adam and Eve: Collected Essays*. Leiden: Brill.

Andriolo, K. R. (1973), 'A Structural Analysis of Genealogy and World View in the Old Testament'. *American Anthropologist* 75: 1657–69.

Arneth, Martin (2007), 'Die noachistischer Gebote (Genesis 9,1-7). Die Priesterschrift und das Gesetz in der Urgeschichte', in R. Achenbach, M. Arneth and Eckart Otto, eds, *Tora in der hebräischen Bibel. Studien zur Redaktionsgeschichte und synchroner Logik diachroner Transformationen*. Wiesbaden: Harrassowitz, pp. 7–25.

Arnim, J. von (1903), *Stoicorum Veterum Fragmenta*, vol. 3. Leipzig: Teubner.

——— (1905), *Stoicorum Veterum Fragmenta*, vol. 1. Leipzig: Teubner.

Attridge, H. W., and R. A. Oden (1981), *Philo of Byblos, The Phoenician History*. Washington, DC: Catholic Biblical Association.

Auffarth, Christoph, and Loren T. Stuckenbruck (2004), *The Fall of the Angels*. Leiden: Brill.

191

Bailey, John A. (1970), 'Initiation and the Primal Woman in Gilgamesh and Genesis 2–3'. *JBL* 89: 137–50.

Baker, D. W. (1992), 'Tarshish'. *ABD* 6: 331–33.

Barr, James (1985), 'The Question of Religious Influence: The Case of Zoroastrianism, Judaism, and Christianity'. *JAAR* 53/2: 201–35.

———— (1988), 'The Authority of Scripture: The Book of Genesis and the Origin of Evil in Jewish and Christian Tradition', in G. R. Evans, ed., *Christian Authority: Essays in Honour of Henry Chadwick*. Oxford: Clarendon, pp. 59–75.

———— (1992), ' "Thou art the cherub": Ezekiel 28:14 and the Post-exilic Understanding of Genesis 2–3', in Eugene Ulrich et al., eds, *Priests, Prophets, and Scribes*. Sheffield: JSOT, pp. 213–23.

———— (1993a), *The Garden of Eden and the Hope of Immortality*. Minneapolis: Fortress.

———— (1993b), *Biblical Faith and Natural Theology*. Oxford: Clarendon.

———— (1999), *The Concept of Biblical Theology*. Minneapolis: Fortress.

Barré, Michael L. (1988), 'The Riddle of the Flood Chronology'. *JSOT* 41: 3–20.

———— (1999), 'Rabisu, רביץ'. *DDD* 682–83.

Barrett, C. K. (1962), *From First Adam to Last: A Study in Pauline Theology*. New York: Scribner.

Bassett, F. W. (1971), 'Noah's Nakedness and the Curse of Canaan: A Case of Incest?' *VT* 21: 232–37.

Bauks, Michaela (1997), *Die Welt am Anfang. Zum Verhältnis von Vorwelt und Weltentstehung in Genesis 1 und in der altorientalische Literatur*. Neukirchen-Vluyn: Neukirchener Verlag.

———— (2001), ' "Chaos" als Metaphor für die Gefährdung der Weltordnung', in Janowski B. and Ego Beate, eds, *Das biblische Weltbild und seine altorientalischen Kontexte*. Tübingen: Mohr-Siebeck, pp. 431–64.

Beeston, A. F. L. (1986), 'One Flesh'. *VT* 36: 115–17.

Begrich, Joachim (1932), 'Die Paradieserzählung. Eine literargeschichtliche Studie'. *ZAW* 50: 93–116.

Ben Yashar, M. (1982), 'Zu Gen 4,7'. *ZAW* 94: 635–37.

Berner, Christoph (2006), *Jahre, Jahrwochen und Jubiläen*. Berlin: de Gruyter.

Betz, Hans Dieter (1973), '2 Cor 6:14–7:1: An Anti-Pauline Fragment?' *JBL* 92: 88–108.

Bird, Phyllis (1981), ' "Male and female he created them": Gen 1:27b in the Context of the Priestly Account of Creation'. *HTR* 74: 129–59.

Black, Matthew (1985), *The Book of Enoch or 1 Enoch: A New English Edition*. Leiden: Brill.

Blenkinsopp, Joseph (1990), 'The Judge of All the Earth: Theodicy in the Midrash on Genesis 18:22-33'. *JJS* 41: 1–12.

———— (1992), *The Pentateuch: An Introduction to the First Five Books of the Bible*. New York and London: Doubleday.

———— (2000), *Isaiah 40–55: A New Translation with Introduction and Commentary* (AB 19A). New York: Doubleday.

———— (2003), 'The One in the Middle', in J. Cheryl Exum and Hugh Williamson, eds, *Reading from Right to Left: Essays on the Hebrew Bible in Honour of David J. A. Clines*. Sheffield: JSOT, pp. 63–75.

———— (2004), 'Gilgamesh and Adam', in *Treasures Old and New: Essays in the Theology of the Pentateuch*. Grand Rapids: Eerdmans, pp. 85–101.

———— (2006), *Opening the Sealed Book: Interpretations of the Book of Isaiah in Late Anntiquity*. Grand Rapids: Eerdmans.

———— (2009), 'Abraham as Paradigm in the Priestly History in Genesis'. *JBL* 128: 225–41.

Bloom, Harold (1990), *The Book of J*. New York: Weidenfeld.

Boardman, John (2000), *Persia and the West*, London: Thames & Hudson.

Borger, R. (1974), 'Die Beschwörungsserie *Bit Mēseri und die Himmelfahrt Henochs*'. *JNES* 33: 183–96.

Bouteneff, Peter C. (2008), *Beginnings: Ancient Christian Readings of the Biblical Creation Narratives*. Grand Rapids: Baker.

Boyce, Mary (1979), *Zoroastrians: Their Religious Beliefs and Practices*. London & New York: Routledge.

———— (1988), 'The Religion of Cyrus the Great', in Amélie Kuhrt and Heleen Sancisi-Weerdenburg, eds, *Achaemenid History*, vol. 3: *Method and Theory*. Leiden: Nederlands Instituut voor het Nabije Oosten, pp. 15–31.

Bremmer, Jan N. (2000), 'Pandora or the Creation of a Greek Eve', in Gerard P. Luttikhuizen, ed., *The Creation of Man and Woman: Interpretations of the Biblical Narratives in Jewish and Christian Traditions*. Leiden: Brill, pp. 34–62.

———— (2004), 'Remember the Titans!', in Auffarth and Stuckenbruck 2004: 35–61.

———— (2005), 'Creation Myths in Ancient Greece', in G. H. van Kooten, ed., *The Creation of Heaven and Earth: Re-interpretations of Genesis 1 in the Context of Judaism, Ancient Philosophy, Christianity, and Modern Physics*. Leiden: Brill, pp. 90–96.

Brett, Mark G. (2002), *Ethnicity and the Bible*. Leiden: Brill.

Brown, Raymond E. (1966), *The Gospel according to John I–XII*. Garden City, NY: Doubleday.

Bryan, David T. (1987), 'A Reevaluation of Genesis 4 and 5 in Light of Recent Studies in Genealogical Fluidity'. *ZAW* 99: 180–88.

Budde, Karl (1883), *Die Biblische Urgeschichte (Gen 1–12,5)*. Giessen: Ricker'sche.

Burkert, Walter (1977), *Griechische Religion der archaischen und klassischen Epoche*. Stuttgart: Kohlhammer.

Burstein, Stanley M. (1978), *The Babyloniaca of Berossus*. Malibu: Undena.

Callender, Dexter E. (2000), *Adam in Myth and History: Ancient Israelite Perspectives on the Primal Human*. Winona Lake, IN: Eisenbrauns.

Carroll, Robert P. (1986), *Jeremiah: A Commentary*. Philadelphia: Westminster.

Cassuto, U. (1961), *A Commentary on the Book of Genesis*, vol. 1. Jerusalem: Magnes Press.

Castellino, Georgio (1960), 'Genesis IV.7'. *VT* 10: 442–45.

Charles, R. H. (1913), *The Apocrypha and Pseudepigrapha of the Old Testament in English* (2 vols). Oxford: Clarendon.

Charlesworth, James H. (1983), *The Old Testament Pseudepigrapha*, vol. 1. Garden City, NY: Doubleday.

——— (1985), *The Old Testament Pseudepigrapha*, vol. 2. Garden City, NY: Doubleday.

Cheyne, T. K. (1897), 'The Connection of Esau and Usōos'. *ZAW* 17: 189.

Clifford, Richard J. (1972), *The Cosmic Mountain in Canaan and the Old Testament*. Cambridge, MA: Harvard University Press.

Clines, David J. A. (1997), *The Theme of the Pentateuch* (2nd edn). Sheffield: Sheffield Academic Press.

Cogan, M., and H. Tadmor (1988), *II Kings: A New Translation with Introduction and Commentary* (AB 11). New York: Doubleday.

Cohn, Norman (1996), *Noah's Flood: The Genesis Story in Western Thought*. New Haven and London: Yale University Press.

Collins, John J. (1993), *Daniel* (Hermeneia). Minneapolis: Fortress.

Coogan, Michael D. (1978), *Stories from Ancient Canaan*. Philadelphia: Westminster.

Copan, Paul, and William L. Craig (2004), *Creation out of Nothing: A Biblical, Philosophical, and Scientific Exploration*. Grand Rapids: Baker.

Coxon, P. W. (1999), 'Nephilim, נפילים'. *DDD* 618–20.

Cross, Frank Moore (1973), *Canaanite Myth and Hebrew Epic*. Cambridge, MA: Harvard University Press.

Crüsemann, Frank (1981), 'Die Eigenständichkeit der Urgeschichte. Ein Beitrag zur Diskussion um den "Jahwisten" ', in J. Jeremias and L. Perlitt, eds, *Die Botschaft und die Boten. Fst. für Hans Walter Wolff*. Neukirchen: Neukirchener, pp. 11–29.

——— (2002), 'Human Solidarity and Ethnic Identity: Israel's Self-Definition in the Genealogical System of Genesis', in Mark G. Brett, ed., *Ethnicity and the Bible*. Leiden: Brill, pp. 57–76.

Cryer, F. H. (1985), 'The Interrelationships of Gen 5:32, 11:10 and 7:6 and the Chronology of the Flood'. *Bib* 66: 241–61.

Dahood, Mitchell (1965), *Psalms 1–50* (AB 16). Garden City, NY: Doubleday.

Dalley, Stephanie (1989), *Myths from Mesopotamia*. Oxford: Oxford University Press.

Davies, Philip R. (1983), 'Calendric Change and Qumran Origins: An Assessment of VanderKam's Theory'. *CBQ* 45: 80–89.

Davila, James R. (1992), 'Shinar'. *ABD* 5: 1220.

Day, John (1985), *God's Conflict with the Dragon and the Sea: Echoes of a Canaanite Myth in the Old Testament*. Cambridge: Cambridge University Press.

Drees, Willem B. (2002), *Creation from Nothing until Now*. London and New York: Routledge.

Drew, Robert (1975), 'The Babylonian Chronicles and Berossus'. *Iraq* 37: 39–55.

Driver, Godfrey Rolles (1954), 'Problems and Solutions'. *VT* 4: 343.

———— (1955), 'Problems in the Hebrew Text of Job'. *VTSup* 3: 72.

Driver, Samuel Rolles, and George Buchanan Gray (1921), *A Critical and Exegetical Commentary on the Book of Job* (ICC). Edinburgh: T. & T. Clark.

Ehrenzweig, Armin (1915), 'Kain und Lamech'. *ZAW* 35: 1–11.

Eichrodt, Walther (1961), *Theology of the Old Testament*, vol. 1. Philadelphia: Westminster. ET by J. A. Baker of *Theologie des Alten Testaments*, vol. 1. (6th edn). Stuttgart: Ehrenfried Klotz Verlag, 1959.

———— (1967), *Theology of the Old Testament*, vol. 2. Philadelphia: Westminster. ET by J. A. Baker of *Theologie des Alten Testaments*, vol. 2. (5th edn). Stuttgart: Ehrenfried Klotz Verlag, 1964.

———— (1970), *Ezekiel: A Commentary*. London: SCM. ET by Cosslett Quin of *Der Prophet Hezekiel* (Göttingen: Vandenhoeck & Ruprecht, 1965).

Emerton, John A. (1988), 'The Priestly Writer in Genesis'. *JTS* 39: 396–400.

Enslin, Martin S. (1967), 'Cain and Prometheus'. *JBL* 86: 88–90.

Eppstein, V. (1968), 'The Day of Yahweh in Jeremiah 4:23-28'. *JBL* 87: 93–97.

Eslinger, Lyle M. (1979), 'A Contextual Identification of the *bene haʾelohim* and *benoth haʾadam* in Gen 6:1-4'. *JSOT* 13: 65–73.

Finkelstein, J. J. (1981), *The Ox that Gored*. Philadelphia: American Philosophical Society.

Fitzmyer, Joseph A. (1974), *Essays in the Semitic Background of the New Testament*. Missoula, MT: SBL Sources for Biblical Study.

Fowler, M. D. (1987), 'The Meaning of *lipnê YHWH* in the Old Testament'. *ZAW* 99: 384–90.

Fox, Michael (2000), *The Book of Proverbs: A New Translation with Introduction and Commentary* (AB 18A). New York: Doubleday.

Freedman, H., and M. Simon (1939), ed., *Midrash Rabbah: Genesis I* (London: Soncino Press).

Gardiner, Alan (1961), *Egypt of the Pharaohs: An Introduction*. Oxford: Clarendon.

Gardiner, Alan (1999), *The Egyptians: An Introduction*. London: The Folio Society.

George, Andrew (1999), *The Epic of Gilgamesh*. London: Penguin Books.

————— (2003), *The Babylonian Gilgamesh Epic: Introduction, Critical Edition and Cuneiform Texts* (2 vols). Oxford: Oxford University Press.

Ginzberg, Louis (1955), *The Legends of the Jews*, vol. 5: *Notes to Volumes I and II*. Philadelphia: Jewish Publication Society of America.

————— (1961), *The Legends of the Jews*, vol. 1: *Bible Times and Characters from the Creation to Jacob*. Philadelphia: Jewish Publication Society of America.

Goldberg, J. (1969), 'Sohn des Menschen oder Sohn der Schlange?' *Judaica* 25: 203–21.

Greenstein, Edward L. (2002), 'God's Golem: The Creation of the Human in Genesis 2', in Henning Graf Reventlow and Yair Hoffman, eds, *Creation in Jewish and Christian Tradition*. Sheffield: Sheffield Academic Press, pp. 219–39.

Grelot, P. (1959), 'Les Targums du Pentateuque: Étude comparative d'après Genèse IV, 3-16'. *Semitica* 9: 59–88.

Groningen, B. A. van (1953), *In the Grip of the Past*. Leiden: Brill.

Gunkel, Hermann (1895), *Schöpfung und Chaos in Urzeit und Endzeit. Eine religionsgeschichtliche Untersuchung über Gen 1 und Ap Joh 12*. Göttingen: Vandenhoeck & Ruprecht.

————— (1997), *Genesis*. Macon, GA: Mercer University Press. ET by Mark E. Biddle of *Genesis* (3rd edn). Göttingen: Vandenhoeck & Ruprecht, 1910.

Gwirkin, Russell E. (2006), *Berossus and Genesis, Manetho and Exodus: Hellenistic Histories and the Date of the Pentateuch*. New York and London: T. & T. Clark.

Harrington, Daniel J. (2000), 'Wisdom Texts'. *EDSS* 2: 976–80.

Hartman, T. C. (1972), 'Some Thoughts on the Sumerian King List and Genesis 5 and 11B'. *JBL* 91: 25–32.

Hayward, C. T. R. (1991), 'Pirke deRabbi Eliezer and Targum Pseudo-Jonathan'. *JTS* 42: 215–46.

Heidel, A. (1949), *The Gilgamesh Epic and Old Testament Parallels* (2nd edn) Chicago: University of Chicago Press.

————— (1951), *The Babylonian Genesis* (2nd edn) Chicago: University of Chicago Press.

Heider, G. C. (1999), 'Tannin, תנין'. *DDD* 834–36.

Heither, Theresia, OSB, and Christiana Reemts, OSB (2007), *Biblische Gestalten bei den Kirchenvätern: Adam*. Münster: Aschendorff.

Hendel, Ronald S. (1985), 'The Flame of the Whirling Sword'. *JBL* 104: 671–74.

————— (1999), 'Serpent, נחש'. *DDD* 744–47.

————— (2004), 'The Nephilim were on the Earth: Genesis 6:1-4 and its Ancient Near Eastern Context', in Auffarth and Stuckenbruck 2004: 11–34.

Herrmann, Wolfgang (1999), 'Baal Zebub, בעל זבוב'. *DDD* 154–56.

Hess, Richard S. (1989), 'The Genealogies of Genesis 1–11 and Comparative Literature'. *Bib* 70: 241–54.

———(1992), 'Nephilim'. *ABD* 4: 1072–73.

——— (1993), *Studies in the Personal Names in Genesis 1–11*. Neukirchen-Vluyn: Neukirchener Verlag.

Holladay, Carl R. (1983), *Fragments from Hellenistic Jewish Authors*, vol. 1: *Historians*. Chico, CA: Scholars Press.

Huffmon, Herbert B. (1992), 'Lex Talionis'. *ABD* 4: 321–22.

Hulst, A. R. (1958), 'Kol Basar in der priesterlichen Fluterzählung'. *OTS* 12: 28–68.

Humbert, Paul (1940), *Études sur le récit du paradis et de la chute dans la Genèse*. Neuchatel: Université de Neuchatel.

Hvidberg, Flemming (1960), 'The Canaanite Background of Gen. 1–11'. *VT* 10: 285–94.

Isaac, E. (1983), '1 Ethiopc Apocalypse of Enoch: A New Translation and Introduction', in Charlesworth 1983: 5–89.

Isenberg, S. (1970), 'An Anti-Sadducee Polemic in the Palestinian Targum Tradition'. *HTR* 63: 433–44.

Izreʾel, Shlomo (2001), *Adapa and the South Wind: Language has the Power of Life and Death*. Winona Lake, IN: Eisenbrauns.

Jacobsen, Thorkild (1939), *The Sumerian King List*. Chicago: University of Chicago Press.

———(1981), 'The Eridu Genesis'. *JBL* 100: 513–29.

Jacobs-Hornig, B. (1978), 'גן, *gan*'. *TDOT* 3: 34–39.

Jacobus, Helen R. (2009), 'The Curse of Cainan (*Jub.* 8.1-5): Genealogies in Genesis 5 and Genesis 11 and a Mathematical Pattern'. *JSP* 18: 207–32.

Jacoby, F. (1957), *Die Fragmente der Griechischen Historiker: Erster Teil A: Genealogie und Mythographie* (2nd edn). Leiden: Brill.

Johnson, M. D. (1985), 'Life of Adam and Eve: A New Translation and Introduction', in Charlesworth 1985: 249–95.

——— (1988), *The Purpose of the Biblical Genealogies* (2nd edn). Cambridge: Cambridge University Press.

Jonsson, G. (1988), *The Image of God: Genesis 1:26-28 in a Century of Old Testament Research*. Lunde: Gleerup.

Kaiser, Otto (1959), *Die mythische Bedeutung des Meeres in Ägypten, Ugarit und Israel*. Berlin: de Gruyter.

Kapelrud, Arvid S. (1980), 'חוה, *chavvāh*'. *TDOT* 4: 257–60.

Kawashima, R. S. (2006), 'A Revisionist Reading Revisited: On the Creation of Adam and then Eve'. *VT* 56: 46–57.

Kedar-Kopfstein, B. (1999), 'עדן, *ēden*'. *TDOT* 10: 481–90.

Kent, Roland G. (1953), *Old Persian: Grammar, Texts, Lexicon*. New Haven: American Oriental Society.

Kikawada, M. (1972), 'Two Notes on Eve'. *JBL* 91: 35–37.

Klein, Ralph W. (1974), 'Archaic Chronologies and the Textual History of the Old Testament'. *HTR* 57: 255–63.

Knierim, Rolf P. (1995), *The Task of Old Testament Theology*. Grand Rapids: Eerdmans.

Knox, Wilfred L. (1937), 'The Divine Wisdom'. *JTS* 38: 230–37.

Knuuttila, Simo (2001), 'Time and Creation in Augustine', in E. Stump and N. Kretzmann, eds, *The Cambridge Companion to Augustine*. Cambridge: Cambridge University Press, pp. 103–15.

Koch, Klaus (1983), 'Sabatstruktur der Geschichte. Die sogenannte Zehn-Wochen Apokalypse (1 Hen 93 1–10, 91 11-17) und das Ringen um die alttestamentlichen Chronologien im späten Israelitentum'. *ZAW* 95: 403–30.

———— (1987), 'P – Kein Redaktor! Erinnerung an zwei Eckdaten der Quellenscheidung'. *VT* 39: 446–67.

———— (1999), 'עָוֹן, ʿāwōn'. *TDOT* 10: 546–62.

Kselman, J. S. (1973), 'A Note on Gen 7:11'. *CBQ* 35: 491–93.

Kugel, James L. (1998), *Traditions of the Bible: A Guide to the Bible as it was at the Beginning of the Common Era*. Cambridge, MA: Harvard University Press.

Kuhl, Curt (1953), *Die Entstehung des Alten Testaments*. Berne: Francke Verlag.

Lambert, Wilfred G. (1965), 'A New Look at the Babylonian Background of Genesis'. *JTS* 16: 287–300.

———— (1967), 'Enmeduranki and Related Matters'. *JCS* 21: 126–38.

Lambert Wilfred G., and Alan A. Millard (1969), *ATRA-HASIS: The Babylonian Story of the Flood*. Oxford: Oxford University Press. Repr. Winona Lake, IN: Eisenbrauns, 1999.

Larsson, G. (1977), 'Chronological Parallels between the Creation and the Flood'. *VT* 27: 490–92.

———— (1985), 'The Documentary Hypothesis and the Chronological Structure of the Old Testament'. *ZAW* 97: 316–33.

Layton, Scott C. (1997), 'Remarks on the Canaanite Origin of Eve'. *CBQ* 59: 22–32.

Lemche, N. P. (1980), 'The Chronology in the Story of the Flood'. *JSOT* 18: 52–62.

Levenson, Jon D. (1985), *Creation and the Persistence of Evil*. San Francisco: Harper & Row.

Levin, Yigal (2002), 'Nimrod the Mighty King of Kish, King of Sumer and Akkad'. *VT* 52: 350–66.

Levison, John R. (1988), *Portraits of Adam in Early Judaism*. Sheffield: Sheffield Academic Press.

Lévi-Strauss, Claude (1969), *The Raw and the Cooked*. New York and Evanston: Harper Torch Books. ET by John Weightman and Doreen Weightman of *Le Cru et le Cuit* (Paris: Plon, 1964).

Lewis, T. J. (1992), 'Belial'. *ABD* 1: 654–56.

Lipiński, E. (1966), 'Nimrod et Aššur'. *RB* 73: 77–93.

Louth, Andrew, and Marco Conti (2001), *Ancient Christian Commentary on Scripture: Old Testament I: Genesis 1–11*. Downers Grove, IL: InterVarsity Press.

Luckenbill, Daniel David (1927), *Ancient Records of Assyria and Babylonia: Part Two*. Chicago: University of Chicago Press.

Luttikhuizen, Gerard P., ed. (2000), *The Creation of Man and Woman: Interpretations of the Biblical Narratives in Jewish and Christian Traditions*. Leiden: Brill.

McEvenue, S. E. (1971), *The Narrative Style of the Priestly Writer*. Rome: Pontifical Biblical Institute Press.

Machinist, Peter (1992), 'Nimrod'. *ABD* 4: 1116–18.

McKane, William (1986), *A Critical and Exegetical Commentary on Jeremiah*, vol. 1: *Jeremiah I–XXV*. Edinburgh: T. & T. Clark.

McNamara, Martin (1992), *Targum Neofiti I: Genesis: Translated with Apparatus and Notes*. Collegeville, MN: Liturgical Press.

Mason, Steven D. (2007), 'Another Flood? Genesis 9 and Isaiah's Broken Eternal Covenant'. *JSOT* 32: 177–98.

May, Gerhard (1994), *Creatio ex Nihilo: The Doctrine of 'Creation out of Nothing' in Early Christian Thought*. Edinburgh: University of Edinburgh Press.

May, Herbert G. (1962), 'The King in the Garden of Eden: A Study of Ezekiel 28:12-19', in B. W. Anderson and W. Harrelson, eds, *Israel's Prophetic Heritage*. New York: Harper & Brothers, pp. 166–76.

Mellinkoff, Ruth (1981), *The Mark of Cain*. Berkeley: University of California Press.

Mendenhall, George E. (1974), 'The Shady Side of Wisdom: The Date and Purpose of Genesis 3', in H. N. Bream et al., eds, *A Light Unto My Path: Old Testament Studies in Honor of Jacob M. Myers*. Philadelphia: Temple University Press, pp. 319–34.

Mettinger, Tryggve (2007), *The Eden Narrative: A Literary and Religio-historical Study of Genesis 2–3*. Winona Lake, IN: Eisenbrauns.

Milgrom, Jacob (2000), *Leviticus 1722: A New Translation with Introduction and Commentary* (AB, 3). New York: Doubleday.

Milik, J. T. (1976), *The Books of Enoch*. Oxford: Clarendon.

Millard, Alan R. (1984), 'The Etymology of Eden'. *VT* 34: 103–106.

Miller, J. Maxwell (1972), 'In the "Image" and "Likeness" of God'. *JBL* 91: 291–93.

Montgomery, James A. (1926), *A Critical and Exegetical Commentary on the Book of Daniel* (ICC). Edinburgh: T. & T. Clark.

Moore, George Foot (1927), *Judaism in the First Centuries of the Christian Era* (2 vols). Cambridge, MA: Harvard University Press. Repr. New York: Schocken Books, 1971.

Muilenburg, James (1961), 'The Biblical View of Time'. *HTR* 54: 242.

Müller, Hans-Peter (1985), 'Das Motif für die Sindflut'. *ZAW* 97: 295–316.

Müller, Hans-Peter, and M. Krause (1980), 'חכם, *chākham*'. *TDOT* 4: 364–85.

Murphy, Roland E. (1958), 'Yēṣer in the Qumran Literature'. *Bib* 39: 334–44.

Murphy-O'Connor, Jerome (1987), 'Relating 2 Cor 6:14–7:1 to its Context'. *NTS* 33: 272–75.

Nicholson, Ernest W. (1988), 'P as an Originally Independent Source in the Pentateuch'. *Irish Biblical Studies* 10: 192–206.

Nickelsburg, George W. E., and James C. VanderKam (2004), *1 Enoch: A New Translation based on the Hermeneia Commentary*. Minneapolis: Fortress.

Nissinen, Martti (2001), 'Akkadian Rituals and Poetry of Divine Love', in R. M. Whiting, ed., *Mythology and Mythologies: Melammu Symposia II*. Helsinki: Helsinki University Press, pp. 93–136.

Nitzan, Bilha (2002), 'The Idea of Creation and its Implications in Qumran Literature', in Henning Graf Reventlow and Yair Hoffman, eds, *Creation in Jewish and Christian Tradition*. Sheffield: Sheffield Academic Press, pp. 240–64.

Novak, David (1983), *The Image of the Non-Jew in Judaism: An Historical and Constructive Study of the Noahide Laws*. New York: Mellen.

——— (1998), *Natural Law in Judaism*. Cambridge and New York: Cambridge University Press.

O'Connell, Robert J., SJ (1969), *St. Augustine's Confessions: The Odyssey of a Soul*. Cambridge, MA: Belknap Press.

Oded, B. (1986), 'The Table of Nations (Genesis 10): A Socio-Cultural Approach'. *ZAW* 98: 14–31.

Oden, R. A. (1981), 'Divine Aspirations in Atraḥasis and in Genesis 1–11'. *ZAW* 93: 197–216.

Oppenhein, A. Leo (1964), *Ancient Mesopotamia: Portrait of a Dead Civilization*. Chicago: Chicago University Press.

Otto, E. (2004), 'שבע, *šeba*'. *TDOT* 14: 336–67.

Otzen, B. (1975), 'בליעל, *běliyyaʿal*'. *TDOT* 2: 131–36.

——— (1990) 'יצר, *yāsar*'. *TDOT* 6: 257–65.

Pettinato, G. (1968), 'Die Bestrafung des Menschengeschlechts durch die Sindflut'. *Or* 47: 165–200.

Pope, Marvin H. (1965), *Job: Translated with an Introduction and Notes* (AB 15). Garden City, NY: Doubleday.

Propp, William H. C. (2006), *Exodus 19–40: A New Translation with Introduction and Commentary* (AB 2A). NY: Doubleday.

Pury, Albert de (1989), *Le Pentateuque en Question*. Geneva: Labor et Fides.

——— (1992), 'Yahwist (J) Source'. *ABD* 6: 1012–20.

Reiner, Erica (1961), 'The Etiological Myth of the "Seven Sages" '. *Or* N.S. 30: 1–11.

Rendtorff, Rolf (1961), 'Genesis 8:21 und die Urgeschichte des Yahwisten'. *Kerygma und Dogma* 7: 69–78.

———— (1990), *The Problem of the Process of Transmission in the Pentateuch*. Sheffield: JSOT. ET by John J. Scullion of *Das Überlieferungsgeschichtliche Problem des Pentateuch*. Berlin: de Gruyter, 1977).

———— (2005), *The Canonical Hebrew Bible: A Theology of the Old Testament*. Leiden: Deo. ET by David E. Orton of *Theologie des Alten Testaments. Ein kanonischer Entwurf*. Neukirchen-Vluyn: Neukirchener Verlag, 2001.

Reventlow, Henning Graf (1985), *Problems of Old Testament Theology in the Twentieth Century*. Philadelphia: Fortress.

Reventlow, Henning Graf, and Yair Hoffman (2002), *Creation in Christian and Jewish Tradition*. Sheffield: Sheffield Academic Press.

Ricoeur, Paul (1967), *The Symbolism of Evil*. Boston: Beacon Press.

Robertson Smith, William (1972), *The Religion of the Semites: The Fundamental Institutions* (based on 2nd edn, 1894). New York: Schocken Books.

Robinson, R. B. (1986), 'Literary Functions of the Genealogies of Genesis'. *CBQ* 48: 595–608.

Rochenmacher, Hans (2002), 'Gott und das Chaos: Ein Beitrag zum Verständnis von Gen 1,1-3'. *ZAW* 114: 1–20.

Rowley, Harold H. (1976), *Job* (NCB, 2nd edn) London: Oliphants.

Runia, David T. (1993), *Philo in Early Christian Literature: A Survey*. Assen: Gorcum.

Rüterswörden, Udo (1988), 'Der Bogen in Genesis 9, militärhistorische und traditionsgeschichtliche Erwägungen zu einem biblischen Symbol'. *UF* 20: 247–63.

Sanders, E. P. (1977), *Paul and Palestinian Judaism*. London: SCM.

Sarna, Nahum M. (1989), *The JPS Torah Commentary: Genesis*. Philadelphia: Jewish Publication Society.

Sasson, Jack (1978), 'A Genealogical "Convention" in Biblical Chronography?' *ZAW* 90: 171–85.

Sawyer, John F. A. (1986), 'Cain and Hephaestus: Possible Relics of Metalworking Traditions in Genesis 4'. *Aram Nahrain* 24: 155–66.

Schäfer, Peter (1971), 'Zur Interpretation von Genesis 1:1 in der rabbinischen Literatur'. *JSJ* 2: 161–66.

Schmidt, Werner H. (1964), *Die Schöpfungsgeschichte der Priesterschrift*. Neukirchen-Vluyn: Neukirchener Verlag.

Scholem, Gershom (1961), *Major Trends in Jewish Mysticism*. New York: Schocken Books.

———— (1971), *Kabbala*. Jerusalem: Keter.

Schüle, Andreas (2006), *Der Prolog der hebräischen Bibel. Der literar- und theologie-geschichtliche Diskurs der Urgeschichte (Genesis 1–11)*. Zurich: Theologische Verlag.

Schwarz, Hans (2002), *Creation*. Grand Rapids: Eerdmans.

Schwarzbaum, H. (1957). 'The Overcrowded Earth'. *Numen* 4: 59–74.

Scroggs, Robin (1966), *The Last Adam*. Oxford: Oxford University Press.

Seebass, Horst (2007), 'Die Gottessöhne und das menschliche Mass: Gen 6,1-4'. *BN* 134: 5–22.

Shattuck, Roger (1996), *Forbidden Knowledge: From Prometheus to Pornography*. New York: St. Martin's Press.

Simons, J. (1954), 'The Table of Nations (Genesis X): Its General Structure and Meaning'. *OTS* 10: 155–84.

Skinner, John (1910), *A Critical and Exegetical Commentary on Genesis* (ICC) Edinburgh: T. & T. Clark.

Smith, Morton (1963), 'II Isaiah and the Persians'. *JAOS* 83: 415–21.

Speiser, E. A. (1955), 'Ancient Mesopotamia', in Robert C. Dentan, ed., *The Idea of History in the Ancient Near East*. New Haven and London: Yale, pp. 35–76.

———— (1958), 'In Search of Nimrod'. *ErIsr* 5: 32*–36*.

———— (1964), *Genesis: Introduction, Translation and Notes* (AB 1). Garden City, NY: Doubleday.

Stern, E. (1982), *The Material Culture of the Land of the Bible in the Persian Period 538–332 BC*. Warminster: Aris & Phillips; Jerusalem: Israel Exploration Society.

Stone, Michael E. (1992), *A History of the Literature of Adam and Eve*. Atlanta: Scholars Press.

Stordalen, T. (2000), *Echoes of Eden: Genesis 2–3 and Symbolism of the Eden Garden in Biblical Hebrew Literature*. Leuven: Peeters.

Stuckenbruck, Loren T. (1997), *The Book of Giants from Qumran*. Tübingen: Mohr-Siebeck.

———— (2004), 'The Origins of Evil in Jewish Apocalyptic Tradition: The Interpretation of Genesis 6:1-4 in the Second and Third Centuries BCE', in Auffarth and Stuckenbruck 2004: 97–118.

Talmon, Shemaryahu (2000), 'Calendars and Mishmarot'. *EDSS* 1: 108–17.

Toy, Crawford H. (1899), *A Critical and Exegetical Commentary on the Book of Proverbs* (ICC). Edinburgh: T. & T. Clark.

Trible, Phyllis (1978), *God and the Rhetoric of Sexuality*. Philadelphia: Fortress.

Tsevat, Mattatyahu (1954), 'The Canaanite God Šālah'. *VT* 4: 41–49.

Uehlinger, C. (1999), 'Leviathan, לויתן'. *DDD* 511–15.

———— (1999), 'Nimrod, נמרוד'. *DDD* 627–30.

———— (2003), 'Bauen wir eine Stadt und einen Turm … !' *BK* 58: 37–42.

Van der Horst, Peter (1990), 'Nimrod after the Bible', in *Essays on the Jewish World of Early Christianity*. Fribourg: Universitätsverlag; Göttingen: Vandenhoeck & Ruprecht, pp. 220–32.

———— (2002), *Japhet in the Tents of Shem: Studies on Jewish Hellenism in Antiquity*. Leuven: Peeters.

VanderKam, James C. (1992), 'Calendars: Ancient Israel and Early Jewish'. *ABD* 1: 814–20.

———— (1995), *Enoch: A Man for All Generations*. Columbia: University of South Carolina Press.

Van der Kooij, Arie (2006), 'The City of Babel and Assyrian Imperialism'. *VTSup* 109: 1–17.

Van der Toorn, Karel (1999), 'Rahab, רהב'. *DDD* 684–87.

Van der Toorn, Karel, and Peter van der Horst (1990), 'Nimrod Before and After the Bible'. *HTR* 83: 1–29.

Van Seters, John (1983), *In Search of History: Historiography in the Ancient World and the Origins of Biblical History*. New Haven and London: Yale.

———— (1992), *Prologue to History: The Yahwist as Historian in Genesis*. Louisville: Westminster/John Knox Press.

———— (1995), 'The Historiography of the Ancient Near East', in Jack M. Sasson, ed., *Civilizations of the Ancient Near East*, vol. 4. New York: Charles Scribner's Sons, pp. 2433–44.

Vawter, Bruce (1977), *On Genesis: A New Reading*. Garden City, NY: Doubleday.

Vermes, Geza (1975), 'The Targumic Versions of Genesis 4:3-16', in *Post-Biblical Jewish Studies*. Leiden: Brill, pp. 95–99.

Von Rad, Gerhard (1934), *Die Priesterschrift im Hexateuch*. Stuttgart: Kohlhammer.

———— (1961), *Genesis: A Commentary*. London: SCM Press. ET by John H. Marks of *Das erste Buch Mose, Genesis*. Göttingen: Vandenhoeck & Ruprecht, 1956.

———— (1962), *Old Testament Theology*, vol. 1: *The Theology of Israel's Historical Traditions*. Edinburgh and London: Oliver & Boyd. ET by D. M. G. Stalker of *Theologie des Alten Testaments*, vol. 1. Munich: Kaiser Verlag, 1957.

———— (1965), *Old Testament Theology*, vol. 2: *The Theology of Israel's Prophetic Traditions*. Edinburgh and London: Oliver & Boyd. ET by D. M. G. Stalker of *Theologie des Alten Testaments*, vol. 2. Munich: Kaiser Verlag, 1960.

———— (1966), 'The Theological Problem of the Old Testament Doctrine of Creation', in *The Problem of the Hexateuch and Other Essays*. Edinburgh and London: Oliver & Boyd, pp. 131–43. ET by E. W. Trueman Dicken of 'Das theologische Problem des alttestamentlichen Schöpfungsglaubens', in *Gesammelte Studien zum Alten Testament*. Munich: Kaiser Verlag, pp. 136–47.

———— (1972), *Wisdom in Israel*. London: SCM. ET of *Weisheit in Israel*. Neukirchen-Vluyn: Neukirchener Verlag, 1970.

Wacholder, Ben Zion (1968), 'Biblical Chronology in the Hellenistic World Chronicles'. *HTR* 61: 451–81.

Wallace, H. N. (1985), *The Eden Narrative*. Atlanta: Scholars Press.
———— (1992), 'Eve'. *ABD* 2: 676–77.
Watson, W. G. E. (1999), 'Helel, הילל'. *DDD* 392–94.
Weimar, Peter (1974), 'Die Toledot-Formel in der priesterschriftlichen Geschichtsdarstellung'. *BZ* n.F. 18: 65–93.
Wellhausen, Julius (1885), *Prolegomena to the History of Ancient Israel*. Edinburgh: T. & T. Clark. ET by W. Robertson Smith of *Prolegomena zur Geschichte Israels* (6th edn). Berlin: De Gruyter, 1883.
Wenham, Gordon (1987), *Genesis 1–15* (WBC) Waco, TX: Word Books.
Wenning, R. (1990), 'Attische Keramik in Palästina. Ein Zwischenbericht'. *Transeuph* 2: 157–67.
West, Martin Lichfield (1985), *The Hesiodic Catalogue of Women: Its Nature, Structure, and Origins*. Oxford: Oxford University Press.
West, Stephanie R. (1996), 'Hecataeus'. *OCD* 670–71.
Westermann, Claus (1961), *Der Schöpfungsbericht vom Anfang der Bibel*. Stuttgart: Calwer.
———— (1978), *Theologie des Alten Testaments in Grundzügen*. Göttingen: Vandenhoeck & Ruprecht.
———— (1984), *Genesis 1–11: A Commentary*. London: SPCK. ET by John J. Scullion, SJ of *Genesis (Kapitel 1–11)*. Neukirchen-Vluyn: Neukirchener Verlag, 1974.
Whybray, R. Norman (1968), *The Succession Narrative: A Study of II Samuel 9–20 and 1 Kings 1 and 2*. London: SCM.
Wilckens, U., and G. Fohrer (1971), 'σοφια'. *TDNT* 7: 465–526.
Wilken, Robert L. (1975), *Aspects of Wisdom in Judaism and Early Christianity*. Notre Dame and London: University of Notre Dame Press.
Wilson, Robert R. (1977), *Genealogy and History in the Biblical World*. New Haven and London: Yale University Press.
———— (1987), 'The Death of the King of Tyre: The Editorial History of Ezekiel 28', in J. H. Marks and R. M. Good, eds, *Love and Death in the Ancient Near East: Essays in Honor of Marvin H. Pope*. Guildford, CT: Four Quarters Publishing Company, pp. 211–18.
———— (1992), 'Genealogy, Genealogies'. *ABD* 2: 929–32.
Wiseman, Donald J. (1961), *Chronicles of Chaldaean Kings (626–556 B.C.) in the British Museum*. London: Trustees of the British Museum.
———— (1983), 'Mesopotamian Gardens'. *Anatolian Studies* 33: 137–44.
Wright, David P. (1996), 'Holiness, Sex, and Death in the Garden of Eden'. *Bib* 77: 305–29.
Wyatt, Nicholas (1981), 'Interpreting the Creation and Fall Story in Genesis 2–3'. *ZAW* 93: 10–21.
Younger, K. Lawson (1998), 'The Deportations of the Israelites'. *JBL* 117: 201–27.
Zadok, Ran (1984), 'The Origin of the Name Shinar'. *ZA* 74: 240–44.

Zenger, Erich (1983), *Gottes Bogen in den Wolken. Untersuchungen zur Komposition und Theologie der priesterschriftlichen Urgeschichte.* Stuttgart: Katholisches Bibelwerk.

Index of Authors

Index of Authors

Index of Subjects

211